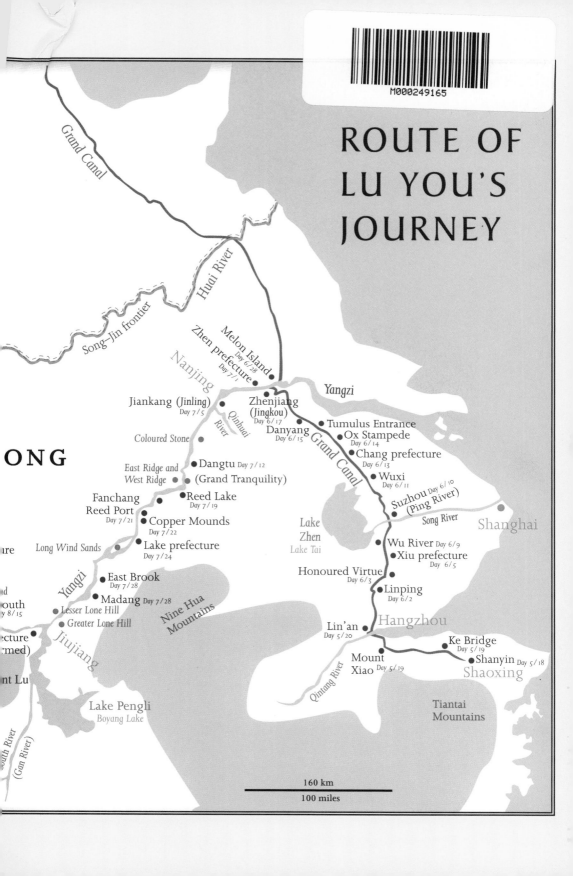

ROUTE OF LU YOU'S JOURNEY

Grand Canal

Huai River

Song–Jin frontier

Melon Island Day 6/28
Zhen prefecture Day 7/1

Nanjing

Yangzi

Jiankang (Jinling) Day 7/5

Zhenjiang (Jingkou) Day 6/17

Tumulus Entrance

Qinhuai River

Danyang Day 6/15

Ox Stampede Day 6/14

Chang prefecture Day 6/13

Coloured Stone

Grand Canal

ONG

East Ridge and West Ridge

Dangtu Day 7/12 (Grand Tranquility)

Wuxi Day 6/11

Fanchang
Reed Port Day 7/21

Reed Lake Day 7/19

Suzhou Day 6/10 (Ping River)

Song River

Shanghai

Copper Mounds Day 7/22

Long Wind Sands

Lake prefecture Day 7/24

Lake Zhen
Lake Tai

Wu River Day 6/9

Xiu prefecture Day 6/5

ure

Yangzi

East Brook Day 7/28

Honoured Virtue Day 6/3

uth
y 8/15

Madang Day 7/28

Lesser Lone Hill

Greater Lone Hill

Nine Hua Mountains

Linping Day 6/2

d

Jiujiang

Lin'an Day 5/20

Hangzhou

Ke Bridge Day 5/19

Shanyin Day 5/18

ecture
med)

Mount Xiao Day 5/19

Shaoxing

nt Lu

Lake Pengli
Boyang Lake

Qintang River

Tiantai Mountains

uth River (Gan River)

160 km

100 miles

GRAND CANAL, GREAT RIVER

GRAND CANAL, GREAT RIVER

THE TRAVEL DIARY OF A TWELFTH-CENTURY CHINESE POET

TRANSLATED WITH A COMMENTARY BY PHILIP WATSON

F

FRANCES LINCOLN LIMITED
PUBLISHERS

Frances Lincoln Limited
4 Torriano Mews
Torriano Avenue
London NW5 2RZ
www.franceslincoln.com

British Library Cataloguing in Publication data
A catalogue record for this book is available from the British Library.

ISBN: 978-0-7112-2719-4

Printed and bound in Singapore by Tien Wah Press Pte Ltd

9 8 7 6 5 4 3 2 1

CONTENTS

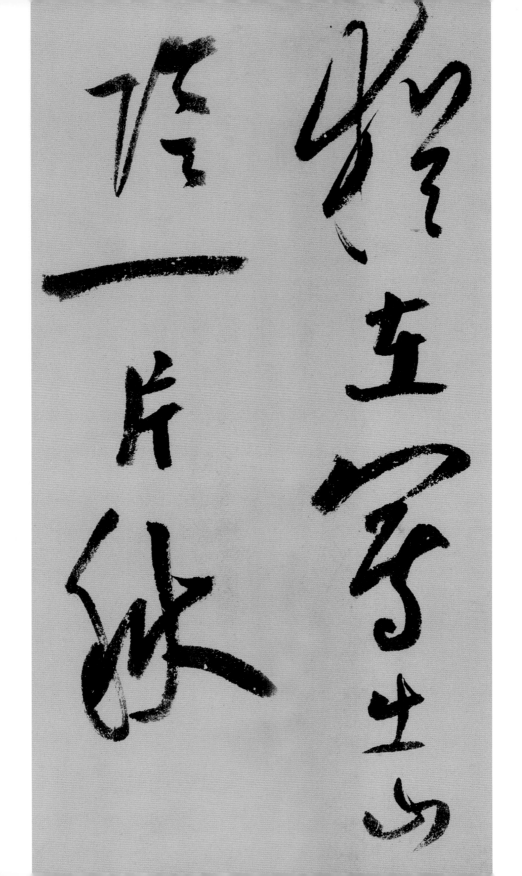

INTRODUCTION

A journey to an unknown world is an exercise in imagination, whether that world be one removed in space or time, or in culture and values. Perhaps you have picked up this book because China interests you, or travel, history, diaries. But across the space of hundreds of years, at the other end of the Eurasian land mass, and in a society whose outlines appear strange and perhaps forbidding, the imaginative effort can seem daunting. You are about to embark in east China on a journey by boat some eight and a half centuries ago, and to travel a section of the Grand Canal, whose claim to be one of man's greatest engineering achievements ranks with those of the pyramids and the Great Wall of China; to emerge onto the Yangzi, one of the mightiest of the world's rivers, and to proceed through the heart of a powerful medieval empire amidst its cities, villages, remote and wild country, past one of nature's most extraordinary features, the Yangzi Gorges, to reach a small walled town in the western province of Sichuan where our journey ends. But as with any travel, our curiosity may wane and our enthusiasm be blunted by the babble of strange tongues, the confusion of currencies, an unaccustomed diet and the habits of strangers which we do not share. The more removed from our experience that journey is, the greater the need for a guide to what is unfamiliar, and indeed to what may at first sight seem familiar but is not. This book, in the person of the diarist and of the translator, attempts to provide such a guide to a world at once remote yet comprehensible.

Other guides have taken us on similar journeys. Travellers of past and present – Marco Polo, Ibn Battuta, Odorico da Pordenone, Isabella Bird, Eric Newby, Michael Palin, Paul Theroux, to name but a few of those who have recorded their exploits – have given us a view of another world previously little known to us. But, distinguished as such writing may be, it shares a common weakness. The guide, like the travellers he leads, is looking from the outside in. He can point out what is unusual, what is worthy of note, he may attempt to explain a foreign custom, remark an extraordinary fact, laugh at a peculiarity of habit or behaviour, but he does so as a stranger. He will pass by largely oblivious of the associations which the landscape may hold for the inhabitants: of battles and heroes and poems and paintings; he cannot interpret the meaning of ceremonials and religious rites which he sees, is largely ignorant of the political background and administrative structure of those towns through which he travels, is oblivious of meaning in place-names. Hardy and extraordinarily brave the ancient travellers may have been; resolute, organized and well-equipped the modern adventurer; but the cultural currency they carry is not accepted locally. If a Chinese wandered round Rome with no more than a rudimentary notion of its Republic and Empire, of its associations with early Christianity, had heard only vague reports of the Renaissance or of Baroque art, we should question

Lu You's calligraphy.

his value as a guide, though we might find his reflections throw an interesting light on the state of Chinese knowledge of the outside world.

There is another drawback to the medieval travellers from the west whose accounts have come down to us. Some at least are unreliable. A few examples will suffice. Marco Polo's travels have longed been questioned. Sir John Mandeville's account of his journey of 1356/7 has been described as the 'lettered explorations of a mental traveller through the known as imagined world of his day'.[1] Samuel Purchas (1577–1626) described that book as 'stuffed with fables'. The situation is little better when we come to such a reputable figure as the Moroccan Ibn Battuta (1304–77). According to Ross E. Dunn,[2] Ibn Battuta's journey to China (he was in the east in 1345 and 1346) 'must be told in a spirit of uneasy skepticism'. His itinerary is vague, his descriptions muddled or patently inaccurate as regards the part in China, there is a lack of personal witness. As for Jacob d'Ancona's *The City of Light*, the purported account of a Jewish merchant's travels to China in the late thirteenth century as the Song dynasty came to an end, it reads like a pastiche informed by Judaic learning rather than sinological experience. We are on much firmer ground with accounts of travel by the Chinese monk Xuanzang who visited India between 629–45 to bring back Buddhist sutras, or of the Japanese monk Ennin who left a detailed daily record of his activities in China from 838–47. They, like the Daoist Changchun whose journey across Central Asia in the early 1220s was recorded by a disciple travelling with him, are largely reliable witnesses. Where even they sometimes falter we must recall the vast tracts of unknown territory, and the unfamiliar customs apprehended only imperfectly across barriers of language. As William of Rubruck (c.1210–c.1270) became aware on his journey of 1253–5, his interpreter 'totum aliud dicebat secundum quod ei occurebat'.[3]

In the journal before us, describing a journey from east to west China made from July–December 1170, we have the advantage that we are led by a citizen of twelfth-century China, and one who is not only working within his own culture but is also an eminent writer. But such guides come, it need hardly be said, with their own baggage, their own blinkers, and do not either literally or metaphorically speak our language. Our guide understands the customs and history of the country, knows the language and is highly educated in the literature of his own and preceding ages; he is indeed the most famous of twelfth-century Chinese poets, an official versed in the intricacies of the politics and government of China, a historian of some repute and a writer of vigorous prose; his interests range widely, as was not uncommon amongst those who had received the education of the scholar class of his time. His name is Lu You (Lu as in 'loo' and You as in 'yo-yo'). He was born in 1125, and lived to the great age for the period of 85, dying in January 1210. But in order to understand his attitudes we need briefly to describe the world which formed him.

China was unified in 221 BC by its first emperor (he beside whose tumulus was found the terracotta army). His dynasty soon collapsed, to be replaced by the Han (206 BC–AD 220), roughly analogous in extent, population, development and dates to the Roman empire. There followed a period of division, barbarian invasion and the spread of Buddhism which remade China, though in contrast to western Europe the standard of material and artistic life remained high. Once more unified by a short-lived dynasty, the Sui (581–618), whose lasting memorial is the Grand Canal, China was ruled by the Tang from 618–907. This dynasty, whose glazed tomb figurines have caught the Western imagination, extended Chinese power from north Korea to the South China Sea, and across the deserts of Central Asia. It was not only the physical extent of this empire but its economic and technological development that marks it out as the leading world civilization of the period.[4] The Chinese had had paper since the second century; the Tang added printing and porcelain; articulated an influential legal code; administered their empire through a bureaucracy whose higher ranks were in part chosen on the basis of examinations; and, with an extensive land and water transport system developed by the ninth century, the makings of a national economy handling more than local products or luxury goods. Cities began to burst their mural bounds, and the administrative structure was obliged to try to keep up with a less tidy world in which, for instance, the city-dweller was no longer shut in at night for his own and the government's peace of mind. Though there was a weakening of central power in the ninth century, and the growth of a form of warlordism, this increasingly disordered world masked developments in attitudes amongst the educated (those alone whose voices are audible today) which have to do with a greater sense of self, of the particular, a concern with material objects and their ownership, and with individual experience. Indeed the ninth century has been described as 'the end of the Chinese middle ages' not just for the shift in economic relationships but perhaps more strikingly for a new outlook. At the apex of society the great aristocratic families gave way to local landowners, gentry, from whom most of the official class derived. There is something here of the Tudor revolution in England.

But these advances were at first played out against a background of political instability, leading to military interventions, as local military leaders defied central government and then declared themselves independent. The period from 907–60 is known as the Five Dynasties and Ten Kingdoms, which sufficiently portrays the confusing array of short-lived regimes. One of the usurping generals managed to seize power in 960, declaring himself emperor of a new dynasty, the Song. He went on to defeat rival kingdoms, though it was not until 978 that his successor had extinguished the last of the other states in central China. Large and populous though the Song domains were, they were much diminished compared to the great empires of the past, the Han and the Tang. Other large and powerful states, of nomadic peoples in differing degrees of sinicization, lay to the north-east and north-west, in what is now Beijing and beyond to Manchuria, and along the so-called Gansu corridor, the route that leads out to central Asia between the Himalayan massif and the inhospitable deserts to the north. Zhao Kuangyin, the general who founded the Song, appears to have been prepared to compromise; neutralising his own leading generals so that they could not threaten his own power as had happened so often during the past half century, while accepting that he could not reassert his authority over large parts of what had previously been the Chinese sphere of influence.

The restoration of centralised government under the Song to most of what geographers call China Proper, with a capital just south of the Yellow River at Kaifeng, led to increasing prosperity for north central China above and below the Yellow River; for the Yangzi basin, westwards to the inland province of Sichuan; but in particular for the area of growing importance at its mouth (though Shanghai did not figure at this time, other cities which are still significant such as Suzhou and Hangzhou most certainly did); and southwards to Canton and other seaports which traded with South-east Asia and beyond. But the traditional Chinese world view of a single source of authority presiding over China and surrounded by barbarians in differing degrees of dependence and tutelage was hard put to it; the Song lived in a multi-polar world. In the early decades of the dynasty they conducted a series of military campaigns which merely demonstrated Song inability to match their illustrious predecessors. Peace was made with the Liao, a Khitan people, in 1004; and with the Western Xia who held the Gansu Corridor in 1006. The terms were felt to be humiliating to the Song but they gave more than a hundred years of peace. The eleventh century in China was a period of prosperity, of re-assessment of the traditional cultural inheritance resulting in what became known as Neo-Confucianism, the development of a self-consciously 'literati' programme in literature and painting which distinguished itself from the artisinal (we shall meet a number of the poets of the period when Lu You quotes their lines); but also of attempts to reform the political and financial bases of the state, indeed its moral base: a series of minor reforms in the 1040s was followed by the major programme of reformation from 1069 onwards of almost every aspect of the Chinese political economy from tax to education to military affairs. Such a wide-ranging programme can be seen as an attempt to address the question why it was that the Song state had not achieved the success and dominance of the great dynasties of the past, but it led to sharp divisions within the political élite, and the seesawing of the careers and fortunes of those who espoused one side or the other. The ramifications of this divide, though it was by no means clear-cut and the political groupings were permeable and subject to family and local loyalties as well as ideological ones, persisted for the next half century.

After a century of peace disturbed only by sporadic and limited wars and localized rebellions the rise of another nomadic group, the Jurchen, appeared to give the Song government an opportunity to overcome the Liao state which controlled a huge area stretching into what is now Inner and Outer Mongolia and across Manchuria. But the rubric 'my enemy's enemy is my friend' proved nearly fatal. The Jurchen defeated the Liao in 1125 but went on to conquer most of north China in the aftermath. The Song capital at Kaifeng was lost in 1127, the emperor and his recently abdicated father, the distinguished painter and calligrapher Emperor Huizong, were captured. This was the end of the Northern Song, so-called from the location of its capital. The terrain of south China, rivers and lakes, checked the advance of Jurchen cavalry and gave time for the Song to regroup under an energetic younger son of Huizong who declared himself Emperor Gaozong. For more than ten years, though, a peripatetic Song government remained under imminent threat from the northern invaders; only in 1138 did Gaozong establish a new capital at Hangzhou, south of the Yangzi, on the Grand Canal and close to the sea. The fiction that the court resided there only temporarily was maintained throughout the rest of the Southern Song, a period appositely named since the dynasty held only the territory south of the Huai River which runs west to east a hundred miles or so to the north, and in parallel with, the Yangzi.

This, then, was the political background against which Lu You grew up; China divided in two, the southern state in which he lived richer, more populous and more technically advanced but less effective militarily than its northern neighbour who styled their dynasty the Jin. The eleventh-century arguments about reform were now translated at the new capital of Hangzhou into a fierce debate on the merits or otherwise of attempting to regain the north. Lu You was born in 1125, at the very end of the Northern Song, and though from a noted gentry family based south of Hangzhou he was throughout his life firmly in the hawks' camp. Indeed, he is remembered in China as a patriotic poet who unswervingly called for the reconquest of the north from the barbarians (though this reputation does less than justice to the wide range of his output in poetry and prose). Unfortunately for him the doves held power for most of his long life, and on those occasions when the Southern Song launched revanchist attacks on the north disaster ensued. Though he was accepted as a distinguished literatus in his lifetime Lu's eminence rested on his poetry and historical writing rather than his attainment of the most senior posts in the bureaucracy. His passion and sincerity in the cause of a united China were not in doubt; they coloured not only his career but his friendships, and appear tangentially even in works such as his 1170 Diary. Lu died in 1210, shortly after another attack by the Southern Song on the Jurchens had ended in failure. It had been promoted by a Prime Minister who has not found favour with traditional Chinese historians, one who had attempted to suppress a faction with whom Lu You was close: an illustration of the complexity of allegiances based not only on family connections, local loyalties, student links, economic interests, philosophical outlook and literary and aesthetic affiliations, but political ideals and programmes as well.

The end of this story, though it has no direct bearing on the Diary, rounds out the picture. The Southern Song continued to resist Jin pressure in the decades after Lu's death, but a new power was rising in the Jurchens' rear which appeared to offer once more the chance to link up with 'my enemy's enemy'. Though he could not have known it, in 1167, three years before Lu's journey across China and the composition of his Diary, Genghiz Khan was born in Central Asia. The Mongols had overrun the state of Jin by 1234, and though the Southern Song military machine, backed by more advanced economic and technical resources, was able to resist for a further four decades, Kubilai Khan's armies overran Hangzhou in 1276 and had finally defeated the Song by 1279. Thereafter, China became for a while part of the vast Mongol conglomerate. This was the period of Marco Polo and more direct contact between the eastern and western ends of the Eurasian land mass.

Such in outline was the world in which Lu You tried to make his way as an official and writer. His career lasted with interruptions from 1158–1203. He had early distinguished himself in the all-important civil service examinations in 1154 but was blocked from immediate advancement, having expressed his revanchist views in the examination papers, not to speak of having been placed ahead of the Prime Minister's grandson. Shortly thereafter the Prime Minister died, and from 1158 until 1166 Lu held a number of minor posts. He then spent a period living at home but by 1169 had decided, apparently for financial reasons, that he would have to resume his official career. This must have been galling since the post to which he was appointed was no more senior than those he had held before, and was moreover in a distant city of no great economic or strategic importance on the Yangzi above the Gorges. As Lu tells us in the Diary, he was not well enough to set off on the long and arduous journey until the summer of the following year; nor was his arrival a matter of urgency. He took one hundred and fifty-seven days, from July to December, to cover a little over 1,800 miles from his home in what is now Shaoxing in eastern China, about seventy-five miles as the crow flies south-west of the modern Shanghai. He proceeded northwards along the Grand Canal via the capital at Hangzhou, then joined the Yangzi and went westwards up-river to his posting in the province of Sichuan. Along this route, travelling at a leisurely pace with his family, he had many diversions, taking the opportunity to visit famous sites and to call on other officials and on educated Buddhists who formed part of the social class to which he belonged; and he suffered a number of delays because of weather or for other reasons. Only occasionally does Lu directly tell us anything of himself: he is moved by the beauty or strangeness or fearsomeness of nature, more than once depressed by his own situation, indignant or concerned at the absence of political will to attack the Jurchen Jin state to the north. But we come to know him and his age obliquely from his qualities as a writer and from his multi-faceted interests. Almost every day of his journey Lu made a diary entry; the subjects he covered included literary criticism, politics and history, epigraphy and calligraphy, bureaucratic and administrative structures, landscape, shipping, commerce, fauna and flora, poetry, religion, architecture, painting, prose style, alchemy, popular customs, the qualities of drinking water, aesthetically attractive stones, local economies and much more. He is always intellectually curious, and keen to display his knowledge, especially of history. He is discerning, a keen observer, and rather a stickler for accuracy with a tendency to score points. We may infer that he was a fond father, and like many Chinese then and now preoccupied with his health. But revelation of his more intimate feelings, mention of family matters, would have been quite out of bounds to a traditional Chinese scholar. We should not expect a Samuel Pepys, whose diaries are in truth remarkable enough for their period even five hundred years after Lu You's. But Lu's observation of people from many levels of society, the blind old scholar, the neglected soldier, women working at water pumps, children with their school books, boatmen and their superstitions, is combined with a sensitivity to scenery and wide knowledge of the landscape of the past, both literary and historical.

As to why Lu wrote a diary, he offers no explanation. Nor do we know his working methods; presumably he made detailed notes as he proceeded on his journey and filled them out and checked some of the references as best he could in the year (1171) he was living in Kui prefecture. I have treated the daily entries as a record made as he went along (the fact that Lu sometimes misquotes other writers adds weight to the hypothesis), putting the English into the present tense as befits a diary made on the spot. The diary form itself was not an innovation. There had early been descriptions of journeys of the spirit, and there were geographic itineraries. In the Tang dyansty a tradition was established of writing about excursions of a day or more to famous beauty spots, monasteries, even remote valleys or caves. These often incorporated descriptions of landscape and sometimes drew a moral from the outing. There are accounts in more or less daily format from the Tang dynasty of travels into exile by officials out of favour. And there were records of travel with a religious colouring, such as that of the seventh-century Buddhist monk Xuanzang who travelled from China to India and back. In the Northern Song there had been travel accounts written in diary form. For instance Zhang Li's *A Record of Travel South of the City Walls* gives an account in diary form of the architectural and cultural relics of the former capital of the Tang dynasty at Chang'an as they were in the eleventh century.[5] In Lu You's own day there were diurnal accounts by Southern Song ambassadors who kept travel journals, in part a kind of political sitrep, which were presumably of use to the court in assessing the state of their enemy to the north. The Song was also a period in which a genre usually translated as *Miscellaneous Notes* (biji) flourished. Lu You wrote such a book himself, a collection of anecdotes, comments, historical asides and so on. It had a freedom from structure which must have attracted writers generally bound to adopt the rhythmic and tonal perfection of Chinese poetry, the rhetorical devices of formal prose, or the established constraints of historical writing. Even short stories, a form increasingly popular with scholars in their off-duty moments, had a structure imposed by the narrative. But the diary, like the miscellaneous notes of which it may be considered to form a sub-genre, was a cumulative process in which the writer could express himself as fully, or as little, as he wished and on whatever topic took his fancy. For a writer as prolific as Lu You (there are nearly 10,000 of his poems extant, and this after he excised most he had written before his forties) the composition of a diary on a long journey would have been a distraction which he enjoyed.

Perhaps (but here I speculate) Lu You saw his Diary as a means of keeping himself in the public eye, the public for this purpose being the court and fellow officials in the provinces. He might be away from the centre of power for a long time (as it turned out Lu spent seven years in Sichuan) in an obscure and unimportant post. He could at least remind policy-makers that he was an able and knowledgeable official as well as a poet of distinction. The Diary was not printed until 1220, but manuscript copies may well have circulated during Lu's lifetime. Such publicizing of his skills and current situation may offer one motive for Lu's writing of the Diary. But in adopting the diurnal format, providing a factual account of the progress of his journey which is neither a fantasy journey through a spiritual kingdom, nor a quest for learning or spiritual knowledge, but rather a product of an individual experience at a specific time and place, Lu You's Diary marks an advance in the genre. It is the longest and most comprehensive specimen of a Diary of its time, and indeed a long while after. Lu has taken the travel journal format and extended it to draw a picture of south central China over hundreds of miles and months on end. He is describing not just one mountain or one expedition, but a continuum; and not just one mood but a personality. This is where his innovation lies.

Perhaps the idea of continuum gives a clue to how we should read the Diary: one may think of it as a Chinese handscroll, one of those long paintings which slowly unroll from right to left through a winding and ever-changing landscape. Such handscrolls were indeed being painted in Lu You's day, and one is tempted to say that in such Song dynasty scrolls water was always the linking motif, whether the Yangzi itself as in Xia Gui's (fl. 1190–1225) Ten Thousand Li Along the Great River or the canal which winds through the masterpiece ascribed to Zhang Zeduan (fl. 1111–26), Qingmingshanghetu (Going Up the River on the Qingming Festival), which shows the suburban fields giving way to the bustle of the city within the walls. So the Grand Canal and the Great River both dictate the course of Lu's journey and provide it with a narrative thread. In many Chinese scrolls we are presented with an ever-changing scene interspersed with an observation or a poem, the calligraphy set on the bare ground of the sky, describing or commenting on the landscape. So in a sense Lu You's frequent use of poetic quotation and reference to historical events provide a counterpoint and bear testimony to the passing scene he records. One thinks how later Chinese novelists use lines of poetry to 'prove', as they put it, the narrative. In the same way Lu employs literary landscape to corroborate the natural landscape through which he leads us, like the painter drawing us along the landscape scroll and explaining and validating it for us. Linda Walton, in an essay[6] on a diplomatic mission to the north of China in 1169–70 written by Lou Yue (1137–1213), explains the writer's digressions on historical geography as an attempt to deal with 'a landscape . . . inscribed with a past that made sense of the present'. Lu You did not have to provide detailed descriptions of diplomatic ceremonial, nor was he gathering intelligence on enemy occupied territory as was Lou Yue, but like Lou's his digressions on historical geography are an attempt to work out the relationship of past and present and to make sense of the vicissitudes of history. But we should not fear that the Diary is abstruse, though it is sometimes erudite: the passage of centuries and the difference of cultures mean we require something in addition to Lu You's unvarnished words to follow him, but his lively and direct style, his curiosity about nature and human affairs, particularly the strange and inexplicable, and the delicacy of his emotional reaction to scenes and historical associations, carry us forward.

I should draw attention to some aspects of the approach I have adopted, no doubt idiosyncratic in some respects and unlikely to satisfy all readers, but which I hope will make the Diary enjoyable and comprehensible – in a (modern) word, 'accessible'; while, on the other hand, being faithful to the meaning and, as far as this can carry across from classical Chinese to modern English, the tone of the original. Firstly, I have used throughout the pinyin system for romanizing Chinese words and names, unless quoting some earlier authority. The example which will immediately strike the English-speaking reader is Yangzi rather than the traditional Yangtze or its other variants. Pinyin is now standard for most publications on China and presents the English speaker with only a few surprises: Q is pronounced as ch (for instance the surname Qin sounds like chin); C is the sound ts as, for instance, in Watson (so that the name Cai is tsai); ZH is like j as in jug, so the surname Zhou is like the English Joe; X used to be represented in older systems of romanization as *hs* which gives a closer approximation of the Chinese sound. We should bear in mind, in any case, that all the transliterations (which I have tried to keep to a minimum) are merely pronunciations of the words as they sound in modern northern Chinese (so-called Mandarin) rather than as they would have sounded to a twelfth-century southerner such as Lu You.

With regard to personal names, I have generally adopted one form rather than using several variations for the same individual as Lu You sometimes does. Chinese of the scholar class traditionally had surnames, given names, courtesy names, and sometimes nicknames, soubriquets, studio names and noble titles as well (in later life Lu You was made Earl of Weinan), not to speak of their posts, ranks and honorific titles, unfamiliarity with which is likely to breed confusion if not contempt. On first occurrence each individual's birth and death dates, where known, are given (absent, of course, in Lu You's original text), and because the cast is well-populated I have provided a list of Dramatis Personae on page 209 with brief biographical details, including the Chinese characters for the names. While on the subject of names I should add that I have made every effort to translate place-names. This is a risky business, but the risk seems to me worth taking to avoid a plethora of transliterated ancient toponyms which are bound to be both unrecognisable and unmemorable to the Western reader, and pretty indigestible. Where necessary I have added the relevant modern names in the Commentary to help identification. In many instances the meaning of a place-name is directly relevant to how a Chinese of the period would 'read' the landscape. This is particularly true of the names of buildings such as monasteries, towers and pavilions. One would miss much of the aesthetic appeal and the historical resonances if one did not make an attempt to seek out the meaning, sometimes allusive, of such names.

Weights and measures present a particular problem. Though well established from literary and archaeological evidence, they could vary with local usage and economic circumstance. I have generally followed the *Hanyu Dacidian*, but provided the rough English equivalents (miles, feet and so on) of Song dynasty values rather than distances that would be obscure to most of my readers. Some such measurements represent journey times rather than physical distance, and should not be taken too precisely. This seems to me to justify the approximation necessarily involved in using a Western system of measurement. And what is lost in authentic Chinese period flavour is I hope compensated for in readability and immediacy of comprehension.

Lu You met a number of his fellow officials in the course of his journey, and since he was writing for an audience of similarly educated bureaucrats, students, scholars and gentry it was of some interest to provide his contemporary readers not only with their names but also their ranks and official positions. This may seem otiose to the modern reader. Chinese themselves seem sometimes to have found the obligation to entertain visiting fellow officials rather tiresome; we see in the Diary that at one town the officials were said to have filled in a landing-stage to escape this burden. But I take the view that in a complete version of the Diary such as this one should give the full text in translation; and that it is confusing, boring and ultimately meaningless to the

Western reader merely to transliterate such nomenclature. Though this is not the place to provide an account of the complexities of the Song government structure and its accompanying ranking system, it is sufficient to say that every such title conveyed a meaning in terms of the honours bestowed, the rank attained, or responsibilities held. I have therefore always given a translation of these terms, and in doing so have followed the line of least resistance by adopting those established by Charles O. Hucker in *A Dictionary of Official Titles in Imperial China*; the translations do not always fall naturally on an English ear, but proceeding in this way has the virtue of consistency and compatibility with other work in the field.

For the modern Western reader a very different society a long way off both in time and space is bound to need explanation. In pondering how best to present a text, which is in itself immediate and readable, but which also needs the prop of explanatory material, I have tried to avoid drowning out Lu You's voice with footnotes and other academic impedimenta. These are kept to a minimum. Instead the entries of the Diary are interlaced with a commentary which picks up various points mentioned by Lu You which may need amplification. To some readers this will seem inadequate, and it could hardly hope to be exhaustive; at the end of the book will be found a brief bibliography intended to point in the direction of further material on the Song period. But I would hope that in the course of reading the Diary some picture will cumulatively have been given, in as painless a manner as possible, of Song dynasty society: of its economy, religion, architecture, social relations and so on. To other readers the Commentary will detract from the immediacy of the Diary. They have it in their power to let their eye glide over the text of the Commentary and to read only the twelfth-century words.

Those who find the Commentary of help will notice that I have called in aid a number of other travellers on the Yangzi. One of Lu's contemporaries, the poet and official Fan Chengda, is quoted on occasion since like Lu he was a diarist, an official and travelled over some of the same route only a few years later. And, to reassure the armchair voyager with guides whose voices have a familiar timbre, the experiences of some nineteenth-century Western authors are recounted either to confirm or contrast with Lu You's account. The stalwart Captain Thomas Blakiston R.N., who explored Canada, mapped the Yangzi in 1859 and went on to live in Japan and the United States; the merchant Archibald Little, keen to prove the viability of steamers ascending through the Yangzi Gorges to Chongqing; perhaps most redoubtable, and certainly best known, Isabella Bird (Mrs Bishop, as she added in her later writings) whose travels in North America, Japan, Korea and South-east Asia made her famous at the end of the nineteenth century and the beginning of the twentieth. Her journeys across China which concluded in 1897 were, she tells us, 'undertaken for recreation and interest solely'. All these travellers on the Yangzi, mapping, photographing, or attempting to prove a commercial point have made observations which provide a useful comparison and measure both of China then and now, and in contrast to the twelfth century; and also an object lesson in perspective: theirs, so much wider an angle of vision in many respects than that of Lu You, and in others so much less aware of the country through which they were passing. We may claim a wider perspective still. With the advantage of a body of sinological work by modern scholars we can attempt to understand how Chinese of eight hundred years ago felt and thought, but our vantage point is an increasingly distant one as China continues to change with ever greater speed. And we certainly have none of the intrepid spirit which took these earlier travellers on long journeys across great distances at risk from all manner of threats, and with little or no outside assistance to call on.

Lu You enters each day under its respective date according to the traditional Chinese lunar calendar; I follow this system where it is necessary to refer to an entry (for instance Day 8/24 means the twenty-fourth day of the eighth lunar month), but have given in addition for each diary entry the date according to the Julian calendar which was in operation in Europe at the time. So far as year dates are concerned, I have used BC for dates before our era, and have given the bald year (e.g. 960, 1151) for dates thereafter.

The illustrations which accompany the Diary are intended, like the Commentary, to illuminate the world it describes. I have attempted for this purpose to show paintings and artefacts which are as relevant as possible to the topics of which Lu You is speaking; both close to his time and demonstrating the sort of scenes and objects with which he would have been familiar. I have eschewed, within the limits of what is available, material which is not of Song dynasty, and preferably Southern Song, provenance. I have also chosen some sketches and photographs from our nineteenth-century authors. Blakiston's illustrator, Dr Alfred Barton, in particular conveys the drama of the Gorges in his day. My own photographs of places along Lu You's route, by comparison, may seem an anti-climax, but like much else in China they show something of the contrasts between old and new, the ugly and the beautiful. The map, without which not even armchair travel should be undertaken in unfamiliar country, contains details which relate to the Diary: Lu You's route, with the names and dates according to the lunar calendar of the principal places he visited in bold; the modern names of these and of other places given in light type to enable readers to get their bearings.

All such explanatory apparatus is and must be subservient to the original text. The history of that text and its editions has been covered by Chang Chun-shu and Joan Smythe in their *South China in the Twelfth Century*, published by the Chinese University Press in 1977; and more exhaustively by Professor Chang in his article 'Notes on the Composition, Transmission and Editions of the *Ju-Shu chi*' published by Academia Sinica in its *Bulletin of the Institute of History and Philology*, Vol.48, No. 3, also in 1977. Discrepancies in the text of the *Ru Shu ji*, whose literal translation is *Record of Entering Shu* (roughly Sichuan province), are small considering the length and age of the work. We owe this to a double piece of good fortune. Lu You, like many authors of the period, was concerned to preserve his collected works which he edited before his death, entrusting the publication of them to his sixth and youngest son Lu Ziyu (1178–1250), and instructing him to include the *Ru Shu ji* with the rest of his prose (though it might otherwise have stood as an independent book) lest it be lost. Ten years after his father's death Lu Ziyu oversaw the printing (we must recall that the Chinese had printed books from the ninth century) when he was an official at Liyang in Anhui in 1220. Secondly, a copy of that 1220 edition of *Weinan Wenji* (*The Collected Prose of the Earl of Weinan*) containing the complete *Ru Shu ji* has survived and is held in Beijing in the National Library of China. Lu You's *Collected Works* were republished in five volumes under the title *Lu You ji* in 1976 by the Zhonghua Shuju publishing house which based its simplified character version of the *Ru Shu ji* on the printed 1220 text, collated with the so-called Hua moveable type edition of 1502 (itself based on a Song dynasty version) and the Jigu Hall edition of the famous seventeenth-century scholar and printer Mao Jin (1599–1659). I have worked from the Zhonghua Shuju edition, checking doubtful readings against versions in the standard collectanea.

Professor Chang, who continued the work of the late Miss Smythe, has also set out various points concerning sources and references, particularly regarding Lu You's quotations and the identification of many places and some of the people mentioned in the Diary, though a planned companion volume on the life and times of the author seems to have been abandoned. Why then another translation? Apart from its intrinsic interest as a historical document and as a milestone in the development of a literary genre, Lu You's Diary is a work of literature. Lu was, as well as the outstanding poet of the twelfth century, a prose stylist in the so-called Ancient Style of classical prose (on which he dilates in the entry for Day 8/26 of the Diary) and, it seems to me, the translator owes Lu the duty of faithfulness not only in accuracy of meaning but also in conveying something at least of the readability, and if possible the distinction, of the original. Professor Chang's translation remains the only complete version until now,[7] but despite the learning which underpins its scholarly apparatus it seems to me deficient in a number of respects. This has emboldened me to undertake the present translation of the Diary. The Chang and Smythe version contains mistakes of comprehension, from which I hope I have learned; and on occasion lacks empathy with the argument or direction of narrative. Its English seldom flows, and gives a poor impression of the spontaneity and richness of the original; sometimes the sense of the English is unclear or infelicitous. Nor have the translators attempted the task of dealing with terms such as official titles; there is much left in transliteration which will confuse and ultimately irritate the reader. Professor Chang wrote of the *Ru Shu ji* that its language was terse, obscure and informal, and that it contained diverse quotations in many styles: 'such a text is hard to follow even for a seasoned Chinese scholar of the field; it is even more difficult to translate into a version that will be intelligible to readers of another culture'. Such an observation is liable to daunt the embarking translator, but provides a source of satisfaction for even partial success. I have drawn on his work and that of other scholars, but made an entirely fresh translation. I can only hope I have not introduced too many blemishes of my own in aspiring to produce for a wider Western audience a translation which should be read for pleasure, a pleasure it has given an educated readership in China for the past eight hundred years.

THE DIARY

Qiandao period, fifth year, day 12/6 (25th December, 1169)

On the sixth day of the twelfth month of the fifth year of the Qiandao period I received notice of my commission as Assistant Prefect at Kui prefecture. Since I'd just been suffering from a long illness and wasn't up to making a distant journey I planned to leave home at the beginning of summer.

In the absence of the Christian method of dating from the birth of Christ, the Chinese devised an elaborate system for referring to the passage of the years. During the Song and earlier dynasties the Chinese designated the years by giving an auspicious appelation to a period on the accession of a new emperor or during the course of a reign when a change of name was felt to be appropriate. Only for the later dynasties (Ming and Qing) is it accurate to speak of 'reign periods', exactly equating to the emperor's period on the throne. In fact the Song emperors changed period names frequently to signal a fresh start or a change of political direction. The years were enumerated from the first of the new period, and Lu You received his commission in the twelfth month of the fifth year of the Qiandao, or Supernal Way, period, which had begun in 1165. The Chinese months were lunar and consisted of either 29 or 30 days. Since the solar year has 365 days it was therefore necessary every once in a while to add another month to keep lunar and solar calendars in step, and it so happens that 1170, the year in which Lu You made his journey, was a year requiring one of these additional 'intercalary' months. One should also bear in mind a further point on the Chinese dating system. The Chinese New Year generally falls in late January or early February by the Western calendar, so that the twelfth month in the lunar calendar often equates to January. For each entry of Lu You's diary I have given the lunar date which he provides and its equivalent in the Julian calendar then in use in Europe. Time throughout the day was marked out in two-hour watches, which were subject to variation according to season and geography, but where these are referred to I provide their rough equivalents in parentheses.

Qiandao period, sixth year, day 5/18 (3rd July, 1170)

On the eighteenth day of the intercalary fifth month of the sixth year we set off in the evening and by nightfall had reached the Monastery of the Dharma Cloud where my brothers gave a banquet for my departure. It was the fifth watch [3–5 a.m.] by the time we said our farewells and I left.

As far as possible I translate the names of monasteries and temples. Place-names are translated where meaning seems clear and the place in question is not, like Hangzhou for instance, sufficiently well known from the geography of modern China. The process involves some risk of misinterpretation but will I hope give the English-speaking reader something more solid than transliteration of Chinese sounds to hold in mind. I should also explain that I have generally translated Buddhist establishments as monasteries, and those of the Daoists as temples or priories according to the Chinese term used; a distinction at once arbitrary but consistent.

Towpath on Looking Glass Lake near Shaoxing.

Lu was starting from his home town of Shanyin, now absorbed into the modern city of Shaoxing in northern Zhejiang province near the coast south of Shanghai. The Dharma Cloud is the Cloud of the Buddhist Law or Dharma, said to cover all with its beneficent influence.

Lu had three brothers, and was the third eldest of them.

Day 5/19 (4th July)

At first light we reached Ke Bridge Guesthouse and met the people who had come to see us off. Around 10 a.m. we arrived at Qianqing and ate in the pavilion where it felt as fresh and crisp as autumn, and I crossed the pontoon bridge on foot with my sons and those seeing us off. The bridge is really solid, and nothing like the old one.

The pavilion is beautifully decorated as well. Both have been built by Grand Councillor Shi Hao [1106–94]. We reached Mount Xiao county after 5 p.m. and rested at the Dream of the Pen post-house. The post-house stands beside the Garden of Enlightenment Monastery which, tradition has it, is Jiang Yan's [444–505] old house. There is a large stele with an inscription by Ye Qingchen [1000–49], while the monastery's horizontal tablet and the placard over the Buddha Hall are both in the calligraphy of Shen Liao [1032–85]. Another stele in Shen's calligraphy is also particularly fine and archaic. And in addition there's a painting of waters by a native of Piling, Qi Shunchen [996–1052], on the great wall by the Buddha's rear dais. When you suddenly see it you feel an alarming sense of waves and breakers swirling and eddying. Some of the older generation called it 'inert water', but that's wrong.

The Assistant Magistrate in provisional charge of the county, Ji Xun, and Commandant Zeng Pan came to call on me. Zeng Yuanbo, whose personal name is Feng, invited me for dinner at his son, Zeng Pan's office. I got back here at the second watch [9–11 p.m.], but then Zeng Yuanbo came over again and we sat together at the doorway of the post-house. The moon was as bright as daylight, but it was very cool. At the fourth watch [1–3 a.m.] the boat cast off and we proceeded as far as West Jing market town.

Lu You was travelling west along the extension of the Grand Canal that runs across northern Zhejiang province. Beyond West Jing market town the canal reaches the southern bank of the Qiantang River, famous for its tidal bore at the equinoxes, and continues from Hangzhou, which lies on the northern bank of the Qiantang, in a north-easterly direction to skirt Lake Tai and onwards to the Yangzi (Yangtse). This is the route that Lu You takes in the ensuing entries.

TOP: Pontoon bridge near Looking Glass Lake in Zhejiang.
ABOVE: The Grand Canal with its towpath at Ke Bridge (Keqiao).

Lu You's audience for his diary was scholar officials like himself, and it was important to establish the identity of those he encountered along his route. This is why when he meets other officials he spells out their full names, the posts they held and their honorific titles. This may try the patience of modern Western readers but reflects the importance of status within his social circle of educated officialdom.

Shi Hao had been governor of Lu You's home town, had recommended Lu for promotion and, like Lu, was an advocate of a revanchist policy to recover the lost territories of northern China.

Jiang Yan, whose house had been turned into the Garden of Enlightenment Monastery, was a leading writer of the fifth century. He had dreamed he was given a multi-coloured writing-brush by a deity, hence the name of the post-house.

Shen Liao was a writer in several genres, prose, song and poetry, and was acquainted with Wang

Light Wind on Lake Dongting, Ma Yuan (fl. 1190–1224).

Anshi and other leading lights of his day. Shen seems to have left, in examples of his calligraphy, evidence of his travels along the Yangzi.

The great eleventh-century writer and painter Su Shi, whom we shall meet many times in the course of the Diary, once wrote of 'lively water' and 'inert water' in paintings, praising a painter friend of his for the vividness of his depiction of movement in water: 'In recent years Pu Yongsheng of Chengdu, wine-bibber and bohemian, whose character is consonant with his painting, started depicting "lively waters".... In the past Dong Yu, and in recent times Mr Qi from Chang prefecture, have painted water and people have handed them down and treasured them; but the works of Dong, Qi and their like may be termed "inert waters" and can't be spoken of in the same breath as that of Pu Yongsheng.'[8]

Day 5/20 (5th July)

At first light we crossed the river, which was calm and waveless, and rested briefly at the Grove of Immortals Monastery where the monks opened up the guesthouse for us and served hot drinks. Then I hired a small boat to go out through the North Gate, and west of the Customs Post at Red Pavilion we went aboard the boat chartered by the Fiscal Commission.

There are no mosquitoes tonight.

Lu You crossed the Qiantang River and was now in Hangzhou, at this period the capital of the Southern Song dynasty following the loss of north China to the invading Jurchen in 1127, shortly after Lu was born. He had not been in the capital for eight years and spent over a week with family and friends.

Qiantang River at Hangzhou, about where Lu You crossed.

In all Lu travelled in five boats during his trip – boats adapted for canals, the broad Yangzi and the dangerous gorges.

Day 5/21 (6th July)
I paid my respects to my third elder brother.

This was probably Lu Song (1109–82) who was Lu You's eldest brother but the third child in the family.

Day 5/22–24 (7th–9th July)
We stayed at my elder brother's house for these days.

Day 5/25 (10th July)
In the evening Vice-Director Ye Mengxi [1122–83], whose personal name is Heng, invited me to dinner. On the table he had placed several plates with piles of alum which looked like snow.

Southern Song bowl, lotus petal design, from Longquan kilns near Lu You's home town.

Ye Heng, who was nearing the peak of his career, was a distinguished official of the Southern Song period who served under emperors Gaozong and Xiaozong. He was an able administrator who made some original proposals for expanding agriculture. Alum came from the Wu area (roughly modern Jiangsu) and was sometimes used in alchemy, though here its display seems to be entirely aesthetic.

Day 5/26 (11th July)

In the evening Director of Studies Rui Ye [1115–72], whose courtesy name is Guoqi, invited me to dinner. Amongst the guests were my elder cousin [Lu] Zhonggao [1113–74]; Senior Writer Zhan Daozi, whose personal name is Kangzong; and Junior Compiler Zhang Shuqian,

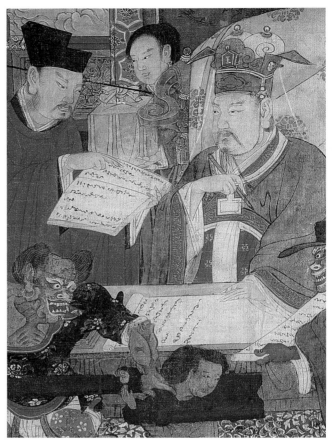

A Chinese judge of the underworld, thirteenth century. Museum fur Ostasiatische Kunst, Berlin.

whose personal name is Yuan. During the party Rui Guoqi told us that when he was recently working in the Fiscal Commission in the Eastern Circuit of Guangnan there was an Intendant of Tea and Salt called Shi Duanyi. He was cruel and heartless, and whenever officials or clerks were arrested and imprisoned he would always put them in a cangue of rock salt wood. This is the toughest and heaviest of woods, and he would often remark that 'Heaven has made a wood called rock salt [Rock's Salt] for my use'. Later Shi was found guilty of some offence and ended up wearing the cangue himself.

Shi, a common surname, means stone or rock. His name and his office with responsibility for the salt monopoly form the basis of the pun. The salt monopoly was an important source of government revenue at this time. Director of Studies Rui Guoqi, who tells the story, was a senior member of the National University based in the capital.

Day 5/27 (12th July)

No entry.

West Lake at Hangzhou.

Day 5/28 (13th July)

I came out through the Hidden Gate with Zhonggao and we hired a little boat to sail on West Lake, reaching Long Bridge Temple. It's been eight years since I was in Lin'an and the bamboos and trees in the lakeside gardens are all luxuriantly green, the tall willows reach to the sky, and the Buddhist monasteries have been refurbished. But most of my old friends have scattered and gone, whilst others are so exalted they no longer keep in touch, for which I heave a heavy sigh.

Lin'an is another name for Hangzhou, whose West Lake remains one of China's most famous tourist sites. About half the corps of senior members of the administrative class of 20,000, or what one might call the high-flyers in contrast to the clerical staff, runners, police and so on, were based in the capital; the other half were on provincial postings such as the one to which Lu You was proceeding.

Day 5/29 (14th July)

Examiner Shen Chiyao [c.1107–c.1190], whose personal name is Shu, invited me to dinner where I ran into Vice-Minister Zhao Dezhuang [1121–75], whose personal name is Yanduan. In the evening I went out by the Gate of Bubbling Gold and followed the city wall alongside the lake back to our boat.

> Zhao Yanduan, to whom we are introduced here by his courtesy name Dezhuang, was a well-known writer of lyrics as well as a junior scion of the imperial family.

Day 5/30 (15th July)

No entry.

Day 6/1 (16th July)

In the early morning our boat was moved out through the locks, but it took practically the whole day before we could get through the three locks; the various craft were as close as the teeth of a comb. It was very hot, and though there was light rain in the afternoon the heat hasn't dissipated. We've moored in front of a grain market.

> A writer with the *nom de plume* Naide Weng describes the scene in his *Duchengjisheng* of 1235: 'Within the northern water-gate of the city [of Hangzhou] there is a stream which flows for several tens of *li* [a *li* is about a third of a mile] (to the) Baiyang Lake. Along its banks rich families have constructed several tens of go-downs, each of which contains over a thousand units of space, or at least several hundreds. They are used for storage of goods belonging to the shops in the capital and to itinerant merchants. They are surrounded on all four sides by water, and so can avoid being set alight by the wind [i.e. blowing flames from other fires], besides resisting the depradations of robbers.'[9]

The Gate of Bubbling Gold at West Lake.

A Corner of West Lake, Xia Gui (fl.1190–1225).
National Palace Museum, Taipei.

Day 6/2 (17th July)

We cast off around midday. A servant from my home township arrived and told me that they were worrying about the rain at home. In the villages every household is pumping out the water. For the past three consecutive years we've had a good crop, but this Spring the old men were saying that the omens for the harvest were worrying. I wonder how things will turn out.

We passed the Well-met Guesthouse at Red Shore and rested a while in the pavilion at the front. Well-met is a place where envoys from the north lodge and are given banquets. It's twelve miles from Lin'an.

In the evening there was a rainstorm and it was quite cool.

We're spending the night at Linping. It's here at Linping that Grand Tutor Cai Jing [1047–1126] buried his father Zhun, with the Qiantang River for water and the Kuiji Mountains as an altar. The hill is shaped like a camel. He buried his father in the camel's ear and built a pagoda on the camel's hump, for the geomancer at the funeral had said that 'the camel which carries a heavy weight will travel a long distance'. But Su Shi [1036–1101] had certainly already stated in a ballad:

> Who compares with the soaring pagoda standing on Linping Hill
> That greets the traveller from the west and sees him on his way?

So in fact Linping has long had a pagoda and it must simply have been added to after the Cai burial, or maybe it was moved. The order demoting Cai Jing to Junior Guardian of the Heir Apparent referred to this when it stated that 'on the pretext of honouring the emperor's birthday he embellished the hill of Linping'.

The boat cast off at midnight.

Zhu Xi, the great Neo-Confucian philosopher who was Lu You's contemporary, noted in a memorial that Shaoxing (Lu's hometown) was over-populated and produced insufficient rice for its needs. Even when the harvest was good it was supplied from neighbouring prefectures.[10] Lu was right to be apprehensive. This year it rained heavily in the area south of the Yangzi, causing extensive

Listening to the Zithern, attributed to Emperor Huizong, who plays the lute while Cai Jing, seated on the left, listens. Huizong's characteristic calligraphy (top right) and signiture (bottom left), and a poem by Cai at the top, date this scroll to the first quarter of the twelfth century. National Palace Museum, Beijing.

flooding, and some districts were exempted from the poll tax.[11]

The name of the guesthouse is *Banjing*, translated here as Well-met, and refers to the story of two friends in ancient China who met by chance on the road and spread twigs (*ban jing*) to sit on as they talked. The expression had been used as the name of a guesthouse to receive foreign envoys earlier in the dynasty when the capital was in Kaifeng, and, with the loss of north China to the Jurchens, this Well-met Guesthouse just north of the new capital of Hangzhou was similarly used to greet their embassies. It was a polite, not to say placatory, name to give to the reception point for the detested Jurchen barbarian envoys.

Cai Jing had passed the high flyers' civil service examination, the *Jinshi*, in 1070 and by 1085 was governor of the Northern Song capital of Kaifeng. He went on, in the complicated politics of the late eleventh and early twelfth centuries, which pitted the followers of the conservatives under Sima Guang against those of the great reformer Wang Anshi, to rise and fall a total of four times. Cai managed to survive until the brief reign of the last emperor, Qin Zong, at the very end of the Northern Song, though much of the infamy of the collapse in the face of the Jurchen invasion was placed at his door. The concept for his father's funeral had been grand indeed: water and hills are geomantic requirements for a satisfactory burial place, but the Qiantang River is a mile or more broad in the vicinity of Hangzhou, and the Kuiji Muntains are far away on the other side of the river in northern Zhejiang. The theories implicit in this passage will be discussed when we come to Day 7/7.

Su Shi, who as we shall see is frequently quoted by Lu throughout his diary, was the leading literary figure of the eleventh century, a major poet, prose writer and arbiter of aesthetic norms, as well as a politician of some significance.

Lu You's journey was now taking him north up the Grand Canal to the junction with the Yangzi (Day 6/17).

Day 6/3 (18th July)

At first light we reached Long River Dam, which is a small market, and where there were plenty of fish and crabs. By afternoon we'd reached Honoured Virtue county in Xiu prefecture. Wu Daofu, the County Magistrate and a junior Gentleman for Loyal Service; Li Zhi, his Assistant and a junior Gentleman for Fostering Uprightness; and Zhang Shi, supervisor of the Xiu prefecture general customs post and a junior Gentleman for Loyal Service, all came to call on me. In the past I've heard Dai Ziwei tell that there was a merchant of Honoured Virtue named Wu Yin who suddenly abandoned his family and went to live in a lodging house. He would sit silently all day in his single room, which contained only a divan, and if visitors came they would sit together with him on the divan. If they brought wine when they called on him he wouldn't rebuff them, but would spend the whole day conversing on philosophical themes. Wu Yin had had no previous education but now, when he occasionally told others of his prognostications based on *The Book of Changes*, there was subtlety in all he said. He could also foretell other people's good or bad fortune, and how long they would live. No one who met him could fathom it. So I took the opportunity of my meeting Magistrate Wu to ask him about this story and he said that it was all true. Wu Yin had now moved out into a village.

This evening we travelled six miles and are staying the night at Stone Gate. There are mountains of flaming cloud so I can tell it will be hot tomorrow.

Alongside the established and organised religions of Buddhism and Daoism, and Confucian social tenets and moral philosophy, there co-existed beliefs in local (and in this period increasingly regional and national) gods – deified heroes and miracle-workers who attracted popular worship; and soothsayers, geomancers, fortune-tellers, and others whose behaviour and abilities appeared to defy rational explanation. Lu You, along with many of his contemporaries, was always interested in such phenomena.

Day 6/4 (19th July)

Intense heat, and only by afternoon was there a slight breeze. In the evening we moored in front of the Monastery of Innate Enlightenment. The temple used to be the Sacred Empyrean Priory. It fell into ruin during the war, and though it was rebuilt after the Jianyan period [1127–30] at present it's still very crudely constructed. But by the western range of the temple there's a lotus pool of an acre and a half with an arched bridge and little pavilions which are most beautifully decorated. There are innumerable turtles in the pool and when they hear people's voices they all cluster round, rows of heads gazing up. My children tried to startle them but they didn't go away.

In the pavilion is a little stele with the Old Drunkard Roundelay written by Guo Xiangzheng [fl.1060s–80s] in the Yuanyou period [1086–93], followed by his own colophon saying: 'Seeing that what Su Shi wrote wasn't much good I composed this piece,' which is pretty astonishing.

Lotus.

The war to which Lu refers was the attack by the Jurchens which led to the loss of north China; during the campaign of 1130 the Jurchens penetrated as far as Hangzhou; their cavalry entered the city and 'set fires and plundered unrestrainedly'.[12] Much of the reconstruction work was not carried out until some years after Lu had written his diary. Lu You cites other examples of Buddhist and Daoist establishments which changed hands between the religions at this period. As a Buddhist monastery the establishment he visited would have had a pool containing turtles since the releasing of turtles or of doves was an act symbolising the giving of life.

Su Shi, whom Lu greatly admired, was considered in his own lifetime and indeed by all succeeding ages to be one of the greatest poets and prose writers. Guo (see Days 7/13 and 7/17) was a minor literary figure and his comment is impertinent.

Day 6/5 (20th July)

In the morning we reached Xiu prefecture and I called on Zhu Ziqiu, Assistant Prefect in provisional charge of the Commandery and a junior Court Gentleman for Comprehensive Duty; Zhao Shikui, Supernumerary Assistant Prefect, a junior Gentleman for Managing Affairs and Auxiliary in the Imperial Archives; and Vice-Director Fang Wude [1102–72], whose personal name is Zi. Fang detained me for a meal, after which I went back to the boat for a little rest. It was extremely hot.

I paid a courtesy call on Administrator Fan Ziqiang and Instructor Fan Zimu (their courtesy names are respectively Guang and Yi, and they are both sons of Fan Maoshi [1102–64] of the Ministry of Rites); and Instructor Wenren Boqing (whose personal name is Fumin. He is the son of Reviser Wenren Maode). The two Fans live outside the city in a very imposing residence which Fan Maoshi built in his latter years. It is still not completed. Across a brook there's a delightful little garden with bamboos and trees growing luxuriantly, and a pool of lotus that stretches away into the distance. By the pool is a hall called the Hall of Study.

I paid a visit to the Jewelled Flower Nunnery, and made obeisance in the shrine-hall to Lu Zhi [754–805]. There was a broken and damaged stele, but here and there one could make out the worn remains of calligraphy by a Prefect of Su prefecture, Yu Di [d.818]. Broadly it said that 'Mr Lu Qiwang, the Director of the Imperial Library, first built a nunnery here, and later the brothers Ba, Chan and Li refurbished it. Later still there was a virtuous younger sister with the courtesy name Yi,[13] for the Lu family used to have daughters who became nuns.' But it says nothing of why Lu Zhi has a shrine here. (Our family genealogy regarding Li is, on the basis of this evidence, mistaken. The person with the taboo name Ba was the father of Lu Zhi.) The elderly nun Miaoji, the Reverend Fachun, and their disciple Jubai detained us to take tea. They said that the shrine-hall has just been refurbished.

The boat was moved to the Propagation of Morality Pavilion at the North Gate. In the evening I visited Fang Wude again for dinner.

The Jewelled Flower, or Deva-flower, is a celestial flower, which appears in Buddhist scripture.

Lu Zhi was a distinguished ancestor of Lu You's who had served as a Grand Councillor in the Tang dynasty. Lu would naturally wish to pay his respects at his forefather's shrine, and the nuns were no doubt delighted to have a visit from a descendant of the man of whose observances they had charge, and whose family had provided nuns. Lu Zhi's father was called Lu Kan and died when Lu Zhi was young so Ba must have been his taboo or childhood name. Lu Qiwang was Lu Zhi's grandfather. The Lus traced their ancestry back to the Western Han (206 BC–AD 8), and more fancifully back to the 'Madman of Chu' who was supposed to have lived at the time of Confucius (sixth century BC); Lu You's interest in genealogy was one widely shared by his contemporaries.

Day 6/6 (21st July)

Lü Yuan, a junior Court Gentleman Consultant and newly appointed Assistant Prefect of Jingnan, called on me. His courtesy name is Yanneng. And the Presented Scholar Wenren Gang came. His courtesy name is Boji and he is employed as private tutor by Fang Wude. He told me he had known Mao Dezhao. Mao, whose personal name was Wen, was from River-hill county in Qu prefecture but he had lived here in Xiu. When I was a boy I studied under him for a long while. Mao was an avid scholar, but in middle age unfortunately he got ill, went blind and died. He had no children. Wenren Gang said that after Mao went blind he would still spend all day sitting bolt upright, reciting to himself thousands of words from the Six Classics without a pause. How poignant.

I attended an official reception at the Assistant Prefect's Bureau, and we sat in the Pavilion of Flowers and Moonlight. There was a small stele with a lyric by Zhang Xian [990–1078], whose courtesy name was Ziye:

Clouds are rent, the moon comes out, and flowers play with their shadows.

It's said the line came to him in this pavilion.

In the evening I went to a gathering of Fang Yiwu's [1133–1201], whose personal name is Dao, at the house of Assistant Magistrate Chen Daguang. The two Fans and Assistant Prefect Lü were all there. Chen's courtesy name is Zichong, and he is a grandson of the Censor Chen Guan [1057?–1122?]. His residence is impeccably elegant, and the jasmine was in full bloom.

Day 6/7 (22nd July)

In the morning I did the round of farewells to all these gentlemen, and went to Fang Wude's for a vegetarian meal. In the evening the boat was moved outside the city walls and we moored in front of the Grain in Abundance guesthouse, which is rather an imposing building.

It's been raining heavily all day without cease.

I summoned Dr Jiang to examine members of my household and Tao.

Tao and Tong – the latter is mentioned a few days later – were the affectionate names of two of Lu You's sons.[14] At this stage of his life Lu had five sons; another was born after the family reached Sichuan, and a seventh in 1178. The eldest boy was born in 1148, the second in 1150, the third about 1151, the fourth in 1156 and the fifth in 1166. They therefore ranged from young adulthood to a small child during the journey to Sichuan. Tao appears to have been suffering from heat stroke (see Day 6/9).

Day 6/8 (23rd July)

The rain has cleared and it's been as chilly as late autumn, but the wind has been set fair so for the first time the boatmen have hoisted the sails. We passed Junction, which has a big population, and in particular a large number of sellers of preserved fish.

Fishermen rowing standing up.

Water wheel (nineteenth-century photograph).

Along the roadside were many herds of military horses. The Grand Canal had burst its banks and the fields of the nearby villages are several feet in water. On either bank they were pumping away the flood water, women and children working flat out, some using water buffalo, the women peddling the water wheels with their feet while with their hands they were still twining hemp which they hadn't put aside.

Passing Level View we encountered torrential rain and high winds and the inside of the boat was completely drenched, but after a short while the sky cleared. We stopped for the night at Eight Feet and heard that some boats that had been en route had capsized and sunk.

Little boats are coming by, banging on the gunwales to sell fish which are really cheap. But the mosquitoes are as fearsome as bees and scorpions.

Day 6/9 (24th July)

It was clear but windy. The boatmen had been scared by last night's bedlam and didn't dare cast off, so it was only when the sun was high that we got going. Since reaching Honoured Virtue we have been travelling through a great marsh, but now we've got here we begin to see the distant mountains by Lake Zhen.

Around noon we reached Wu River county and crossed the Song River. The wind had dropped completely. At the Emaciated Retreat the bamboos and trees are growing densely, but the owner has died.

Guan Chong, the County Magistrate and a junior Gentleman for Discussion, and Zhou Yan, the Commandant and a junior Gentleman for Meritorious Achievement, came to call on me. In the county offices there's a stone engraving of poems by Mr Zeng Ji [1084–1166] called 'On Illustrations of Fishermen's Implements' which the former county magistrate Liu Ying [twelfth century] had had engraved. 'Fisherman's Implements' is said to include ten items more than is recorded in the Collection of Songs from Songling.

I troubled Commandant Zhou to call a doctor, Zheng Duancheng, to take the pulses of Tong and Tao who are both suffering from the summer heat.

There was quite delectable preserved fish on sale in the market.

In the evening we cast off and from mid-stream I looked back at the many storied pagodas of Long Bridge, and the misty waves stretching far away; it really was like a painting.

xxx Nguyệt Lạc, ô đề, sương mãn thiên
Giang phong Ngư hoả đối sầu Miên
Cô Tô thành, Ngoại Hàn Sơn Tự
Dạ bán chung thanh đáo Khách thuyền –

Trương Kế –

We are spending the night at Yin's Bridge, and I've been up onto it to gaze at the moon.

The *Collection of Songs from Songling* was named after the Song (or Wu or Wusong) River, past which Lu You was just travelling, and was composed by a group of ninth-century poets. Song in this place-name means Pine Tree, but is (or was) well known to foreigners by its transliterated name (Sung Creek) where it flows out into the Huangpu River, intersecting the Bund at Shanghai. It seems otiose to translate it here. In the Southern Song dynasty it was the major watercourse draining the area east of Lake Tai (known to Lu as Lake Zhen) and had as its tributary the insignificant Huangpu. Dyke building during the eleventh and twelfth centuries, which turned the Yangzi delta into a prosperous agricultural area and important producer of grain, led to sedimentation which eventually reduced the Wusong to its present insignificant state, while the water which man had impeded gradually opened the Huangpu into the major river which one now sees at Shanghai. One must, in other words, understand the river which Lu You was crossing at this point as one of the major commercial arteries of Song dynasty China, along which goods passed for trade with the south China coast and to foreign countries. Such commercial activity did not prevent the Song River from producing a well-known variety of fish for supply to the capital at Hangzhou.[15]

Zeng Ji, scholar and poet, had been Lu You's mentor and Lu in his own poetry shows great fondness for Zeng.

Day 6/10 (25th July)

We reached Ping River but didn't enter because of sickness there, skirting the city walls past the Platter Gate. I gazed at the buildings and pagodas on Martial Mound Hill which are just like those on Precious Woods in my home town, and that made me melancholy.

We are spending the night in front of the Maple Bridge Temple, about which the Tang dynasty poet wrote:

αxx Dạ bán chung thanh đáo Khách thuyền –

The tolling of the midnight bell reaches the traveller's boat.

Ping River is the modern Suzhou (Su prefecture), also known in Lu You's time as Gusu. It was a major city on the Grand Canal. We shall encounter it again as the place of origin of some of those Lu meets on his journey and as the place to which the boatmen return to purchase sails. Burton Watson, who translated this passage, thought the sickness was on Lu You's boat; Chang and Smythe don't commit themselves. But Lu's passengers were suffering from nothing worse than heat sickness so I believe the illness must have been in the town.

There are many elegant bridges over the Grand Canal. Isabella Bird, the late-nineteenth-century traveller, found that 'China is a land of surprising bridges . . . we entered nearly every city under a fine arch, from fifteen to thirty feet in height, formed of blocks of granite cut to the curve of the bridge, the roadway attaining the summit by thirty-nine steps on each side. . . . Part of the route is along the Grand Canal, that stupendous work, wonderful even in its dilapidation, which connects Hangchow [Hangzhou] with Tientsin [Tianjin]. This part of it, which connects Imperial Hangchow

Early thirteenth-century bridge in Shaoxing, Lu You's home town.

with the flourishing port of Chinkiang [Zhenjiang] on the Yangtsze, was cut in AD 625, but never mapped till the work was undertaken by our own War Office in 1865.'

Zhang Ji (*fl.*742–80) wrote the quatrain from which comes the line Lu You quotes, one known to most educated Chinese. As he passed the same spot Lu wrote a quatrain which echoes the original while pondering the journey that lies ahead from the Buddhist monastery (*vihara*) by the busy Grand Canal to the remote Ba mountains of Sichuan:

Spending the night at Maple Bridge
It's seven years since I've been to Maple Bridge vihara;
As ever to the traveller's pillow comes the midnight bell.
But even such romantic scenes can't allay my sorrow:
Ba's mountains lie a thousand ranges further on from here.[16]

Day 6/11 (26th July)

At the fifth watch [3–5 a.m.] we set out from Maple Bridge and during the morning passed Waterside Villa, which has a large population, to reach Lookout Pavilion where we had a brief rest. From here on both sides of the canal were lined by long mounds with high embanking, mostly planted with beans and millet in dry fields; or with shrubs and clumps of bamboo. It has a mean, cramped air and bears no comparison with the land east of Maple Bridge. Only as we approached Wuxi [No Tin] county did it became a bit flatter and more open.

Tonight we've moored at the county post-house. Near the city is the tin-bearing Tin Hill; at the end of the Han dynasty a prophecy was recorded that:

> Where there's tin the world's at war,
> No tin and the world is pure.
> For when there's tin the world will spar,
> But no tin and the world's secure.

To this day if tin should come to light people always cover it up again, and no one dares take it.

> Waterside Villa (Hushu) is a place in Jiangsu. Wuxi (No Tin) remains an important town on the Grand Canal near Lake Tai.

Day 6/12 (27th July)

In the morning I paid a courtesy call on Director Yu Zicai [d.1180], whose personal name is Chu. It's said that when Yu comes to bid farewell he is carried in a sedan chair by two fellows, doesn't take a folding chair with him, and personally hands out his visiting cards.

Wu Li, the magistrate and a junior Court Gentleman Consultant called on me.

We travelled through the evening and by the <u>fourth watch</u> of the night [1–3 a.m.] have arrived outside the city walls of Chang prefecture.   *canh' tú '*

> This mention of Director Yu is, I suppose, intended to draw attention to his unaffected manners. Yu, a well-known scholar, was showing respect to those whom he bade farewell by travelling in a light sedan of the simpler sort and not using his folding chair. Chairs were becoming popular by the Song dynasty in preference to sitting on a mat on the ground (a custom which the Japanese retained),

Sedan-chairs, detail from the *Qingmingshanghetu*, Zhang Zeduan (fl.1111–26). Palace Museum, Beijing.

but mats were still common and sitting on a folding chair would have been a statement of superiority when others were on the floor. Director Yu's gesture was underlined by giving out his visiting cards in person. W.E. Geil, an American traveller on the Yangzi, did not get quite such flattering treatment. He described in his book *A Yankee on the Yangtze* of 1904 an interview with the local Viceroy who seemed anxious to be helpful, and 'before we left the wharf a messenger from His Excellency hastened on board and presented me with the Viceroy's card as a final expression of good-will and esteem.'

Day 6/13 (28th July)
In the morning we entered Chang prefecture and moored at the Jing Creek guesthouse.

Tonight the moon makes it seem like day-time, and I've been strolling in the moonlight with my family outside the post-house.

Tao is beginning to get a bit better.

Day 6/14 (29th July)
In the morning I called on Li Anguo, the Prefect and a junior Grand Master for Court Audiences; Jiang Yi, Assistant Prefect and a junior Gentleman for Court Service; and Zhang Jian, Supernumerary Assistant Prefect and a senior Grand Master for Closing Court. Zhang Jian is a son of Zhang Gang [1083–1166], whose posthumous name was Wending. Chen Boda, Instructor and a senior Gentleman-litterateur; Shen Ying, Supernumerary Instructor and a senior Gentleman for Government Participation; and Xu Bohu, Revenue Manager and a junior Gentleman for Government Participation, came to call on me. Chen Boda's courtesy name is Jianshan, Shen Ying's is Zishou. I had not met either of them before, but

A waterway off the Grand Canal at Chang prefecture (Changzhou).

The Grand Canal north of Chang prefecture.

Shen still produced a volume of his recent works. Xu Bohu's courtesy name is Ziwei. He's an old friend of mine from my youth when we were fellow students.

We went to the Temple of the Eastern Sacred Mountain to see the ancient juniper trees which are several hundred years old, and also had a short rest at the Celebrating Victory Monastery to enjoy the cool air. Then the boat cast off and by about 8 p.m. had passed the Ox Stampede Lock. When Shen Huaiming was despatched by Emperor Ming [r.465–72] of the [Liu] Song dynasty to attack Kong Ji [fl.466] he reached Ox Stampede and here it was he built a rampart. The water surges through the lock with a terrific din. Then we got to Lü City lock. From our founding emperor onwards there have been only four places in the empire where military forces have been deployed at locks, Lü City and Jingkou being two of them.

Lu You was already a well-known literary figure and clearly vulnerable to aspiring writers and their unsolicited offerings.

Lu uses the expression, translated above as 'fellow student', 'old friend of the writing-brush and ink-stone'. Ink-stones were and are used to grind the ink-stick with a little water as preparation for writing or painting with a brush.

Shen Huaiming was sent on his expedition by Emperor Ming in 466. The Song dynasty referred to here lasted from 420–79, and is commonly known as the Liu Song after the name of its ruling family. It is not to be

Song dynasty ink-stone, National Palace Museum, Taipei.

Emperor Taizu, founder of the Song dynasty, unknown artist. National Palace Museum, Taipei.

confused with the more illustrious and enduring Song dynasty under which Lu You was living, and whose founding emperor Taizu (r.960–75) he alludes to in the same paragraph. Lu refers to the Liu Song and other short-lived dynasties of the fifth and sixth centuries in the next day's entry.

Jingkou, the mouth of the Jing, is the modern Zhenjiang which lies at the intersection of the Grand Canal with the Yangzi.

Day 6/15 (30th July)

In the morning we passed the Lü City lock, and for the first time saw small carts with a single-shaft. Passing Tumuli Entrance we saw large stone animals, now worn and damaged, which have fallen prone by the wayside. They are from Southern Dynasties mausolea. This is the Tumulus Entrance where Wang Jingze [d.498], having risen in revolt during the reign of Emperor Ming [r.494–8] of the Qi dynasty, wept bitterly as he passed by. A while ago I went to the tumulus of Emperor Wen [r.424–53] of the [Liu] Song dynasty. The roadway was still very broad, and there were stone pillars with bowls on top for gathering dew, with unicorns, griffins and such-like all in place. On the pillars were carved the eight words 'Spirit Way of the Great Ancestor Emperor Wen'. I also went to the tumulus of Emperor Wen [r.550–1] of the Liang dynasty, father of Emperor Wu [r.502–49].[17] This too has a couple of griffins still preserved, one of them entwined in creeper as though it were shackled. But one can no longer make out the tumulus. To the side is a Monastery to the August Enterprise, though this is referred to in the historical record as the Monastery to the August Foundation; I suspect the change was

Six Dynasties griffin (bixie or Ward-off Evil), Luoyang Museum.

made to avoid a Tang dynasty taboo. The two tumuli are situated in Danyang, over ten miles from the county town. A gentleman of the commandery, Jiang Yuanlong, whose courtesy name is Ziyun, told me: 'When Mao Dake was governor someone was selling golden pomegranates and apples. He was arrested on suspicion of having stolen them, and it duly turned out that they'd been obtained by excavating the Liang dynasty tumuli.'

By nightfall we have arrived at Danyang, anciently referred to as Qu'a, or else Yunyang. Xie Lingyun [385–433] has the lines:

> With the dawning sun we set out from Yunyang,
> In the setting sun we reached Zhufang.

They must refer to this place.

Lu You was travelling northwards on the Grand Canal near to the point at which it joins the Yangzi. The area was rich in historical associations from the period of north–south division known as the Northern and Southern Dynasties when a number of minor dynasties followed each other in quick succession. The period began in 420 and was concluded when China was reunified under the Sui dynasty in 589.

Tumulus Entrance (Lingkou) lies to the east of the Grand Canal, Danyang town to the west. Tomb robbing has been common in China as elsewhere from early times.

Xie Lingyun was a leading writer of the early fifth century, a poet of nature and reclusion.

Day 6/16 (31st July)

In the morning we set out from Danyang, drawing water from the Jade Milk Well. The well is in the Monastery of the Goddess of Mercy beside the highway, and its name is listed in the 'Classification of Waters'. The colour of the water resembles cow's milk, and it's so sweet and cold it sets one's teeth on edge. The horizontal tablet by the well was written by Chen Yaosou [961–1017] in Eight Part style in chased jade. In front of the monastery there's also the Light of Lian Pavilion from which you look down over the Lian Lake; a beautiful spot, and very close to the government highway, yet passing travellers seldom go there.

Today I saw *Magnolia pumila* which are just blooming. In the hills at home they finished flowering over a month ago, such is the contrast in climate.

We passed the Flanking Mounds where there are two stone figures standing erect on the top of the mounds. They are popularly known as the Stone Elder and the Stone Matron. Actually they are effigies in front of an ancient mausoleum.

Before the Liang and Chen dynasties [the period 502–87] there was no waterway connecting Jingkou with the Qiantang. It was under Emperor Yang [r.605–17] of the Sui dynasty that a canal was first dug for two hundred and seventy miles with a width of one hundred feet throughout. The flanking mounds, like a line of hills, must be the spoil that was piled up at the time. It's only because of this canal that our court is able to reside at Qiantang. We owe both the Bian canal and this one to the efforts of the Sui, and it is surely Providence that our own Song dynasty has benefited.

We passed New Feng where we rested briefly. Li Bo [701–62] has the lines:

Mounds alongside a waterway off the Grand Canal, presumably created from excavation spoil.

> In southern lands the New Feng wine,
> In eastern hills the little geishas' songs.

And another Tang poet wrote the lines:

> Once more I enter New Feng market,
> And still I smell old wine's bouquet.

They are both referring to this place rather than to the New Feng in Chang'an, though that too had a famous wine as appears in the poetry of Wang Wei [c.699–761]. To this day the residents and the market are pretty flourishing here.

By nightfall we've arrived outside the city walls of Zhenjiang. Today is the first day of autumn.

One of the subjects for the Tang and Song scholar's connoisseurship was the quality of water, whether for drinking or brewing tea. A number of works were produced enumerating and classifying the empire's springs and wells; the 'Classification of Waters' is one of two such lists to be found in a work entitled *Record of Waters for Boiling Tea* by the ninth-century writer Zhang Youxin.[18] Lu You, as we shall see, regarded himself as something of an expert on the subject. The Eight Part style of calligraphy was an intermediate style between Small Seal Script and Clerical Script which tradition has it was invented in the third century BC, but appears actually to have been devised in the first century BC.

The Poet Li Bo, Liang Kai (c.1140–1210), National Museum, Tokyo.

The Liang and Chen dynasties, together covering most of the sixth century, were superseded by the Sui (589–617), who constructed the Grand Canal. This, the lasting achievement of the Sui dynasty, ran north from the Yangzi to the capital of the Northern Song at Kaifeng, a sector known as the Bian Canal; and southwards from the Yangzi to Hangzhou on the Qiantang (by which name the city of Hangzhou was also sometimes known). It is this latter section from the Yangzi to the Qiantang River, in other words the route he had just traversed, to which Lu is referring when he speaks of Jingkou and Qiantang. With the loss of Kaifeng and the rest of north China in 1127 only the southern extension of the Grand Canal to Hangzhou remained under Song control, but it was of huge economic and strategic significance. The fiction was maintained that the Song removal south was a temporary expedient and Lu You is careful to speak of the court residing in Hangzhou rather than the transfer of the capital.

This is our first mention of the Tang dynasty poet Li Bo (sometimes referred to as Li Taibo, Li T'ai-p'o, Li Bai or Li Pai). He and his contemporary Du Fu are regarded as the greatest of Chinese poets; Lu You quotes Li Bo frequently throughout the Diary because he admired him greatly, but also for the more prosaic reason that Li had travelled the Yangzi in the 720s and again in the last years of his life, leaving a number of occasional poems which provided strong associations of place for later generations. The image of inebriated eccentric, which appealed to one aspect of the educated Chinese, is certainly reflected in the bravura, spontaneity and fantasy of much of Li's poetry. Wang Wei was another of the great poets, as well as a painter, of the so-called High Tang period of the mid-eighth century.

We encounter New Feng again on Day 8/9. The little town still exists, though the first character used to write the name has changed. The route of the Grand Canal is more complicated than perhaps its name would suggest; in Lu You's day the main waterway, whose course can still be made out, branched off to Zhenjiang (otherwise known as Jingkou) rather than proceeding directly north to the Yangzi. Lu was therefore taken straight into the south-east of the city rather than arriving on its waterfront with the Yangzi. Normally autumn would begin in the seventh lunar month but this year had an intercalary fifth month inserted so that autumn started in the middle of the sixth lunar month to bring it into line with the solar year and actual turn of the seasons.

Day 6/17 (1st August)

We entered Zhenjiang as it was getting light and the boat was moored at the Western Post-house. I called on Cai Guang (courtesy name Ziping), who is County Magistrate, a junior Grand Master for Closing Court and an Auxiliary in the Imperial Archives; Cheng Min, Campaign Commander with the Qingyuan Army Military Commission; Zhang Wen, Assistant Prefect and a junior Grand Master for Court Audiences; Tao Zhizhen, a junior Gentleman for Court Service; Xiong Ke, Instructor at the prefectural school and a junior Gentleman-litterateur; and Shi Mizheng, whose courtesy name is Duanshu, Administrator in the Overseer-General's department and a junior Gentleman for Attendance.

Zhenjiang stands, as we have seen, near the confluence of the Grand Canal and the Yangzi. Lu You spent the next eleven days in the area calling on fellow officials, visiting famous Buddhist sites and admiring the scenery of the Yangzi on which he was now about to embark. He gives no description of the city itself; it was commercially and strategically important since it commanded the route east and west along the Yangzi, and north and south along the Grand Canal, but had been under threat only nine years before when the Jin launched an attack south (Day 6/25). By the time of Lu's visit it was prosperous once more. This contrasts with the scene nearly seven hundred years later when the Royal Naval officer Captain Thomas Blakiston (1832–91) visited in February 1861 after the Taiping rebels had been repelled and Qing imperial forces were once more in control: 'But what a scene was below us! – Chin-kiang [Zhenjiang] in ruins. Within the large extent of city wall, or among the heap of débris which marked the site of a once populous suburb, hardly a roof was to be seen. A pheasant rose at our feet, out of a ditch which had formed part of one of the numerous entrenched camps used in the successive sieges, the remains of which may be seen crowning the top of every rising ground around the place; and as we descended to get a nearer view of this desolation, we disturbed a hare and some quail, where human life ought to have been buzzing in jostling crowds. Passing a fine triumphal arch, erected no doubt to some benefactor of his species, but now partly destroyed, we walked for near a mile through the ruined suburb before we reached one of the city gates. The Imperialists at this time held the place, and the presence of our ships of war in the river gained us ready admission. The only difference between the inside and outside of the walls was, that, while the latter was deserted, and had the appearance of a number of Irish villages after the famine clustered together, the former, although in ruins, was inhabited in part by refugees. Reed huts and brick hovels held these starving wretches; everywhere filth abounded, and I had never seen anything so horrible and revolting. After vainly endeavouring to purchase some fowls or a sheep, we

Captain Thomas Blakiston.

left the city by a gate nearer the water, where a party of half-starved soldiers with gaudy banners were on guard, and made our way to our respective vessels. That night, I fancy, with each and everyone of the party the subject uppermost in his thoughts was the scene I have given a faint idea of: it was so in mine.' But thirty years later again Zhenjiang was bustling, as Isabella Bird found, with a fine bund, prosperous-looking foreign houses, well-kept Concession roads policed by Sikhs, the hum of business, throngs of traffic and the Grand Canal choked with junks. There was a British consulate, Chinese-made machinery was in use, and the Germans had started a factory to get albumen from duck eggs for photographic purposes, the yolks being packed for use in confectionary and bar-rooms (she adds in respect of the last, with an evident sniff of disapproval, that 'My informant, Consul Carles, is silent on the use to which they are then applied, but doubtless it is well known to frequenters of such establishments').

Day 6/18 (2nd August)

I was called on by Ge Xun, a junior Court Gentleman Consultant and Notary of the Administrative Assistant to the Military Commissioner; Xu Wuzi, Surveillance Circuit Judge and a junior Gentleman-litterateur; Yang Chong, Adjutant Revenue Manager and a senior Gentleman for Meritorious Achievement; the Venerable Dinghuan of Jiao's Hill Monastery; and the Venerable Huazhao of Ambrosia Monastery.

> Much of the riverside in this area is low-lying, but there are three significant rocky obtrusions beside the River at Zhenjiang; going down-river these were Golden Mount, Mount Beigu and Jiao's Hill, each of which had its complex of Buddhist monasteries. Beigu, which was crowned by Ambrosia Monastery, also had historical associations with the Three Kingdoms period (220–65).

Day 6/19 (3rd August)

The Venerable Baoyin [1109–90] of Golden Mount came to call on me. His courtesy name is Tanshu and he comes from Jia prefecture. He says there are innumerable rapids west of Xia prefecture. This is what Bai Juyi [772–846] meant in his lines:

> From White Dog as far as Yellow Ox,
> The rapids come as often as the notches on bamboo.

I attended Governor Cai's luncheon at the Danyang Building. It was extremely hot, and though there were piles of ice by every seat there wasn't a hint of coolness. Cai personally brewed the tea, at which he is quite skilled, but it was of exceptionally poor quality. Instructor Xiong, who was a fellow guest and comes from Concordia,[19] said: 'The tea from Concordia used to be mixed with rice flour. Then they changed to using taro, and over the past two years they've changed again to using the shoots of the paper mulberry. These blend well with the flavour of the tea and make it very milky, though after the rainy season it will no longer have much zest. Unless you're a connoisseur it's not easy to detect them.'

After 5 p.m. the boat was moved through the three locks, up as far as the Tidal Lock.

Jia prefecture, the modern Leshan, is in Sichuan in the far west of the area then controlled by the Song. It is famous for its giant Buddha carved in the rock face above the river. Coming from the west the Venerable Baoyin would have been familiar with the route Lu You was about to travel, and the perils of the gorges and rapids, of which White Dog and Yellow Ox were two. Baoyin was an erudite layman who tired of the mundane world, was ordained and made a profound study of Buddhist teaching, presiding in the course of his career over a number of widely dispersed monasteries of which Golden Mount was one. Ten years after this meeting with Lu You he was summoned to an audience with the emperor, a mark of high honour for a monk. On his death in 1190 Lu wrote Baoyin's epitaph.

Tea drinking was widespread in the Song dynasty, its principal areas of production being Sichuan and Fujian provinces, respectively in the west and the east. Tea leaves were boiled rather than infused, and

A distant view of Jiao's Hill from Ambrosia Monastery.

Southern Song porcelain pot

clearly the styles of tea could be very different from modern usage.

Bai Juyi (sometimes written Po Chü-i as in Arthur Waley's biography of him) was and is one of the most widely known of poets of the Tang dynasty, admired for the simplicity of his language, his popular themes, and for his friendship with his fellow poet, Yuan Zhen (779–831). In his political career he incurred imperial displeasure with his outspoken remonstrances (always a good mark in the eyes of later Confucian critics) and was banished from the capital in 815. He later rose to be governor of Hangzhou, a provincial city in Bai's time though the capital of the Southern Song through which Lu You had passed on his journey (Day 5/20 and following); and of Suzhou, but retired to the city of Luoyang (in his time a subsidiary capital) where he created a garden and in his last years turned to Buddhism. We shall meet him once more on Day 8/8 when Lu visits the site of his Thatched Hall. Yuan Zhen edited Bai's poems in 825 and Bo himself added to the collection thereafter and went to some trouble to ensure its preservation, though as we shall see Lu You notes that the authenticated version of the *Collected Works* had only narrowly survived.

Day 6/20 (4th August)

We have transferred to a boat belonging to Wang Zhiyi of Jia prefecture. There is a light rain, and it's very cool.

This marks Lu's transition from a canal boat to one suited to the Yangzi, or Great River, or simply the River.

Day 6/21 (5th August)

No entry.

Day 6/22 (6th August)

There was an official reception in the rear garden of the Duke of Wei Hall. The only addition to its previous state is the Steeped-in-Scent Pavilion. Half-way through the party we went up to the Monastery of Universal Radiance at Longevity Hillock to finish the banquet. Longevity Hillock was the residence of Emperor Gaozu [r.420–2] of the [Liu] Song dynasty, and one of its ancient wells still exists. The monastery was originally called Extending Blessings but in the Longxing period [1163–4], when we recovered Si prefecture, a monk from the Monastery of Universal Radiance there presented an image of Sengjia [628–710] when he came over to us. He took up lodging here, and in consequence it was granted the name Universal Radiance and became the place to which the Sengjia chapel was relocated.

Towards the east the Jing Hills run round in an unbroken line as a continuous wall, with official buildings, monasteries, edifices and abbeys on them like a painting. And to the west one gazes out at the Great River, most grand and imposing in aspect.

The Duke of Wei Hall was called after Li Jing (571–649) who had been ennobled with this title. He was one of the generals who helped to found the Tang dynasty.

Bodhisattva in painted and gilded wood, Song dynasty.

The Buddhist monk Sengjia came from Central Asia to the Chinese capital at Chang'an during the reign of Emperor Gaozong of the Tang (r.650–83), and travelled in the Yangzi region where he performed wondrous deeds. He built a monastery in Si prefecture (just north of the Huai River and therefore in Lu You's day an area contested between Song and Jin) for which the emperor wrote the name placard, and was summoned to court to be questioned about Buddhist Law in 708. After his death he was reputed to have been an incarnation of the bodhisattva Avolokiteśvara (Guanyin in Chinese, by this time a thoroughly feminized image in Chinese iconography). From Lu's comment it appears that some Buddhist monks who remained loyal to the Song dynasty took opportunities to move away from the area controlled by the Jin invaders, bringing images and relics with them such as this one of Sengjia from the monastery in which he had lived.

Day 6/23 (7th August)

We reached the Ambrosia Monastery and made a contribution for the feeding of the monks. Ambrosia is on Mount Beigu. The 'Goat Stone' here is held by tradition to have been sat upon by Emperor Zhaolie [r.221–3] of the Han dynasty and the Great Emperor of the Wu [r. 229–52] as they conspired together against Cao Cao. This stone has long since been lost, but the monks of the monastery always fetch another to replace it, and while their visitors are stroking the stone and heaving deep sighs the monks and their young servitors are often sniggering to themselves.

I paid my obeisances at the shrine to Li Deyu [787–849] and climbed the Panorama Building. The building is not on its old site, but was built by the abbot, Huazhao. It looks down over the Great River and I could make out the plants and trees in Huainan. The views from this mirador are actually much better than those of the former building.

I bumped into Xu Rong, a senior Gentleman for Meritorious Achievement and newly appointed Instructor for Grand Tranquillity prefecture. Xu's courtesy name is Zigong and he comes from Quan prefecture.

These mountains have many sheer cliffs, as though they had been cleft, yet they are all made of soil. The *National History* takes them for rock faces, but is mistaken.

Iron Pagoda at Ambrosia Monastery. The two storeys shown here were cast in 1078.

Ambrosia is the Sweet Dew, or amṛta in Sanskrit, which a Buddha or bodhisattva bestowed. The monastery of this name, which was said in the Song dynasty to have five hundred monks, was probably founded in the sixth century and transferred to the top of Mount Beigu by Li Deyu in 825–6 when he built a pagoda there. Li was a leading statesman in the early ninth century, becoming Grand Councillor in 833. His connection with the area Lu You was now visiting stemmed from his time as prefect. Unfortunately Lu tells us nothing of the iron pagoda which had been cast in 1078 to replace Li Deyu's earlier brick one which had collapsed.

To feed Buddhist monks was to perform an act of grace.

Towards the end of the Han dynasty, whose formal fall occurred in 220, China had split into three centres of power which jostled for supremacy, the battles and shifting alliances of the heroic contenders being the stuff of later romances. Emperor Zhaolie is better known as Liu Bei (he only styled himself emperor from 221); his power lay in what is now the westerly province of Sichuan. The Great Emperor, Sun Quan, controlled the middle and lower Yangzi estuary and the territory southwards. They met to co-ordinate their plans for defeating Cao Cao who held north China, and tradition had it that they sat together on the Goat Stone. The stone's history continued to be tortuous and the present stone dates from 1890. Cao subsequently launched an invasion across the Yangzi in 208 in which his much larger force was defeated by his enemies' fire-ships at the battle of Red Cliff. The site of this battle is uncertain, as Lu himself comments on Day 8/19.

The late nineteenth-century Goat Stone.

Huazhao, it will be recalled, had come to see Lu You on Day 6/18. Lu credits him with the rebuilding of the Panorama Building which lay within Ambrosia Monastery, but this does not seem to accord with other records which suggest that the prefect Chen Tianlin rebuilt it in 1170, the very year of Lu You's visit. Perhaps the prefect instigated the reconstruction and the abbot oversaw the work.[20]

Numerous poems were written about panoramic views and the divided state of China, and in Lu You's time the view from this tower inspired sad thoughts of the wish to recover lost lands. But Lu seems to have been in cheerful mood during his visit with his amused observation of the way in which the monks mocked their tourists' gullibility. At any rate he did not take the opportunity for maudlin reflections on the view north towards the Huai river frontier either in his diary or the poems he wrote on the journey.

It may be surprising to read in the final paragraph of this entry of mountains with sheer cliffs, for Lu You was still in the lower reaches of the Yangzi. But as Blakiston found when conducting his exploratory survey of 1861 the topography is varied even in the lower reaches: 'Why China should ever have been called a "vast plain" or "enormous fertile valley" is to me inexplicable. More variation of surface perhaps does not occur in any country; and where we should be most inclined to look for such features, namely, on its great artery, there it is diversified enough to please the most exacting of tourists. Commencing at the mouth of the Yang-tsze Kiang, there is naturally a considerable extent of flat alluvial land, the delta of the river, where once no doubt the ocean held its sway;

The Yangzi, whose main channel is faint in the distance, from the modern Panorama Tower.

but soon we come to hills and high lands, and at Chin-kiang [Zhenjiang] one is delighted with the steep and rugged cliffs. About Nanking [Nanjing] the country is prettily broken into ridges and hills, and, before reaching far above this, mountains shut in the river on either hand. In fact, I think the scenery between Wu-hoo and An-king (usually spelt Ngan-king) equal to that of almost any part of the river. It is, of course, not such bold and near scenery as is found on the upper waters; but the fine ranges of mountains, well removed from the river, whose broad expanse is now broken by low islands, and now widens into lake-like form; the beautiful, partially wooded slopes of the mountains reaching down into the highly cultivated lower land; the occasional village; the collection of reed huts gathered on the immediate bank, as if in doubt whether the ground were as safe as the water; the distant pagoda, marking the site of a town approachable only by some narrow canal-like creek; and then, life made apparent by numerous boats with their white cotton wings; the fisherman attending his ingenious dip-net; some coolies trotting along an embankment which raises them above their fellows who are working away in the irrigated paddy-fields below, while two of a more favoured class are being wheeled along a paved pathway in those best of wheelbarrows; – the objects serve to remind one – the country, of the lake scenery of the Old World, – the river, of the New; but the people, of China, and China only.'

A number of nineteenth-century British travellers noted that the hills which I have tentatively translated as made of soil were of 'conglomerate'; my own observation is that Jiao's Hill and Golden Mount are indeed composed largely of earth, but that Mount Beigu is volcanic in origin with a sheer rock face towards the River. The *National History* in which they received notice was an official work in progress which gathered materials which could later be drawn on in the more elaborated Dynastic Histories. Lu You seems to have used this *National History*, together with local gazetteers, as his guidebooks for the journey.

Day 6/24 (8th August)
No entry.

Day 6/25 (9th August)
In the morning I paid my respects with a sacrificial pig and a flagon of wine at the shrine of the Heroic and Numinous Prince who Aids Favourable Outcomes. This is the so-called Downstream Water Palace of the River God. The shrine belongs to the Golden Mount Monastery and is usually tended by two monks without any other officiant. Yet the notice-board states 'Offerings of Pig's Heads belong to this Temple by Order'. Everyone who sees this smiles.

Previously, at the end of the Shaoxing period [1161], when Wanyan Liang [1122–61, r.1149–61] invaded and ravaged the area, Mr Ye Yiwen [1098–1170] of the Bureau of Military Affairs, who was Inspector-General of the Army, was defending the River. He offered prayers at the shrine of the Water Palace Monastery, pleading that if peace were restored he would petition that the god be promoted to the rank of emperor. But nothing came of this. In the Longxing period [1163–4], when the enemy invaded again, a close imperial adviser raised the matter once more, but the experts argued that the Four Watercourses were only enfeoffed as princes and that the Water Palace shouldn't be superior to the Four Watercourses, so it was merely given a fancy appellation.

In the temple I met a military man, Wang Xiu. He told me he comes from Bo prefecture and is aged fifty-one. At the time that Wanyan Liang was ravaging the border he joined the irregular forces north of the Yellow River, attacked and took Daming, and awaited the arrival of our imperial armies. But following his return he had received no citation, and says he's without influence and has no way of making his case known. He sobbed and sighed without cease.

This evening I'd wanted to go out onto the River but the boatmen declined to do so on the grounds that the tides were wrong; so we are spending the night at the entrance to the River.

The offering of food at temples was commonplace, and as we shall see in the course of our journey pigs and other animals were presented by Lu You and the boatmen in particular abundance as the dangers of the River increased with the approach of the Yangzi Gorges. A pig's head was no doubt an acceptable delicacy for the temple officiants. The joke was that Buddhist monks were supposed to devote themslevs to lives of purity, eschewing the material world. Instead the Golden Mount Monastery had taken over the shrine of another cult together with its offerings, offerings of meat moreover from which monks were supposed to abstain, and announced the fact publicly.

Lu's contemporary Hong Mai (1123–1202), in his collection of anecdotes *Tolerant Study Notebooks*,[21] tells the story of two merchants who go to a temple. One is going overland and wants clear skies, the other is travelling by water and wants rain. The first promises to offer a pig's head to the deity if his wishes are granted, the other a sheep's head. The god cynically remarks to an underling: 'What's to stop us eating pig's head when it's clear and sheep's head when it rains?' The Downstream Water Palace of the River God was matched by an Upstream Water Palace which Lu passes on Day 7/28 though he, or the text we have of the Diary, mistakenly refers to this also as the Downstream Palace.

Following the loss of north China to the Jurchen Jin dynasty there had been sporadic fighting throughout the 1130s. The Song established their new capital at Hangzhou in 1138 and in late 1141 signed a humiliating peace treaty with Jin which required the payment of tribute by the Song. The border was established between the two territories along the Huai River which runs roughly parallel with the Yangzi and one to two hundred miles to the north. Peace was maintained between the two states through the 1150s, but in 1161 Prince Hailing of the Jin (who reigned as emperor), or Wanyan Liang as Lu calls him without dignifying him with a title, invaded with a large army in order to complete the Jurchen conquest of the south of China. After initial success Hailing was defeated in 1161 and murdered by his own officers; the Jin invasion was repulsed by 1162. Emperor Gaozong, who as a young prince had effectively seized the throne and ensured the continuation of the Song when it appeared that the Jin would press forward into south China, now abdicated in favour of his adopted son who became Emperor Xiaozong (r.1162–89). The new emperor initially took a more aggressive posture than his father, abrogated the treaty with Jin and launched an attack to regain the lost territories in the north. This ended with Jin victory at the Battle of Fuli in 1163 and the renewal of the peace treaty, albeit on milder terms than previously.

The fighting of the early 1160s had been accompanied by uprisings in the area of Jin control as groups of guerrillas loyal to the Song tried to exploit the situation. The Southern Song poet and soldier Xin Qiji, for instance, was a northerner who raised his own forces in Shandong province and when it was clear that the Song was incapable of regaining north China was obliged to make his way south into friendly territory. Wang Xiu, mentioned here by Lu You but otherwise unknown to history, was another of those who had made trouble behind enemy lines, in his case in the vicinity of the modern Beijing; but no liberating armies came and he managed somehow to get south again. (His fifty-one

Soldier as a Heavenly Guardian at the tomb of Emperor Renzong (d.1063).

sui would equate to an age of about fifty in Western terms since the Chinese traditionally counted their age by the number of calendar years in which one had lived, rather than by the anniversary of one's birthday). Lu's sympathy for Wang, and the implied criticism of the Song authorities, is unspoken.

The military trial of strength with the Jin had political implications at the Song court. The principal issue facing the Southern Song was how to deal with their Jurchen neighbours: appeasement or revanchism. The fortunes of the opposing groups were subject to frequent change; national defence policy was bitterly contended, and the success of the Jin in penetrating to the Yangzi showed that the danger of a collapse of the Song state in the face of enemy attack was real. Ye Yiwen was a distinguished censor who firmly opposed the 'peace party' of Qin Gui, though when Ye was appointed to a military command in 1160 he made a mess of it and was quickly moved to another post. Lu You, as we have had occasion to note, was firmly in the revanchist camp and his career as an official reflects the ups and downs of the larger political picture. As poet and prose writer he was and is known for his 'patriotic' stand, and throughout this diary of his journey to Sichuan there is an undercurrent of sympathy with those who espoused a robust policy towards the Jin. Though he was being sent off to a minor post in the west it turned out that in fact the years he spent in Sichuan from 1170–8 were to be the most exciting of his official life, engaging with the military in northern Sichuan near the border with Jin.

Day 6/26 (10th August)

At the fifth watch [3–5 a.m.] our boat set forth. Today is the first time the boatmen have sounded the drums. We then visited Golden Mount and I climbed to Jade Looking Glass Hall and Wondrous High Terrace, both of which are utterly magnificent, and far better than they once were. 'Jade Looking Glass' is taken from a poem by Su Shen [c.996–1043]:

> Monks are seated in jade looking glass' rays,
> A traveller is trudging up golden turtles' backs.

Su Shen did indeed end up as a member of the Hanlin Academy, and at the time this poem was considered prophetic.

The newly constructed gateway of the monastery is also very majestic, and has a horizontal tablet in Seal Script calligraphy by Zhai Qinian, whose courtesy name is Boshou. But one isn't allowed to moor boats at the gateway; all those who arrive at the monastery come through the Condescension Gallery. The Venerable Baoyin says that the old horizontal tablet was in the Flying White imperial calligraphy of Emperor Renzong, but when it was displayed wind-tossed waves would swirl about with dragons and alligators plunging in and out. In consequence it was stored in the monastery's gallery, though it now no longer exists. Baoyin has lived on this hill for nearly ten years and the construction work has all been due to his efforts. The monastery has two pagodas. Originally Grand Councillor Zeng Bu [1036–1107] had built them out of his salary from the Bureau of Military Affairs so that offerings could be made to his forefathers. Then in the Zhenghe period [1111–17] the monastery became the Sacred Empyrean Priory and the Daoist priests removed the nine wheeled insignia on the top of the

Dragon, one of a pair of hanging scrolls, Muxi, early thirteenth century. Cleveland Museum of Art.

pagoda and turned it into living quarters, calling it the Terrace of the Uttara Empyrean. Only now, over fifty years later, has Baoyin made it a pagoda again, and what's more is adding to its embellishments. The work is not yet completed.

On the highest summit of the hill is Swallow the Sea Terrace, derived from the idea that its atmosphere is swallowing a vast sea. I climbed up and gazed at the exceptional views. Whenever envoys from the north come on diplomatic missions it is usual to invite them to this pavilion and serve them tea.

Golden Mount and Jiao's Hill face each other; both are famous Buddhist Sangharama and are always competing for pre-eminence. Jiao's Hill of old possessed an Imbibe the River Pavilion, which is a most lovely place. So this one was named Swallow the Sea to go one better. How comic!

Tonight the wind-blown waters are buffeting the boat with a thud.

The Hanlin Academy, the most prestigious of the learned bodies that assisted the emperor, had audiences in a hall the steps to which were decorated with turtles, and hence appointment to the Academy was known as 'mounting the turtles'. Su Shen's future distinction was seen to have been foreshadowed by the lines in this poem of his that Lu You quotes. The monks in the parallel couplet were, of course, caught in the light of the water with its jade-like surface. Since Lu's time there has been much silting of the River in front of Golden Mount and it is now no longer an island.

In Flying White calligraphy the hairs of the brush separate so that the strokes are no longer solid black, but contain streaks of untouched ground. The effect is of speed and lightness; Baoyin's description is a tribute to the energy and exhilaration of the Emperor Renzong's calligraphy.

Zeng Bu and his elder brother the poet, prose stylist, historian and admired public official Zeng Gong both took the Jinshi examination in 1057; their examiners were the outstanding literary men of the period, Ouyang Xiu and Mei Yaochen. Zeng Bu was at first a firm exponent of reformist policies and a confidante of their architect Wang Anshi, though he later criticized aspects of the

View from Golden Mount towards the distant Yangzi. Much silting has occurred in past centuries. The suspension bridge to Melon Island is just visible in the background.

reform programme and was dismissed to provincial posts where he remained while the conservatives repealed the New Policies. But Emperor Zhezong, who had been on the throne since 1085, took charge of government in 1093 after a regency and restored the reformists to favour. Zeng returned to hold senior posts, and on the death of Zhezong in 1100 further strengthened his position by backing the successful candidate amongst the imperial brothers (Zhezong had no surviving sons) who became Huizong, the artistic but politically inept emperor whose reign led to the fall of the Northern Song. Zeng Bu's career prospered in the early years of the twelfth century as he once more promoted reformist policies repealed under the Regency, but he fell out with Prime Minister Cai Jing (who it may be recalled later lost favour and was criticized for his father's lavish funeral) and was once more in the wilderness. Zeng died in Zhenjiang, the point Lu You had now reached on his journey.

As we have seen above (Day 6/4) it was not uncommon for religious complexes to change hands between Daoists and Buddhists at this period. A Sangharama is a Buddhist monastery, or the park of a monastery.

The diplomatic missions from the north refer to embassies from the Jin. Similar missions went in the other direction; for instance Fan Chengda's to Jin mentioned on Day 6/28.

Wheeled insignia on the roof of the Buddhist Yonghe Gong in Beijing, eighteenth century.

Day 6/27 (11th August)

We've stayed on at Golden Mount. It's very chilly. The Venerable Baoyin tells me that the egrets from Mount Liang Military Prefecture in Sichuan are the foremost in the world.

Day 6/28 (12th August)

I rose early and watched the sun emerging from out of the River, sky and water both crimson, a truly magnificent sight. Then we climbed up to the Condescension Gallery to view the two islands. The one on the left is called Falcon Hill and there's an old tradition that falcons nested there, though there are none now. The one on the right is called Cloud-base Island. Both rise up on their own and aren't joined to other hills. They are popularly said to be Guo Pu's [276–324] tomb.

Fan Zhineng [1126–93], Ambassador to Jin and Imperial Diarist, has arrived at the Mount[22] and sent a servant to invite me to a meal at Jade Looking Glass Hall. Zhineng's personal name is Chengda. We were colleagues in the imperial government but have been apart for eight years. Now he tells me that, as an Acting Grand Academician of the Hall for Aid in Governance, State Supervisor of the Longevity Monastery and Reader-in-Waiting, he has been made Supplication and Solicitation Envoy to the state of Jin.

Around noon we were passing Melon Island. The River was smooth as a looking glass, and from the boat I was watching the buildings and towers on Golden Mount rising one upon another. It was exceptionally pretty. But in mid-stream a great wind rose, thunder rolled and lightening flashed, striking the surface of the River just ten feet or so from the boat. The hawsers were urgently attached, but presently the skies cleared and we then got to Melon Island.

Since we reached Jingkou we've had no mosquitoes, but tonight there are lots and we've put up our mosquito nets again.

Guo Pu was a diviner, naturalist, alchemist, commentator and lexicographer. We shall encounter him again later in Lu's journey.

Fan Chengda, whom Lu refers to here by his courtesy name of Zhineng, was, together with Yang Wanli (1127–1206) and Lu You himself, one of the leading poets of the twelfth century. Fan wrote in many modes including patriotic anti-Jin pieces, but he is best known for his bucolic poetry, descriptions of peasant life in all its diversity of season and occupation. This achieves its effect because the poet's own personality is largely suppressed, and critics have drawn attention to the influence of Zen Buddhist concepts of sudden enlightenment and the employment of 'shock techniques' in the work of Fan (and Yang). But Fan Chengda was also a successful official who rose to higher posts in the government hierarchy than Lu You ever achieved, including the embassy mentioned here whose purpose was to renegotiate humiliating protocol conditions imposed on the Song in earlier treaties (for instance, the Song emperor was not happy that he was required to stand up to receive personally formal state documents from Jin envoys) and to discuss the return of the area in which stood the imperial mausolea of the Northern Song.[23] Fan's mission was unsuccessful. He also wrote a gazetteer of his home town of Suzhou and, like Lu, travel journals. His embassy to the Jin court, which took him through the enemy territory of north China, was one such journey he recorded in diary form. Fan had started out on 30th July; his diary does not record this meeting with

Lu You. But his diary of 1177 when he came down-river from Sichuan provides some parallels with Lu's journey up-river.

There were various means of propulsion for boats. In shallow waters poles could be employed; out on large rivers or deep lakes when the weather was reliable masts were raised and sails hoisted; often boats went along the banks of rivers where they could be hauled on ropes, sometimes huge hawsers several hundred feet long, by gangs of men known to the Victorians as trackers. This was effectively the only safe means of locomotion against the stream in the Yangzi gorges. In tight spots it might be necessary to put the rope aboard a smaller boat which was used as a tug. Sometimes the boatmen were reduced to hauling themselves along with grappling irons. Rowing was possible in stretches; the Chinese rowed standing up and facing forwards. They had also invented an 'oscillating oar' extending over the stern like a sternsweep which enabled boats to manoeuvre in tight spaces. It was even possible to drift with the current, for instance

TOP: Sternsweep in action, detail from the *Qingmingshanghetu*, Zhang Zeduan (fl.1111–26). Palace Museum, Beijing.
ABOVE: Trackers in the 1930s.

where large rafts of timber were being transported. The Song had in addition developed the paddle boat; these had been used to engage the Jurchen enemy in 1130 in a battle on Lake Dongting, though Lu You makes no mention of it.

Day 6/29 (13th August)

We moored at Melon Island. The weather was clear and crisp, and looking south to Jingkou the Lunar Tower, Ambrosia Monastery and the Temple of the Water Palace all appeared very close by. Golden Mount was so near I could make out the features on people's faces. But you can't go directly across the River here; you can only get across if you set out by boat a little further to the west, which is why all those who cross take such a long time to get back again.

Because our sails were worn out the boatmen had been in Gusu buying some more, and have just arrived back here today. (Our mast is fifty-eight feet high and the sail of twenty-six sections).[24] Over these two days I've been observing the people who have been crossing back and forth, and there were a good thousand. The great majority were soldiers.

Tonight we watched the lamps in the pagodas on Golden Mount.

Melon Island was not, or at any rate is not now, an island but an area of the Yangzi's northern shore just up-river from Zhenjiang. A fine modern suspension bridge has simplified the crossing of the Yangzi at this point. Lu You was now looking back south-eastwards to Golden Mount and the other places he had just left.

Gusu is the modern Suzhou, by which Lu You had passed on Day 6/10 though they had not entered because of illness.

Zhen prefecture, the forlorn modern Yizheng City, which the prosperity of modern China has as yet passed by.

Day 7/1 (14th August)

At first light we left Melon Island and, with wind set fair, hoisted the sail. By evening we had reached Zhen prefecture where we moored at Scour the Distance Pavilion. The prefecture was originally, under the Tang dynasty, White Sands market town in Yangzi county of Yang prefecture. But during the period that Yang Pu [r.920–37] possessed Huainan Xu Wen came from Jinling to have an audience with Yang at White Sands, and so the name was changed to Receiving the Imperial Carriage market town. Some people think that when Emperor Shizong [r.955–9] of the Zhou dynasty was campaigning in this Huai area his generals all received him and paid their respects here, but this is not so. In the Qiande period [963–8] of our own dynasty it was promoted to become the Jian'an Military Prefecture; and in the Dazhongxiangfu period [1008–17] the Priory of Jade-like Purity and Luminous Response was established, and a foundry sited on the little hill to the north-west of the Military Prefecture. Here statues of the four sage imperial personages, the Jade Emperor, the Sage Ancestor, Taizu [r.960–76] and Taizong [r.976–97] were cast. When they were completed Ding Wei [966–1037] was sent as Receiving Officer, with Li Zonge [964–1012] as his deputy. On reaching the capital the Imperial Carriage came out to receive them, a general amnesty was proclaimed, and it was established as a Military Prefecture under the name Zhen prefecture. On the site of the former foundry the Yizhen Abbey was built. In the Zhenghe period [1111–18], when the Illustrated Gazetteer of the Nine Provinces was composed, the town was even referred to as Yizhen Commandery.

Formerly, because it lay at a crossroads by water and land, it served as the seat of the Supply Commissioner, but this has now been discontinued.

Animals along the Spirit Way at the tomb of Emperor Taizu (d.976).

In addition to his imaginative writing Lu You was also a historian; he was in particular expert in the brief period of division between the end of the Tang dynasty in 907 and the start of the dynasty under which he lived, the Song, in 960. This half century is known as the Five Dynasties and Ten Kingdoms, an appellation which sufficiently conveys the brevity, insecurity and complexity of the political institutions of this period. Lu's historical references in the Diary, though wide-ranging, are weighted towards the Five Dynasties and early Song eras. It was Taizu, then plain General Zhao Kuangyin, who brought the period to an end when in 960 he seized the throne of the Later Zhou dynasty that he was supposed to be serving and founded the Song; Taizong his brother who succeeded him. The Jade Emperor was the Emperor of Heaven; the Sage Ancestor the ancestor of the reigning dynasty who by conventional courtesy was retrospectively and posthumously raised to imperial rank.

Jinling was another name for Nanjing, a major city on the Yangzi which has served as capital of China in several periods of history, and most recently up to 1949.

Day 7/2 (15th August)

I called on Wang Cha, the Prefect and a junior Gentleman for Court Service. The market-town and its official buildings are in a much more prosperous state than they were a few years ago.

I took Tong to visit the Eastern Park which lies about half a mile outside the east gate. Following the war damage of the Jianyan period [1127–30] it fell into utter neglect and ruin. The Fiscal Commission let it to commoners and it brought in an income of several thousand pounds a year. This place, whose former grandeur and beauty had reverted to a wilderness of brambles and weeds for over forty years, is at last being restored as a park. But an examination of the records suggests that only the Pure Brew Hall, Brush Against Clouds Pavilion and Sifted Void Gallery have been restored roughly to their former state; and the Clear Pool to the right and the High Terrace to the north are still in existence. But as for the reference to 'flowing water which runs across in the foreground', this has silted up into a mere trickle. And of the

Dream Journey over XiaoXiang (detail), handscroll, ink on paper, c.1170 Li of Shucheng, illustrating the Chinese conception of 'level distance'. National Museum, Tokyo.

fourteen-acre park, more than half is still abandoned to vegetable patches which really does seem a pity. We climbed up to the terrace and gazed towards the mountains of Xiashu which merge delightfully into the level distance, and lingered for a long while.

We visited the Monastery of Recompensing Kindness and Glorifying Filial Piety, where we stopped briefly. In the troubles of 1161 Yizhen was burned to the ground and this monastery alone survived. There are a hundred monks in the community. The Venerable Miaotuan is from Chang prefecture.

Lu You was on the north bank of the Yangzi, gazing across the river to the Xiashu mountains on the other side. Level distance (*pingyuan*) is a term of art bearing on perspective in Chinese painting. It was defined by the Northern Song monumental landscape artist Guo Xi (*c*.1020–90) as follows: 'to look up at the top of a mountain from its base, with pale mountains in the background, is called "high distance"; to see from the front of a mountain through to its rear is called "deep distance"; to see from the side of a mountain across to low-lying mountains is called "level distance".[25] 'Level distance' produces an effect of hazy recession. As Valerie Malenfer Ortiz remarks, '"level distance" traditionally reminded the viewer of autumn, of the late hours of the day, and, by association, of the melancholic feeling due to time that passes.' It has thus been interpreted as an allusion to exile. And Alfreda Murck describes the type of level distance landscape as the representation of 'the Confucian aesthetic of equilibrium-harmony. It suggests a visual sensation of restfulness in the boundless expanse of space in which man will be able to find peace with himself and the universe, as against the Taoist [Daoist] penchant for the romance and drama of height.'

The troubles of 1161 refers to the Jin general Prince Hailing's invasion of that year (see under Day 6/25).

Day 7/3 (16th August)

Wenren Yaomin, a junior Gentleman for Meritorious Achievement and Supervisor of Taxes, came to call on me. He is the son of Reviser Wenren Maode's elder brother and entered government on a 'preferential degree'. The Venerable Yunchang of the Yongqing Monastery on North Mount called on me.

There was an official reception at the Equable Hall and I went all over the Limpid Waves Gallery and Such Delight Pavilion, and then came back via Grand Spectacle. Grand Spectacle used to possess a piece of rhyme-prose by Mi Fei [1051–1107] inscribed on stone, but this is now lost.

I had previously asked Governor Wang how far the Yizhen Abbey is from the city walls, and he had told me it was about a third of a mile or so to the south. At the time I'd been surprised that this differed from the statement in the *National History*, so having got back here I rushed off to it and found it really is south of the city walls. An old Daoist priest aged over seventy came out to greet me, and said that he was a native of Lu prefecture and that he was able to relate the whole history of Yizhen. The old monastery had indeed been at the foot of a little earthen hill a few miles north-west of the city walls. The gilt-bronze statues that were cast in the Dazhongxiangfu period [1008–17] had been thirty feet high including their pedestals, and they were received into the capital with yellow streamers and the complete paraphernalia of Daoist banners and insignia, all of which accords with the *National History*. So a song of the time went:

> Metal moulded into a likeness to express our solemn reverence;
> Edifices take the shape of avian flight.
> Myriad, the numinous spirits shielding, auspicious vapours wafting;
> Midst the willows on the dykes gleam our yellow streamers.

The Daoist priest also said that the abbey had been granted the title 'Auspicious Response to a Blessed Place', which is not recorded in the histories. The place that is nowadays referred to as the Yizhen Abbey is simply a Daoist cloister where the 'yellow cowls' used to stay when they went into town.

This evening there are strong winds, and the boatmen have increased the number of hawsers.

In the Song dynasty degrees could be awarded, on the recommendation of family members who were officials, outside the normal system to candidates who had taken only the lower levels of examination. Wenren Maode was mentioned on Day 6/5.

Mi Fei was both poet and calligrapher, as well as connoisseur, but is best known as a painter. He was one of a group of eleventh-century artists who introduced a style of painting which consciously distinguished itself from the artisanal tradition, using dots and ink washes which eschewed fine detail for impressionist effects. This marked a profound, though by no means absolute and unbridgeable, distinction between court painting and other forms of figurative representation on the one hand and that of the literati who strove for atmosphere and mood on the other.

Rhyme-prose (sometimes translated as prose-poetry), the genre in which Mi Fei is said to have written the missing lapidary inscription, takes many forms: its use of rhythmic and metrical elements mark it out from prose, but it has none of the discipline of most Chinese verse forms with their strict tonal and rhyme patterns. The great age of

Misty Hills, attributed to Mi Fei. Freer Gallery of Art.

richly descriptive rhyme-prose was the Han dynasty (206 BC–AD 220), but the genre had had a revival in the Song in a more discursive form, often illustrating a moral point.

Yellow was a colour associated with the Daoists and 'yellow cowls' one of several informal ways of referring to Daoist priests.

Day 7/4 (17th August)

The wind was set fair so the hawsers were untied, the sail hoisted, and we set out from Zhen prefecture. Alongside the bank a great many boats were setting out one after another, and their sails in the mist gleamed against the hills, hazy as in a painting. After a short while the wind became brisker and the boat moved forward very fast. We passed Melon Jetty Mountain which writhes and snakes up and down, with small crests rising precipitously over the River. On the highest summit stood a temple to Emperor Taiwu [r.423–52] of the Toba Wei dynasty, with mighty trees in front of it that must be about three hundred years old. Tradition has it that the disused well was dug by Taiwu, but there is no way of telling. In the twenty-seventh year of the Yuanjia period [450] of Emperor Wen of the [Liu] Song dynasty Taiwu made an incursion southward as far as Melon Jetty. Since Jiankang was closely guarded Taiwu cut through Melon Jetty Mountain to make a winding road and at the top he erected a felt tent and held a general assembly of his ministers. I suspect this may be the very place. It's referred to in the line by Wang Anshi [1021–86]:

> The shrine in the copse at Melon Jetty denotes a former dynasty.

And Mei Yaochen [1002–60] wrote lines on this temple as follows:

> Emperor Wu of Wei, defeated, fled for home,
> His army forsaken at the mountain's summit.

But I note that Taiwu never had been defeated; Mei Yaochen had mistakenly taken Emperor Wu for Cao Cao.

These mountains produce agate, but they're full of man-eating tigers and leopards and in times past General Liu Bao [twelfth century] would often recruit men to catch the tigers hereabouts. When Emperor Shizong of the Zhou dynasty launched an expedition against the Southern Tang dynasty the Prince of Qi, Jingda [tenth century], crossed the River from Melon Jetty and made an encampment seven miles from Liuhe. That took place here too.

We entered a channel and proceeded for some miles. The gardens and fields along the banks were rich and fertile, with huts and cottages set amidst flourishing bamboos and trees. For the most part they are farms belonging to the Long-reed Monastery, and when we emerged from the channel we could see the buildings and pagodas of Long-reed rising one above another. During the ravages of war in the Yangzi and Huai River areas not a single official building or private house escaped damage; this monastery alone maintained undiminished the prosperity it had enjoyed in settled times. To this day it has a constant monastic community of several hundred.

The surface of the River stretches boundlessly away and is absolutely awe-inspiring. Li Bo had a pertinent couplet:

> The boat is tethered when we reach Long-reed,
> And my gaze is swept to the misty clouds on high.

In the evening we moored at Bamboo-shoot Port where there are more than twenty households living. It's ten miles from Jinling.

The Yangzi, as the main line of communication between east and west in southern China, and the main barrier between north and south, had many sites of battles, encampments and military fortifications along it. But its route was not straightforward and, as we shall see, at some points involved travelling by side-channels for many miles. These often provided more intimate scenes than the huge vistas of the River itself. At some points Lu You was unable to see the main River; at others he speaks of coming out onto the broad sweep of the Yangzi's main channel.

Wang Anshi, the dominant reforming statesman of the eleventh century whose programme of measures was of Gladstonian proportions, was also a considerable poet and prose writer. His older contemporary, Mei Yaochen, represented the new wave of poets who with Ouyang Xiu initiated what has been called 'the new realism' which came to be characteristic of Song literature. Some of his poetry contains social criticism. He also wrote about the small and the particular, the ugly and trivial; he said there was no subject unsuitable for poetry and rose to a friend's challenge to write about lice. The plainness of style, the detail and realism of description, marked a new departure, but Mei's poetry was not easily digested. Ouyang Xiu (in Burton Watson's translation),[26] described Mei's verse thus:

> His recent poems are dry and hard;
> Try chewing on some – a bitter mouthful!
> The first reading is like eating olives,
> But the longer you suck on them, the better the taste.

Lu You, who admired Mei's poetry and quotes him a number of times in the Diary, here as so often delights in correcting the scholarship of other literati.

Jinling, as we have seen above (Day 7/1), is the modern Nanjing.

Day 7/5 (18th August)

Strong winds. Towards daybreak I covered myself with a padded bedcover, and when I got up in the morning it was as chilly as late autumn.

We passed Dragon Bay where the waves surged like mountains. I looked across to Stone Top Hill which is not very high but rises steeply out of the River, winding along like a wall. All shipping to Jiankang goes beneath it, so when there are disturbances in the lower reaches of the Yangzi the first thing to do is secure Stone Top. It's a point of real strategic importance.

From the New River we entered Dragon Radiance Gate. On the city wall [of Jiankang] there has long been the Pavilion to Gladden the Heart; and White Egret Pavilion stands at the right of the gateway. Recently they've also constructed the Two Rivers Pavilion to the left of the gateway. It's a truly impressive sight; but Gladden the Heart has been obscured by the other two pavilions and has rather lost the fine views it had when one climbed up to it in the past.

We moored at the Pavilion of the Qinhuai River. Geomancers considered that the Zhongfu mountains occupied the *gen* position [representing the rise of a new dynasty], and that if water were found occupying the *geng* position it would serve as the waters of an imperial ancestral temple. So the Qin

Gateway, detail from the *Qingmingshanghetu*, Zhang Zeduan (fl.1111–26). Palace Museum, Beijing. The camels suggest a city in north China.

dynasty's excavation of the [Qin]huai was essentially intended to shatter any royal ethos emanating from Jinling; though, as it turned out, the waters occupying the *geng* position proved a good augury [of better times under the Han dynasty]. Truly, human efforts are powerless in face of events.

I called on Tang Zhuan, [a member of the subsidiary capital's] Regency, a junior Grand Master for Court Audiences and Senior Compiler in the Imperial Archives; and Pan Shu, Assistant Prefect and a junior Grand Master for Closing Court.

The Auxiliary Palace in Jiankang is situated north of Celestial Ford Bridge. The bridge is of polished granite and most finely worked. I think it dates from the Southern Tang dynasty [937–75].

This evening there has been light rain. Wang Xuan, a junior Gentleman-litterateur and Supervisor of Military Granaries, called on me. Wang said: 'The people of Jingkou celebrate Seventh Night on the sixth of the seventh month. The Southern Tang dynasty seems to have set great store by the Seventh Night festival and a son of the emperor, who was normally governor of Jingkou, would always first perform his devotions to the Spinning Maiden on the sixth before next morning rushing into Jiankang to attend the palace banquet. That's why it has been the custom there, down to the present day, to observe the festival on the sixth.' However, in the time of Emperor Taizong an imperial edict was issued forbidding the sixth from being celebrated as the Seventh Night, so the same custom prevailed in the north. Wang's explanation is, I fear, unfounded.

Emperor Taizong (r. 976–97), brother of Taizu. Song dynasty portrait. National Palace Museum, Taipei.

Jiankang (or Jinling, otherwise known as the modern Nanjing) was and remains a major city on the Yangzi. As Shiba Yoshinobu notes, it consumed large amounts of rice and was the central market at which merchants from the upper reaches of the Yangzi congregated. Liu Zai (1166–1239) tells us: 'Jinling [Nanjing] is the ancient seat of emperors and a place where goods and people gather. There are many consumers, few producers.' Lu You visited one of the famous sites of Nanjing at this time, the Pavilion to Gladden the Heart, which had been built in the early eleventh century and in which a famous painting was exhibited on a screen, though he makes no mention of this. A few days later Lu's boat moored below this pavilion (Day 7/9). Under the Southern Song dynasty Nanjing retained its status as a subsidiary capital, and that is why Lu refers to a call on a member of the Regency rather than the usual prefectural structure of government.

I am indebted to Chang and Smythe for my understanding of this passage about the Zhongfu mountains, though I have adapted their translation. Lu You's point here is that the city of Nanjing, which possessed all the attributes of an imperial capital according to the geomancers, appeared to threaten the imperial claims of the Qin dynasty (221–07 BC) (best known to a Western audience for the terracotta warriors at Xian); the Qin took steps to disrupt this auspicious conjunction of geomantic features by excavating the Qinhuai River, which is only a few miles long, but to no avail because after a short time the Qin was replaced by the long-lasting Han dynasty (206 BC–AD 220). We shall shortly, on Day 7/7, meet the pseudo-science of geomancy again.

The Seventh Night festival, which fell on the seventh day of the seventh month of the lunar calendar, celebrated the love affair between the cow-herd and the weaver maid who meet once a year on this night. Astronomically this was when Altair was in Aquila and Vega in Lyra. It was a festival for women in which supplications were made for skill in spinning and weaving. The Southern Tang dynasty had had its capital at the modern Nanjing which Lu happened to be approaching as the Double Seventh festival drew near. Lu, as we have seen, was something of an authority on the tenth century and wrote the *History of the Southern Tang Dynasty*. His dismissal of Wang Xuan's explanation of Jingkou's (the modern Zhenjiang, which Lu had reached on Day 6/17) early celebration of the Seventh Night festival seems well-founded. Emperor Taizong, the second Song emperor, reigned 976–97 and in the newly re-unified country his edicts would have run in both north and south, so the custom of celebrating this festival on the sixth was not confined to Jingkou.

Day 7/6 (19th August)

I called on Shen Xia, a senior Grand Master for Closing Court, Vice-Minister in the Court of Imperial Treasury and Overseer-General of Revenues for the Two Huai; and on Guo Zhen, Military Commissioner for the Wutai Command and Campaign Commander for the Jiankang armies. He Zuoshan, a junior Court Gentleman for Instruction and Magistrate of Jiangning; and Chu Yi, a junior Gentleman-litterateur and Surveillance Circuit Judge, came to call on me. He Zuoshan has the courtesy name Baixiang; Chu Yi's is Chengshu. In the evening I called on Vice Director Qin Bohe, whose personal name is Xuan. He is the grandson of the former Grand Councillor Qin Gui [1090–1155], Duke of Yi. He invited me to sit in his hall of paintings which is a vast and beautiful structure looking out at the front on a large lake. Beyond the lake is the Gallery of Imperial Calligraphy. The mansion was an imperial gift.

Members of my household are suffering from boils and I troubled Magistrate He to summon a doctor, Liu Zhongbao, to examine them.

Qin Gui, whose grandson Lu encounters here, was a stalwart champion of the need for compromise with the Jin. He served as Grand Councillor (in effect Prime Minister) from 1138–55 and contributed to the stabilisation of the dynasty in its reduced territory with its new capital at Hangzhou. But Qin had had to accept peace terms which required the Song to pay large quantities of tribute to Jin and to employ humilific, and humiliating, language in its diplomatic dealings with

Cast-iron statues of Qin Gui and his family apologizing at the temple to Yue Fei's mother outside Jiujiang (River prefecture).

its northern neighbour. Qin also recalled the dashing and charismatic young general Yue Fei (1103–42) from the north, where he had achieved some military successes against the Jurchen, and had him executed as a sop to the Jin. Such appeasement earned him the lasting hatred of Chinese, a hatred given fresh wind in the modern period by those who saw parallels with China's ninteenth- and twentieth-century humiliations at the hands of foreigners. Lu You's views on handling the Jin were anathema to the 'peace party' and he had personally, albeit inadvertently, run into trouble with Qin Gui. In 1154, when Lu took the civil service examinations, he had advocated a revanchist policy and been placed first ahead of Qin Gui's grandson Qin Xuan. Normally success in the examinations was a guarantee of early promotion in the bureaucracy, but the grandfather ensured Lu You's career was blocked, though Lu was fortunate that Qin Gui fell from power and died the following year. It is interesting to see Lu punctiliously calling on Qin's grandson and being treated courteously; and a few days later (Day 7/9) Qin Xuan (Bohe) arranges for a doctor to call on Lu's family, and sends some medicines. Taking the capital examinations together was generally a strong bond.

Day 7/7 (20th August)

In the morning I visited Heaven's Blessings Abbey which lies at the foot of the Foundry City Mountains. Geomancers believe the connecting veins of this hill come from Mount Jiang, but there is no way of telling. City walls and ramparts of the Wu and Jin eras [third and fourth centuries] mostly followed the line of the hills.

To the west of the abbey is the Temple of the Loyal and Heroic which is dedicated to Bian Kun [281–328], but in which Ji Shao [253–304] and Bian's two sons Zhen and Xu share in the offerings. Ji Shao died in the reign of Emperor Hui [r.290–306] and before Bian Kun, and besides had nothing to do with the Lower Yangzi, so to give him a cult ancillary to Bian Kun is wrong. Behind the temple is a thick grove of trees which tradition has it is the tomb of Bian Kun. There's also a very spacious pavilion to the north-east of the tomb called the Pavilion of Loyalty and Filial Piety. This was originally, under the Southern Tang dynasty, the Loyal and Devoted Pavilion, but was later changed to avoid a taboo. Loyal and Devoted was Bian Kun's posthumous name. The modern name of Loyalty and Filial Piety combines the death of his two sons with the calamity that befell the father.

The Daoist priest of the religious house, Chen Dexin, whose courtesy name is Kejiu, comes from Gusu and is a man of great perception. He accompanied us up the hill for the view and we stayed there a long time. I then left by the west gateway to visit the Clear and Pure, Broad Compassion Monastery. The monastery is a third of a mile or more from the town and is situated on Stone Top Wall, overlooking the Great River and facing south to Ox Head Mountain. It has a very majestic atmosphere, though it has been damaged by sword and fire. In front of the Dharma Hall once stood the Virtue's Blessings Hall, the placard of which was in the Cloth Brush calligraphy of the Last Ruler of the Southern Tang. A stone inscription of this still exists, but the hall itself has been moved over to the western side. There is also a funerary oration to the Zen Master Wukong which says: 'In the the ninth month of the ninth year of the Baoda period, the year *xinhai*, His Imperial Majesty performed the ceremony of making an offering of a milky potion of scented tea to the Zen Master Wukong of the Clear and Pure Monastery

Stone Top Wall, Nanjing.

under the Court of State Ceremonial.'[27] I note that Emperor Yuanzong [r.943–61] of the Southern Tang dynasty succeeded to the throne in the year *guimao* [943], and changed the reign period to Baoda. This equated to the eighth year of the Tianfu period of Emperor Chudi of the Jin dynasty. As for the *xinhai* year, this was indeed the ninth year of the Baoda period, equating to the first year of the Guangshun period of Emperor Taizu of the Zhou dynasty. So it was Emperor Yuanzong who made the offering to Wukong. *The Jiankang Gazetteer* believes it to have been the Last Ruler [of the Southern Tang dynasty], but it was not.

The Venerable Baoyu, a native of Chu prefecture, detained me for lunch and presented me with an ink-rubbing of the placard from the Virtue's Blessings Hall. After eating we climbed up to Stone Top together. To the west we could see the Xuanhua ferry-crossing and the mountains of Liyang. It is truly a place with great natural advantages. If at some future date the capital were established at Jiankang Stone Top would still serve as a place of strategic importance. Some people think that now the city wall has been shifted south there's no advantage in defending Stone Top; they haven't thought the matter through. For though with this shift southwards the Qinhuai river bisects the walls so that measures such as establishing forts and blockading navigation undertaken in the Six Dynasties [222–589] can no longer be implemented in an emergency, nevertheless the Great River is a natural barrier, the city walls overlook it, and our 'iron-clad battlements and scalding moats' are more effective than those of the Six Dynasties. We would surely not need to rely on the [Qin]huai River for our security?

Liu Wei, a senior Gentleman for Meritorious Achievement and newly appointed Commandant of Wukang in Hu prefecture; and Li Ying, a junior Gentleman for Meritorious Achievement and Director of the Audit Bureau, called on me. Liu Wei is a protégé of Qin Xuan. He said that the decline of the Qin family was poignant; they were even reduced to repeated pawning of their possessions, and their revenues were meagre as well. I asked what their annual income was, and he said it was only seventy thousand bushels of rice!

We have already encountered geomancy, a form of divination concerned with the configuration of the earth which has been defined as 'the art of adapting the residences of the living and the dead so as to cooperate and harmonise with the local currents of the cosmic breath'.[28] This pseudo-science, often referred to in English as feng-shui from the Chinese for 'wind and water', remains important in some parts of the Chinese world. On the advice of the geomancers regarding the siting of tombs, towns and indeed cities in relation to hills, watercourses and heavenly bodies depends the

The polluted Qinhuai River near its junction with the Yangzi, Nanjing.

fortune of families and dynasties. This was why Cai Jing (Day 6/2) was concerned to ensure his father's tomb conformed with geomatic requirements; and why the Qin dynasty took alarm at the thought that Jinling (Nanjing) might be a more auspicious seat of power than their own capital (Day 7/5). In the passage above Lu You appears to see a connection between the putative veins of the mountains and the lines of the ramparts along the hills. There was, to quote Needham,[29] 'in general a strong preference for tortuous and winding roads, walls and structures, which seemed to fit into the landscape, rather than to dominate it; and a strong objection to straight lines and geometrical layouts'.

Bian Kun lived in the early fourth century and served the Jin dynasty (no connection with the dynasty occupying north China in Lu You's time) with great loyalty, dying in battle along with his two sons. Ji Shao served Emperor Hui of the same dynasty and also died in battle in the service of his emperor, but otherwise they had no connection. Valerie Hansen[30] has drawn attention to the way in which some gods at this period escaped their local roots and became regionalised or even national. Other literati besides Lu You objected to this process, but it was a reflection of the increasing propensity for merchants and others to travel and to take their local cults with them.

The stone inscription which came from the Virtue's Blessings Hall need not, despite Lu You's confusing litany of dynasties and dates, detain us long. Lu is demonstrating his mastery of the Five Dynasties period. Setting the calendar was always in China an important function demonstrating the legitimacy of a dynasty, and in this period of competing claims each petty regime had maintained its own concurrent and conflicting calendar. Lu points to a mistake in the local gazetteer which assumed that the Imperial Majesty referred to in the inscription is the poet-emperor, known as the Last Ruler, who lost his Southern Tang kingdom and was taken prisoner (and probably poisoned) by the first ruler of the Song dynasty; but the Last Emperor only came to the throne of his doomed state in 961, after the official founding of the Song dynasty which still had some mopping up of rivals to do. As Lu argues, the man who offered the ceremonial tea to the Zen Master in 951 must have been Emperor Yuanzong, the father of the Last Ruler. The milkiness of the tea refers to the colour and consistency of the potation rather than the use of cow's milk. More interesting, perhaps, is the reference to Cloth Brush calligraphy, a style of calligraphy said to have been invented by the Last Ruler of Southern Tang in which a piece of rolled cloth, rather than a brush, is used as the instrument of writing.

The Jiankang Gazetteer was written in 1169 by Shi Zhengzhi, an admiral on the Yangzi who wrote of paddle ships.

When Lu climbs to Stone Top with the Buddhist monk Baoyu he is prompted to a strategic observation with political connotations palpable to contemporary readers. In arguing for the strategic importance of the Yangzi in the area of Nanjing he is also advocating a more forward policy. He had in fact submitted a paper to government on this subject in 1163, advocating the transfer of the capital to Jiankang (Nanjing). In the Diary he maintains that a capital on the Yangzi and nearer to the front-line would be defensible, by implication suggesting that a capital withdrawn to its 'temporary' site at Hangzhou on the Qiantang River is a defeatist posture. Nanjing had been a national capital on a number of occasions in Chinese history, and as he looks at the situation on the ground Lu's argument is that the expansion of Nanjing to include the area beyond the Qinhuai River, a small tributary of the Yangzi, need not render its defences weaker than they were in earlier periods, though Stone Top would be a vital element in its defence.

We met Vice Director Qin Bohe, whose personal name was Xuan, the grandson of the late Prime Minister, in the previous day's diary entry. To provide some sense, however tentative, of what 70,000 bushels of rice meant at this time we can make some comparisons. A thirteenth-century writer, Fang Hui (1227–1307) tells us that a reasonably well off tenant farmer family in the Yangzi delta in his time consisting of five members would consume 36 bushels of rice per annum. In the Southern Song there were in Suzhou estate-owners with several hundreds of thousands, or even a million, bushels (of rice) in their granaries. Given the Qin family's recent prominence Lu You was no doubt genuinely surprised at their relative impoverishment.

Day 7/8 (21st August)

In the early morning we reached the pagoda to Master Zhenjue of the True Way Forest on Mount Zhong, where I burned incense. The pagoda stands above the Ascendant Nation in Grand Tranquillity Monastery, and Baozhi [419–514] is buried there. Inside the pagoda is a gilt-bronze image of Baozhi with an inscription on its breast written when Wang Anshi was governor of Jinling. The monks say that the ancient image was taken off and installed in the Qisheng Cloister in the Eastern Capital. At the inception of our dynasty, whenever prayers were offered the services would be conducted at both the Qisheng Cloister and this pagoda. (I've looked into this and it's true).

To the south-west of the pagoda is a little balcony called Tree Tops. Beneath it there are great pine trees everywhere, whiskered and scaly, writhing like serpents and dragons, often hundreds of years old. Tree Tops must have been named by some later person after that line of poetry by Wang Anshi:

On northern hills above the treetops clouds are drifting by.

The *Jiankang Gazetteer* states that Wang himself gave it the name, but this is wrong.

To the rear of the pagoda there's also the Dinglin Retreat. In the past I've heard my late father say that Li Gonglin [1045–1105/6] painted Wang's portrait on a wall of the Elegance Extolled Chapel in this Retreat. He was wearing cap and sash, and his bearing was life-like. After Wang Anshi's death the chapel was generally locked and barred, though if important visitors came the monks of the monastery would open the doors and then, suddenly seeing the image, the visitor was sure to be flabbergasted at how close to life it was, such was the brilliance of the portrait. But now, since the Retreat suffered a fire, not so much as a foot of rafter remains. I once came here alone in the rain in the autumn of 1165 and left some writing on the walls. Later on someone had this carved on the rock-face. I heaved a sigh when I read it, for some five or six years have passed.

On the return journey I visited Half Hill and stopped for a while. On Half Hill is Wang Anshi's old house, known as the Requited Peace Zen Cloister. This is half-way from the city as you climb Mount Zhong, which is why it's called Half Hill. The Cloister is extremely dilapidated.

West of the monastery there's a hill of soil which is nowadays called the Hummock. This is another instance of someone later taking the name from a poem by Wang Anshi where it says:

> West of the ditch I hired some workmen
> To heft the soil and make a hummock.

At the rear of the monastery there's also Xie An's [320–85] grave-mound, which a poem of Wang Anshi's tells us is north-east of Foundry City. This is the very place.

Baozhi was a distinguished monk of the fifth century whose sudden peculiar behaviour – he had irregular mealtimes, grew his hair long, ranged around and so on – brought him for a time under government suspicion, though he was later revered as a holy man and given the title Bodhisattva Zhenjue of the True Way Forest. Mount Zhong, where he was buried, is now within the Nanjing municipal area. His image had, as Lu You tells us, been brought from Jinling (Nanjing) in the early 980s on the instructions of Emperor Taizong who greatly revered Baozhi. The emperor had founded the Qisheng monastery, where the image was installed, shortly before. In the course of the eleventh century it became one of the leading Buddhist establishments of the

Vimalakirti, attributed to Li Gonglin. National Museum, Tokyo.

Nothern Song capital at Kaifeng. Another image for Baozhi's tomb had clearly been made in the eleventh century to replace the original taken to the capital.

Wang Anshi, as we saw on Day 7/4, was the leader of a reforming group who advocated the so-called New Policies, a set of reforms to the administrative, financial and military structure of the state. He served as Prime Minister from 1069–74 and again through most of 1075–76. His policies were fiercely opposed by the conservatives under the historian and statesman Sima Guang. Both Sima and Wang were writers in various genres; Wang was a considerable poet, Sima a historian. Wang, who had been governor of Jinling (Nanjing) in 1074–5, died in 1086; Sima was brought back as Prime Minister in that year but he too died a few months later. Their followers in various combinations and alliances alternated in power until the calamity of invasion by the Jurchens in 1127 brought an end to the Northern Song.

There was amongst many literati an easy intercourse between on the one hand Confucian values and the career structure of bureaucratic service to the state, and on the other Buddhism with its quite different set of values. Buddhist monks were often highly educated and in many instances shared the cultural values of the class from which they sprang; artistic endeavour, whether in painting or poetry, was common to both and many officials had monk friends.

During the Northern Song the main centre of administration and seat of the imperial court at Kaifeng was referred to as the Eastern Capital.

Lu You's father Lu Zai must have been born around 1088. He died in 1147. He had a fairly successful official career, but most notably was a well-known book collector of the period. He had over 13,000 volumes, or rather fascicules as the Chinese counted their books.

Li Gonglin was a leading figure painter of the Northern Song. As Michael Sullivan remarks:[31] 'Li moved in an intellectual circle at court that included the poet Su Dongpo and the historian Ouyang Xiu, while it is recorded that even the great statesman Wang Anshi, who was "careful in choosing his friends", condescended to visit him. In early life he was a famous painter of horses – until, so the story goes, a Daoist told him that if he continued much longer in this vein he would become like a horse himself, whereupon he switched to other themes. He was thoroughly eclectic, spending years in copying the old masters, and though his own technique was restricted largely to ink-line his subject-matter included everything from horses and genre scenes (a delightful Breughelesque handscroll of peasants dancing was formerly in the National Museum, Peking) to Daoist fairy landscapes, Buddhist figures – a splendid example is a Vimalakirti in Tokyo – and many paintings of Guanyin amid rocks, of which he created an ideal conventional type.'

The Dinglin Retreat was an important monastery founded in 424. It had associations with a number of famous scholars of the Song period, including Wang Anshi, Mi Fei and Li Gonglin. Lu You speaks of his

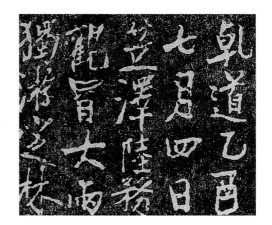

LuYou's inscription at Dinglin, from *Wenwu* No. 9 (1976).

earlier visit here in 1165. He had been on his way from Zhenjiang to an appointment as Sub-prefect of Longxing Military Prefecture and had passed through Nanjing in the seventh lunar month of that year, his respect for the memory of Wang Anshi having brought him here through the rain. The few words that he wrote on that earlier visit to record the event were lost but someone had carved his calligraphy on the rock face, and it was this that Lu saw on the present occasion. The inscription seems to have been overlooked in succeeding centuries, but remarkably was rediscovered in 1975. It reads: 'On the 4th day of the seventh month of the *yiyou* year of the Qiandao period Lu Wuguan of Lize braved heavy rain to visit Dinglin by himself.' The date in question equates to 12th August 1165; Lu Wuguan is Lu You and Lize is Lake Tai from which his ancestors hailed.

Day 7/9 (22nd August)

We reached the two monasteries Preserving Peace and Altar of Abstinence, at the former of which are the Phoenix Terrace and the Pavilion of Light Amassed. Of the terrace, Li Bo's poem says:

> Three Hills half sunk beyond the blue sky,
> Two rivers dividing at White Egret Island.

The terrace has now been abandoned and turned into an armoury for the Great Army. Only the pavilion has been rebuilt on its old site, and it is very imposing. Monks from the monastery told me that the pavilion's notice-board was originally in the Clerical Script of Zhu Dunru [1081–1159], but some ignoramus has altered it. Behind the Dharma Hall is a stone slab with the lustre of black jade. This has a poem by Song Qiqiu [c.886–959] on it with the title: 'The Pavilion at Phoenix Terrace Mountain. Offered to the Minister of Works by Presented Scholar of the Township Song Qiqiu.' The Minister of Works was Xu Zhigao, who later changed his name to Li Bian and became Emperor Liezu of the Southern Tang dynasty. Song Qiqiu was one of his senior ministers. There follows another inscription which states: 'In the third year of the Shengyuan period [939] this stone was carved in respectful accordance with an imperial order.' So presumably Liezu, having taken possession of the state and musing on the origins of this relationship between ruler and minister, had it brought to public notice. Liezu and Song Qiqiu are barely worthy of mention, but nevertheless in a period of struggle for power, and of division and dislocation, had it not been for such a relationship between ruler and minister they wouldn't have achieved even partial success.

The horizontal tablet at the Altar of Abstinence reads: 'Mighty and Victorious Monastery of the Altar of Abstinence'. In olden days it was called the Tiled Coffin Monastery. It has a gallery which follows the line of the hillock at a height of a hundred feet, and is referred to by Li Bo in:

> Where Mount Zhong faces Northern Hu,
> And [Qin]huai River enters southern lushness.

He also wrote the lyric 'Heng River' about it:

> A wind for three days that blows the hills down,
> With white waves higher than Tile Coffin's gallery.

In the time of the Last Ruler of the Southern Tang our court sent the military man Wei Pi [919–99] here as an envoy. The Southern Tang supposed he wasn't literate, so at the banquet in this gallery they asked him to write a poem. Wei seized a brush and composed a piece, the final line of which was:

> Don't prompt the thunder and rain to damage your foundations.

The Last Ruler and his ministers all turned pale. When the Southern Tang fell the gallery was burned down by the soldiers of Wu-Yue. But though our dynasty had enjoyed peace for two hundred years, and Jinling is a major metropolis whose Buddhist monasteries and Daoist abbeys competed in architectural embellishment, yet still we were never able to restore this gallery. Then in the Shaoxing period [1131–62] monks from the north came to live here and lectured on the *Vijñāptimātratāsiddhi-śāstra*. They took an oath to resurrect the gallery, and sought mighty timbers from the region of the rivers and lakes. They were repeatedly on the point of completing the task when the construction of palace buildings intervened, and time and again officials would invariably appropriate the materials. But the monks' resolution wasn't shaken on this account and they worked with yet more determination, finally completing the Vairocana Gallery. It stands seventy feet above the level ground, and outstrips everything in this area south of the Yangzi for grandeur and beauty. The foundations of the old gallery are less than a couple of hundred paces away,[32] but these are now abandoned and turned into a military encampment.

Qin Xuan sent doctor Chai Angong to examine a member of my family's boils. Chai is from Dragon Hill in Xing prefecture.

In the evening Chu Chengshu called on me. As Commandant of Minqing in Fu prefecture Chu had captured brigands and according to regulations should have obtained a job in the capital, but he couldn't bear to benefit personally from the death of others so he declined and didn't take up the post. Up till the present time he's been awaiting promotion or assignment. Someone else who was serving as Commandant of another town also captured brigands, strove energetically to gain a reward, and was finally given a job in the capital. He was about to relinquish his then post and leave, but whenever he went into the commandery city and passed the execution ground he would shield his eyes and give a great cry, and it was several days before his spirits were restored to normal. Later, when he reached his new commandery town he saw there was a stone pillar on the main thoroughfare. He asked what it was for and those accompanying him said that this was a place of execution. He screamed out in terror, almost falling from his carriage. From that time on, wherever he went he would take a circuitous route to avoid places of execution. People shouldn't have such fastidious consciences!

The boat was moved and moored beneath the Pavilion to Gladden the Heart. Qin Xuan sent over some medicines.

Lu you wrote the *History of the Southern Tang Dynasty*, which contained biographies of both Emperor Liezu and his minister Song Qiqiu. The Southern Tang, which adopted the Tang moniker to bolster its spurious claim to a legitimacy deriving from the preceeding and much more distinguished Tang dynasty (618–907), had, whatever its political failings, a reputation for culture; its last ruler was an accomplished poet who surrounded himself with writers, musicians and painters. In an age of military disturbances they saw their kingdom in the softer civilized south as a bulwark of cultural values. Humiliating crude soldiers from their enemy the Song was expected to be good sport, but the effete court had its come-uppance when the soldier was able to turn out a poem with a pointed message for the Southern Tang. Wei Pi's mission can be dated to the eleventh lunar month of 964.

The fighting at the end of the Southern Tang involved one of the smaller states from the lower Yangzi region called Wu-Yue; Lu You manages to exonerate the Song from the destruction of the gallery while expressing some surprise that during the two centuries of peace under the Northern Song no attempt was made to reconstruct the gallery. The monks who later battled against high-handed officials seizing their materials were promoting the *Vijñāptimātratāsiddhi-śāstra*. This is the Buddhist teaching of 'Idealism and the Hundred Divisions of Mental Qualities'. Vairocana, after whom their gallery was named, is interpreted variously according to the different sects, but is counted as the first of the five celestial Buddhas and is the essence of wisdom and purity, and the embodiment of truth.

The position of Commandant was something like police chief and there are a number of instances at this period of officials who made their name by successful suppression of brigands. Promotion was one reward for success, but a posting in the capital where something like half the senior bureaucracy was concentrated, and where entertainment and culture were a great deal more vigorous than in a distant provincial posting far from family and friends, was always an attraction. The brigands themselves could be anything from common criminals to peasant leaders with political demands. The settled condition of Song society was always threatened by a downturn in the economy, but the problem was generally localised.

Day 7/10 (23rd August)

In the morning we went out through the city walls of Jiankang to reach Stone Top where we picked up a favourable wind. The sails were hoisted and we proceeded, but the harbour is shallow and narrow and so our progress was very slow.

We spent the night at Big Wall Knoll. Jinling is full of knolls and hillocks, such as Plum Cliff Knoll, Rocky Knoll, and Old Lady She (read as Sher in the character for 'snake') Knoll which are among the best known. Several dozen households live here, and there are shops.

Lu You and his party now leave the Nanjing area.

Day 7/11 (24th August)

In the morning we emerged from the channel and proceeded along the Great River, passing Three Hills Promontory, Pungent Island, Compassionate Mother Promontory and Coloured-Stone market town, to moor in the river mouth at Grand Tranquillity Prefecture. Both Xie Tiao [464–99] in his 'Climbing Three Hills and Looking Back to the Capital', and Li Bo in 'Climbing Three Hills and Gazing Towards Jinling', wrote poems hereabouts.

All the mountains that give onto the River are called 'promontories', their waters churning furiously, and it's only with a concerted effort of the men working on the poles that one can get up stream. This year, however, autumn is early because of the intercalary month and the water has already dropped several feet, but one can imagine what it must be like at the height of summer. When you look at Three Hills from Stone Top or Phoenix Terrace it's so faint there's just the merest hint of it, yet when you pass beneath it you are only seventeen miles from Jinling. This was the place where, during the Jin attack on Wu, when Wang Jun's [206–85] fleet was passing by Three Hills, Wang Hun [223–97] wanted him to confer. But Wang Jun hoisted sail and said: 'The wind's in our favour; we shouldn't moor'.

Today the wind has been set fair so we proceeded with drums sounding and the sails hoisted. There were two large boats which had been heading down-river east-wards and which had moored by the riverbank because of the headwinds. When they saw us they were furious, and kept on stamping and cursing. Our boatmen didn't reply, they just clapped, roared with laughter and drummed even more energetically, looking delighted. In river travel it's normal to have hold ups and bursts of speed. When those the winds favour brag and those the winds frustrate get angry we may think them both at fault. But I suppose there's a lot of things that happen in the world of this sort, and I record the incident to raise a smile.

Pungent Island lies in the middle of the River. It has a small hill on it called Pungent Hill with very dense vegetation, and there's a shrine to a deity on the hilltop. Compassionate Mother is the most vertiginous of the promontories. Xu Fu [1086–1140] wrote a poem called 'Compassionate Mother Promontory', the preface to which states: 'The promontory and The Gazer Rock face each other and really can be considered a matching pair, but poets have never so much as alluded to them.' So his poem went:

> The departing male phoenix speaks only of boudoir regrets;
> Who grasps the feelings in her eyes as the cow licks her calf?

But Mei Yaochen, when he was escorting his mother's coffin back home to Wanling, said in his poem 'Setting out from the Mouth of Long Reed River':

> Mountains and rivers of the south haven't changed at all:
> Compassionate Mother rends my heart, promontory known of old.

Coloured-Stone, one of the outcrops of high ground along this stretch of the Yangzi.

Xu Fu had simply happened to forget this. Mei Yaochen also wrote poems entitled 'Passing Below Compassionate Mother Promontory' and 'The Bamboo Canes on the Cliff-face of Compassionate Mother Hill'. They are both splendid pieces, and chime well with this hill.

Coloured-Stone is also called Ox Isle. It stands on the opposite bank to He prefecture. The River is narrower here than at Melon Island and that's why, when in the Sui dynasty Han Qinhu [538–92] conquered the Chen dynasty, and in our own Cao Bin [931–99] brought down the Southern Tang, they both crossed at this point. But the slightest breeze will always make it impassable because of the waves. Liu Yuxi [772–842] said:

> In reed and rush the evening wind is stirring,
> And scales appear upon the autumn river.

And Wang Anshi said:

> The faintest flutter of a breeze and every boat is stalled.

They are both referring to this promontory.

It was in regard to this promontory that Fan Ruobing [943–94] of the Southern Tang dynasty submitted his policy recommendation to build a pontoon bridge where our imperial armies could cross. Fan had previously failed in his ambitions under the

Lis, so as a ruse he shaved his head and became a monk, living in a lodge on Coloured-Stone Hill. He chiselled into the rock to make holes, and set up a stone stupa. On moonlit nights he would tie a rope to the stupa and hastily row a little boat across, stretching a rope over to the north side of the River to measure its width. When he had practised until he was sure there was no mistake he fled to our capital and sent in a submission. Later, when our imperial armies crossed south, the pontoon bridge was accurate to the inch.

I note that during Emperor Yang [r.604–17] of the Sui dynasty's campaign against Liao he had used this same scheme to cross the Liao River. Three pontoons were constructed on the western bank which, when completed, were pulled across to the eastern bank. But the bridges didn't reach because they fell short by over ten feet, so the Sui army had to get into the water to join battle while the Koreans could strike at them from the vantage of the riverbank. Only after Mai Tiezhang was killed in battle did the Sui pull back their forces and draw in the pontoons over to the western bank. Fresh orders were issued for He Chou to link up the bridges; in two days this was completed, and then they were used to cross. But it must have been the will of Heaven that in the end the Sui couldn't conquer Korea while our own dynasty brought down the Southern Tang; what did that owe to Fan Ruobing's efforts! For when Fan fled north the whole of south China was aware that he was submitting a proposal for a campaign against the south. Some asked that Fan's mother and wife be executed, but Li Yu didn't dare. He merely had them placed in confinement at Chi prefecture. Later on Fan Ruobing himself made a declaration that his mother and wife were in south China, and the court ordered Li Yu to provide an escort [north] for them. Li was incensed but in the end he dared not disobey and sent them on their way with munificent presents. But neither the holes in the rock that Fan had chiselled nor the stone stupa were destroyed, and our imperial armies used them after all to secure a pontoon bridge. From this you may see how dim and apathetic the dynasty of the Lis was, ruler and ministers alike. Even had there been no Fan Ruobing, would it not have fallen? When Zhang Lei [1054–1114] wrote his treatise on the pacification of the south he suggested that 'Fan should have been arrested and sent to Li Yu as a sop; or else his crime of treachery against his ruler should have been redressed by executing him as an example to the world. Would that not have been striking?'. Zhang Lei's view is received opinion.

I have been ill since we were in Jinling, and only today am I feeling a bit better, though I still can't eat. It's raining tonight.

I have perhaps taken liberties with the translation of some of these place-names. Pungent Island could be taken as Brisk Island; I have found no source to establish how the name was understood, but the reference to dense vegetation inclines me to pungent.

Xie Tiao was a writer best known for his landscape poems, though he worked in many forms and styles. He made his name in the Southern Qi court but was eventually brought down by its politics and landed up in prison where he died.

Wang Jun was ignoring Wang Hun's orders to hold back; the former continued down-river to

Temple on a Mountain Flank, Xiao Zhao (fl. c.1130–60). National Palace Museum, Taipei.

Nanjing and that very day brought an end to the Wu dynasty which had its capital there.

Liu Yuxi was a distinguished prose writer and poet of the latter part of the Tang dynasty, as famous in his time as his contemporary Bai Juyi (see Day 6/19). Liu's influence was felt in poetry of the succeeding Song dynasty; Lu quotes from him in later entries of the Diary.

Once again Lu You displays his knowledge of the tenth century with his account of the pontoon bridge built across the Yangzi by the Song in 974 when they launched their campaign to annihilate the Southern Tang, in which they succeeded the following year. The other campaign to which he alludes was the attempt by the Sui dynasty, which had re-unified China in the late sixth century, to reassert Chinese control over the Korean peninsula. The Liao River runs through what is now China's north-east (Manchuria). The campaign of 612 under General Mai Tiezhang ended in failure, though by the second half of the seventh century, when the Tang had replaced the Sui dynasty, Chinese forces established at least nominal suzerainty over the whole Korean peninsula.

We shall meet Zhang Lei later in the Diary when Lu quotes from his poetry. The story of Fan Ruobing presented Lu You and his contemporaries with a dilemma. Fan had contributed to the fall of the Southern Tang in the 970s and the final victory of the Song under whom they lived, but his loyalty should have lain with the regime of which he was a subject based around the Yangzi and south China. The paradoxical parallel with the Southern Song, similarly based on the Yangzi and the south and facing pressure from the north, cannot I think have been lost on Lu and explains his unwillingness to credit Fan with the merit of helping the foundation of the Song dynasty.

Day 7/12 (25th August)

In the morning the boat was moved and we sailed up the Gushu Creek for two miles, mooring at the Pavilion of Martial Training. I had earlier questioned the boatmen, who told me that the moorings at the mouth of the river were seven miles from the town walls and we would have to enter on foot. But having reached the Pavilion of Martial Training we were actually stopping right outside the town's outer rampart. Zhou Yuante, whose personal name is Cao, and who is an Auxiliary Academician of the Hall of Exemplary Conduct, a senior Gentleman for Court Audiences and Prefect, heard I was ill and came with a doctor, Guo Shixian, to attend me. It has now been eight years since we parted from one another in the capital.

Grand Tranquillity prefectural town was originally Dangtu county under the jurisdiction of Jinling, but in the time of Emperor Shizong of the Zhou dynasty, when Emperor Yuanzong of the Southern Tang dynasty lost the area south of the Huai River, He prefecture was transplanted here and it was called New He prefecture. This was then changed to the Heroic Expeditionary Military Prefecture. But in the eighth year of our dynasty's Kaibao period [975] we gained the submission of south China and it was changed to the Pacified South Military Prefecture, though it only had authority over the solitary city of Dangtu. In the second year of the Taipingxingguo [Ascendant Nation in Grand Tranquillity] period [977] it was made a prefecture and Reed Lake and Fanchang were brought under its jurisdiction, with Dangtu as the administrative centre. The Ascendant Nation Military Prefecture was established at the same time; the names deriving from the two halves of the reign period.

Lu You was travelling up the Yangzi in a west-south-westerly direction, and had now reached Dangtu (both the ancient and the modern name) on the south bank. But as Lu, with a keen interest in historical geography and administrative history, points out it had undergone numerous changes of nomenclature and administrative reorganisations. When the Song took over this area in the late tenth century their victory and the period name were enshrined in these toponyms, for the relevant reign period, as we have seen, was Taipingxingguo which means Ascendant Nation in Grand Tranquillity; so one military prefecture was called Taiping (Grand Tranquillity) and the other Xingguo (Ascendant Nation).

Reed Lake, the modern city of Wuhu, which Lu mentions here, was in a parlous state by the time that Blakiston visited it after the Taiping rebels had left: 'One square – I think the ruins of a temple – was literally filled with beggars lying in filth, and but partly covered by some cotton rags alive with vermin. One or two were lifeless, others breathing their last gasps of the noisome stench that pervaded the den. Most were afflicted with virulent skin disease, and all had the verdict stamped unmistakeably on their countenances, "Died from starvation".' Isabella Bird found Reed Lake the ugliest of all the Yangzi ports, but not unprosperous. Here too the Germans had started an albumen factory, feathers from the ducks being sent back to Germany for the making of feather beds.

Day 7/13 (26th August)

Ye Fen, Assistant Prefect and a junior Gentleman for Court Audiences; Qian Tong, whose courtesy name is Zhonggeng, Supernumerary Assistant Prefect and a senior Gentleman for Court Service; Zhao Ziming, Military Supervisor and a senior Gentleman-litterateur; and Wang Quan, Magistrate of Dangtu county and a junior Court Gentleman for Comprehensive Duty, called on me.

In the afternoon I went into the prefectural town to call on Zhou Yuante. He summoned Dr Guo and sat with us while the doctor felt my pulse and discussed the medicines I should be taking.

The prefectural town lies directly on the north side of Gushu Creek, which the locals call simply Gu Creek. The water is pure green in colour, but as limpid as a looking glass. You can count the tiny fish as they go back and forth. Fishermen's houses cover the south side of the creek; a secluded and enchanting scene. There are two pontoon bridges, both outside the city walls, one leading to Xuan City, the other to Zhezhong. The Gushu Hall is highly renowned for its fine views of the creek and mountains, but just at the moment guests are staying in it so I wasn't able to go there. There's also a tavern where I went upstairs to look out at the splendid scene. These are both south of the city wall. In times gone by the creek divided and one branch passed through the town, but it has long been silted up; and though in recent years it was dredged and put to rights it's only passable for a short while at the turn of spring and summer. We're now in the seventh month and it has stopped flowing already.

In the *Collected Works* of Li Bo there are the 'Ten Paeans of Gushu'. A paternal kinsman of mine, Lu Yanyuan, once said that when Su Shi was returning home from Huang prefecture and passed through Dangtu he read these songs, clapped his hands and guffawed, saying: 'What fakes! How could Li Bo have written such words?' Guo Xiangzheng disputed this, maintaining Su was mistaken. Su Shi laughed again and said: 'Well then, I'm afraid they must have been written by some re-incarnation of Li Bo!'. Guo Xiangzheng felt very indignant. In his youth Guo's verses had an easy elegance, and some amongst the older generation had approved of them, considering him a 're-incarnation of Li Bo'. Guo had then become rather pleased with himself, which was why Su Shi was joshing him about it. Some say that the 'Ten Paeans', 'Homebound', 'Laugh', 'The Monk's Song', and 'Song of Huaisu's Draft Script Calligraphy' didn't appear in the old version of Li Bo's *Collected Works*. When Song Minqiu [1019–79] was re-editing them he fell into the error of over-zealousness in his efforts to find pieces.

> Zhou Yuante and Dr Guo Shixian had ministered to Lu's medical needs the previous day.
>
> The poet Guo Xiangzheng, whom we met on Day 6/4, came from Grand Tranquillity prefecture; he is mentioned again as a deity on Day 7/17. Guo was a friend of Su Shi's and of the painter Li Gonglin (see Day 7/8 and illustration on page 72).

Day 7/14 (27th August)

The evening is clear so we've opened the southern windows and are looking out at the creek and hills. There are vast numbers of fish in the creek, and from time to time they break the water's surface and leap out, the slanting sunlight glinting on them as if they were silver knives. Wherever one looks fishermen are plying rods or hauling nets, and consequently the price of fish is very low. The likes of servants gorge on them every day. The locals say the lush waters of the creek are ideal for fish, and when I drank some it was indeed sweet. Can it be true that its lushness accounts for the quantity of fish?

South-east of the creek are a number of peaks resembling kohl for eyebrows. They must be the Black Mountains.

Fishermen's Flutes in a Tranquil Setting, Xia Gui (fl.1180–1230). Nelson Gallery of Art, Kansas City.

Day 7/15 (28th August)

In the morning I was called on by Wu Bogu, whose courtesy name is Minshu, Instructor at the prefectural school and a senior Gentleman-litterateur; and Yang Xun, whose courtesy name is Xinbo, Supernumerary Instructor and a senior Gentleman-litterateur. When we'd had a meal we visited the Temple of the Eastern Sacred Mountain and the Monastery of Abundant Blessings on Mount Huang, and thereafter we climbed to the Terrace that Chills in Sultry Summer. The architecture of the Temple of the Sacred Mountain is very grand. It was originally called the Director's Temple on Mount Huang, but I don't know what deity this Director was. It seems to be have been a heretical shrine, but now that it's been turned into the Temple of the Sacred Mountain the Director's cult has been lodged instead in a side chapel to receive its offerings. The Abundant Blessings used to be the Monastery to the Longevity of the Sage-like Emperor, but in the *renwu* year of the Shoaxing period [1162] the horizontal tablet was changed by imperial edict. There are twenty or more dilapidated rooms, and the last three or four monks; it's as forlorn as an ancient post-house. The abbot, Huiming, is from Pingyang in Wen prefecture. The Terrace that Chills in Sultry Summer is exactly similar to the Phoenix and Rain Blossom terraces, and was named specifically on account of its hilltop position. It was built by Emperor Gaozu of the [Liu] Song dynasty. The terrain is a wide open space, emerging high above the dusty atmosphere. To the south one looks out on the peaks of the Black Mountains, the Dragon Mountains, and the Nine Wells Mountains as though they were right at one's elbow. The Dragon Mountains are where Meng Jia [mid-fourth century] 'climbed high up and his hat fell off'. On the Nine Wells Mountains is Huan Xuan's [369–404] Altar of Usurpation. Slightly to the west two small hills in the River face each other; these are called East Ridge and West Ridge. Beihu looks down over the new city walls of He prefecture, and I could distinctly make out the watch-towers since it's only some four miles to He prefecture from the far side of the river. There's a poem of Li Bo's about this place entitled 'At the Terrace that Chills in Sultry Summer on Mount Huang, Seeing off my Young Paternal Kinsman on His Boat Journey to Huayin'. At the rear of the terrace is a pagoda, and behind that a pavilion called Pondering the Past.

When I first arrived in Dangtu and drank water from the Gushu Creek I was delighted by its sweet smoothness. But later, having drunk water throughout the town, I find it's all sweet. It seems to be a wonderful network of springs.

I do not know why an ancient post-house should be a by-word for the forsaken and neglected. Buddhist monasteries and Daoist temples had suffered much damage during the fighting of the previous forty years and their buildings were sometimes in a poor state, though as Lu reports many were being repaired and rebuilt by the 1170s.

The Phoenix and Rain Blossom terraces were where the Buddhist monk Yungang (sixth century) is said to have preached so well that the heavens rained flowers.

Meng Jia's hat fell off in a draft when he was attending a banquet in the Dragon Mountains on the Double Ninth festival, when by tradition people would go up to high places, but he didn't notice. When he went to the lavatory his host told another of the guests to write a short note making fun of Meng and put it with the hat back in Meng's place. Meng returned from the lavatory to find himself the butt of the joke, but rose to the occasion by writing an elegant riposte which won universal praise; an example of the sprited and quick-witted gentleman.

Huan Xuan, who has had a bad press from the historians, declared himself emperor a few miles from Gushu in 403.

Day 7/16 (29th August)

There was an official reception at the Daoist Cloister, and we then went on to visit the pavilions and gazebos on the city wall. The Sit Whistling Pavilion is particularly well suited to surveying the scene from on high, and there are lotus flowers growing all over the moat round the city wall.

Tonight the moonlight is as white as day, and its reflection in the creek shimmers like a jade pagoda. Now I understand how marvellous is that line by Su Shi:

> A jade pagoda rests upon the ripples.

Day 7/17 (30th August)

There was an official reception at the Black Mountains shrine hall to Li Bo, in which the two Instructors took part. The shrine is to the north-west of the Black Mountains, but still five miles from them. Li's tomb is behind the shrine where hillocks, which must be a spur of the Black Mountains, undulate. The origins of the shrine are unknown, but it has a funerary inscription written by Liu Quanbai [fl. second half of the eighth century] of the Tang dynasty; and in recent years the Drafter Zhang Zhenfu has written a 'Stele for the Repairs to the Shrine'. Li is depicted in black head kerchief, white gown and brocade coat; the servitor at his side in Daoist hat and feather-trimmed fur cape who enjoys the same sacrificial offerings is Guo Xiangzheng.

When the morning meal was over we visited the Black Mountains. South of the mountain is a little settlement with the site of Xie Tiao's former residence. A family called Tang now lives there. As you gaze south there's a level plain as far as the eye can see, but all around the house are flowing springs and unusual rocks, green woods and speckled bamboos. It's a most beautiful place.

We then climbed up the mountain behind the house on a very precipitous path, but after about a mile and a half there were two Daoists amongst the pines and rocks proffering hot drinks to restore us. And after a further third of a mile or so we came to a retreat from which an old Daoist of over seventy came out to greet us. His surname was Zhou and he came from Wei prefecture, but has lived in these mountains for thirty years. His cheeks were ruddy and his beard and temples had not a hint of white. There was also an Old Mother Li who is eighty. She has acute hearing and sight, and chatted and laughed without any signs of age, telling us that she had acquired the occult arts from a person of strange powers.

In front of the retreat is a little pool called Mr Xie's Pool. The water tastes sweet and cold, and it doesn't dry up even at the height of summer. On the topmost summit there's another little pavilion and this too is called after Mr Xie. As we looked down on the mountains all around they seemed to resemble serpents and dragons hurtling about in a race to the river valleys. They're extremely like the Shun Mountains of my home district, except that the summit of the Shun Mountains is fertile, flat and broad as though it were level ground, and in this respect these mountains can't compare. To the north of the pavilion you directly face Liyang. Mr Zhou told me that when Wanyan Liang raided the area the sound of his battle drums reverberated through these mountains.

By the time we got back to the mooring at night it was already past the first watch [after 9 p.m.]. Yang Xun, who was amongst the company, mentioned that Huan Wen's [312–73] tomb lies near by on the outskirts of the town. It has stone beasts and stone horses of the finest workmanship. There is also a stele on which are carved carriages, horses, clothes, headgear and so on of the period, which is well worth seeing. I'm sorry I can't get there.

As we have seen, Li Bo was a High Tang poet (eighth-century) whose reputation through the ages has been only a little less than that of Du Fu (whom we shall encounter in his own right, as it were, on Day 8/1 and several succeeding entries of the Diary). Li is the wild romantic, free-ranging and bohemian to Du's more cerebral and controlled persona. Guo Xiangzheng, a minor poet of the eleventh century, had a reputation for a while for writing in the style of Li Bo and, as we were told by Lu You on Day 7/13, was regarded as a 'reincarnation of Li', of which he was proud. The creators of the shrine to Li Bo had clearly taken this into account when they arranged a principal altar to Li with a side-shrine to Guo as his alter ego and servitor. Such composite shrines, in which family members or others connected with the principal deity were worshipped together, were then becoming common. Lu You (Day 7/7) was critical of such arrangements when deities without appropriate historical or familial links shared a shrine.

Feathered costumes such as Guo Xiangzheng wore in this image were characteristic of the Daoists. The Daoists sought corporeal immortality through alchemical processes and, increasingly by the Tang and Song dynasties, spiritual techniques which were conceptualized as a kind of 'internal alchemy'. The Daoists that Lu You meets as he climbed the mountain behind the house of the fifth-century poet Xie Tiao suggest by their health and vigour success in these arcane pursuits.

Another of the branches of arcane knowledge to which not only Daoists but Confucian scholars such as Lu You directed their attention was geomancy, which we discussed in the commentary to Day 7/7. His description of the plasticity of the topography through which he was passing give us some sense of the way in which he regarded mountains, their contours and sense of movement, in a geomantic as well as aesthetic light, as well of course as physical barriers significant for trade, communication and military strategy.

We have met Wanyan Liang before (Day 6/25): he was the Jin Emperor, otherwise known as Prince Hailing, leader of the Jurchen forces which were seeking to extend their conquest of north China and to finish off the Southern Song. Lu You's concern about the court's foreign policy was not academic; only nine years earlier, in 1161, the Jin with their battle drums had reached the point he was now passing.

Huan Wen, whose tomb Lu had to omit, had been a general of the fourth century Eastern Jin dynasty.

Day 7/18 (31st August)

In light rain we cast off and emerged from the Gushu Creek to proceed along the River. Where River and creek meet there is no mixing of their clear and turbid waters. For ten miles we were towed through the channel to reach the mouth of the Daxin where we moored. From here one emerges onto the main River, but you need a favourable wind to proceed and one can often be held up by the wind for days on end. Two small hills flank the River, to whit East Ridge and West Ridge; the other name for them is Gates of Heaven Hills. In a poem of Li Bo's he says:

> On either bank black hills emerge opposite each other;
> From out the sun approaches a solitary sail.

And Wang Anshi has a poem:

> Rocky peaks of Gates of Heaven Hills,
> The River's waters circling round their base.

Mei Yaochen said:

> East Ridge like a rearing silkworm,
> West Ridge like a swimming fish.

Xu Fu has:

> Southerners and northerners, their boats from morn till eve;
> East Ridge and West Ridge, hills throughout the ages.

They were all writing lines inspired by this place.

There were crowds of young lads along the water's edge selling water caltrops and lotus roots.

At night I walked on the embankment and gazed at the moon. The mouth of the Daxin is referred to as the mouth of the Daixing by Ouyang Xiu [1007–72] in his *Memoirs of an Official Career*,[33] but I haven't checked which is right. *Memoirs of an Official Career* was composed when he had been banished to Yiling.

On his way down-river Fan Chengda, writing in 1177, had observed the way that the waters of the Han River remained a clear reflective blue for a third of a mile after they joined the Yangzi, before being overcome. He had an explanation. When rivers run slowly they can clear themselves while rushing rivers can't help but be turbid.

Ouyang Xiu was a leading writer and politician of the mid-eleventh century whose influence on his younger contemporaries was pervasive. He brought on the rising Wang Anshi, poet and reformer of institutions; was a patron of one of the greatest Chinese prose-writers of the eleventh century, Su Che, brother of the poet Su Shi; and was a major contributor to the re-assertion of Confucian values that we know as 'neo-Confucianism', both reaction against and incorporation of Buddhist thinking, which reached its full flowering under Lu You's contemporary Zhu Xi (1130–1200). Ouyang was also, as we noted in the commentary to Day 7/8, a historian; and his classical knowledge was widely admired. In addition he wrote essays and miscellanea which contain political anecdotes of his period. Lines of his poetry are quoted by Lu You in numerous later entries of the Diary; and Lu on Day 8/26 gives an account of Ouyang's place in the revival of 'ancient style' prose which would be accepted by modern critics. His *Memoirs of an Official Career*, written in 1036, is an earlier but far less ambitious form of the travel journal.

Day 7/19 (1st September)

The wind was set fair and we passed the Greater and Lesser Fustian Mountains Promontories with their strange rocks soaring up. The fishermen were leaning on the rocks to haul in their nets, just as one sees in paintings.

We passed Baleful Owl Promontory which sticks straight up out of the Great River. Daoists have built a lodge on it. In the Zhenghe period [1111–17] this was granted the name of the Calm Depths Abbey. An old story has it that there are malign owls which harm people on Baleful Owl Promontory; hence the name. When the prefectural and county authorities, who disliked the name, submitted a request for a horizontal placard for the abbey, they stated that the promontory was in the midst of the waters which regularly washed over the rocks, and so it was called the Inundated Promontory. The abbey buildings now consist of more than twenty rooms, but there is only one Daoist priest living there. It's said that if there are two of them then one is sure to die, so no one else dares go there.

We reached Reed Lake county and moored at Waves of Wu Pavilion. Lü Zhaowen, the magistrate and a junior Court Gentleman for Comprehensive Duty, called on me.

I note that in the Han dynasty there was a Reed Lake county in Danyang Commandery, and that Lu Xun [183–245] in the Wu dynasty was stationed there. Furthermore, in Du Yu's [222–84] annotation of the *Spring and Autumn Annals* regarding the Viscount of Chu's expedition against Wu and conquest of Jiuzi, he also refers to the event occurring at Reed Lake. But by the time of the Eastern Jin dynasty [317–420] the name had been changed to At The Lake. I don't know where this came from. When Wang Dun [266–324] rose in revolt he made his camp by At The Lake and its ancient walls still exist. There's also a Flourish of the Whip Pavilion which is another vestige of that period. Wen Tingyun [798–868?] of the Tang dynasty wrote a 'South of the Lake Song' which narrates those events. In more recent times Zhang Lei maintained that where the *History of the Jin Dynasty* refers to 'the emperor arriving at the lake and secretly spying out the camp and fortifications' one should take 'at the lake' as a grammatical unit [rather than a name], and that Wen must have misread it. So Zhang wrote his 'At The Lake Song' to refute him. Liu Yuxi in his poem 'Writing of Events at Liyang', describes incidents associated with his route as follows:

> Gazing out for her husband she turned to stone;
> He dreamed by day the Emperor circled his camp.

It was probably when Liu Yuxi was transferred from Kui prefecture to be prefect of Liyang that he passed through this town.

The townspeople say that a few years ago there were robbers in the environs of the town who dug up a large tomb. The inner and outer coffins had already decayed but they found a great number of looking glasses and knives, swords and the like. On a fired brick were the four words: 'Tomb of the General'. Some people suspect this may have been Wang Dun's tomb.

Lu You's historical and philological antennae are alert to any discrepancies in the record, and he can bring to bear a formidable range of classical learning, though there is no evidence to indicate the extent to which he relied on memory or may have added to or corrected the text of his diary after his journey was over. In the passage above Lu contends that Reed Lake (Wuhu) and At the lake (Yuhu) were one and the same place. This points up the richness of historical associations which the route of Lu's journey possessed for an educated Chinese, and which he is able to call in aid of his argument: the Viscount of Chu, a state which dominated the central Yangzi basin from the ninth to the third centuries BC, launched his attack downstream against the kingdom of Wu (the Wu referred to here is not the same as the Wu dynasty to which Lu Sun belonged, mentioned in the previous lines) and conquered Jiuzi in 570 BC; the event is described in the *Spring and Autumn Annals* which covers the years 771–481 BC. The fall of the Han dynasty in 220 led to the instability of the period in which Lu Sun and Wang Dun flourished; Liu Yuxi (whom we met on Day 7/11), poet and promoter of the ancient prose style which a chronicle such as the *Spring and Autumn Annals* exemplified, lived under the re-unified empire of the Tang in the early ninth century, as did the poet Wen Tingyun; and Zhang Lei, whom we also encountered on Day 7/11 as the critic of the renegade Fan Ruobing, was a considerable literary figure of the eleventh century.

Day 7/20 (2nd September)

Chen Bing, Recorder of Grand Tranquillity county in Secured-nation and a senior Gentleman for Meritorious Achievement, came to call on me. I took a small boat to go and say goodbye to him, for he is lodging in the sub-cloister of the Calm Depths Abbey, having come on instructions from the Judicial Commission to oversee the collection of cash and bolts of silk as a Commissioner for Grand Ceremonials. The Calm Depths Abbey is on the Baleful Owl Promontory across the Great River, so the sub-cloister has been set up in the vicinity of the town. There are a dozen Daoists in it and fine altars, buildings, images and appurtenances. The abbot, He Shoucheng, has now been chosen to reside at the Supreme Unity Priory.

Chen Bing has the courtesy name Dexian and comes from Yiwu in Wu prefecture. He says that his aunt on his father's side found the True Way and in the time of Emperor Huizong [r.1101–25] was awarded the title Adept of Wonderful Calm. She built a lodge beneath the Immortal Ge's Peak, and throughout her life took no cooked food but simply drank wine and consumed raw fruit. She would predict people's fortunes and how long they would live without the tiniest discrepancy. Whenever the weather was clement she would always shut herself up all alone, and if you eavesdropped on her from outside the door it would sound as if there were a couple of children in there, now singing and now laughing. Often this would go on until the middle of the night. No one could fathom her. On New Year's Day of the year in which she became ninety she said she had a long journey to make on the eighth day of the fourth month, and sure enough on that day she took up the meditative position and passed away.

She had often said to Chen Bing that he had the bone structure of an immortal and was bound to encounter a person of exceptional powers. Later, when he was enfeebled by illness, a Mr Xu from the Wan Hills came and dispensed drugs for him to take and his illness subsided that very day. So Xu stayed on and taught him the arcane secrets of abstinence from grains. Chen Bing's parents had hopes of his making a name for himself and firmly forbade him from pursuing this path. Nevertheless, from then on he gave up fine foods, and only ate plain noodle soup and rice every day. He went on in this way for six years, and felt his body becoming lighter and lighter so that he could walk seventy miles in a day. But when he passed the civil service examinations and took a wife he reverted to being a meat-eater. So Xu then took his leave, but as he was about to go he said to Chen: 'In twenty-four years' time you will have to pursue these matters with me once more.' Chen saw him off as far as the creek, but just as he was about to call for a boat to take him across Xu gathered up his gown, walked hastily over the water, and was gone. And though Chen called out to him he gave no further response. To this day Chen feels a sense of regret and thinks of giving up office and going into the Qian and Wan Hills.

I then visited the Eastern Monastery and climbed up onto Wang Dun's wall before returning. The wall runs in parallel with the Great River, and creates a grand and impressive effect.

The town produces the moss terrapin and uncountable numbers of people came to our boat to sell them.

Towards noon we cast off and passed by Three Hills Promontory. On the promontory was a newly built shrine to the River Dragon. A half-drunk Daoist was standing on the most precipitous part of the moss-covered cliff gazing down at the passing boats. It gave one the shivers just to look at him. He was a remarkable fellow.

In the river ten or so freshwater dolphins kept appearing and disappearing. Some were black and some were yellow. Then after a while I saw a creature several feet long and bright red, resembling a huge centipede. It braced its head against the current as it went upstream, churning the water a couple of feet high. It was terrifying.

We spent the night at the mouth of the Guodao.

The Immortal Ge, after whom the peak mentioned here was named, was the historical figure Ge Hong (283–343). Unsuccessful in politics, he turned to the role of literary recluse, seeking immortality through Daoist alchemical practices. Ge was the author of the *Baopuzi* (*He Who Embraces Simplicity*) which was finished around 320. Chen Bing was clearly torn between an official career and the esoteric arts of the Daoists, but such tensions were common to many of Lu You's contemporaries. Lu's own interest in matters occult and in Daoism are evident in this passage; elsewhere we see his easy relations with educated Buddhists, his Confucian sense of civic duty and his cultural chauvinism, all entirely normal for Chinese officials of this period.

The Qian Hills, also known as the Wan Hills, to which Chen wished to escape are in the modern province of Anhui.

Wang Dun was the early-fourth-century general whose tomb had perhaps been opened up by grave robbers a few years previously (Day 7/19).

It is not clear whether Ly You is referring here to dolphins, which are pale in colour, or to porpoises. The Yangzi dolphin was declared effectively extinct in December 2006, a victim of China's industrialization. The freshwater porpoise is facing the same fate.

Day 7/21 (3rd September)

We passed Fanchang county. This was established in the Southern Tang dynasty and at first came under Xuan City, but with the establishment of Grand Tranquillity prefecture was split off again and made subordinate to it.

In the evening we moored at Reed Port and I went for a stroll on top of the embankment, visiting the River Dragon Temple. There was an old Daoist looking after it who was from Xianju county in Tai prefecture. He said he had lived here ten years and that

A Daoist god, Song dynasty.

he cut two bundles of firewood every day to sell, by which means he maintains himself; in rain and snow he begs from others. He has had no other employment. I also went to a retreat where a Buddhist monk told me that across from the port lies the boundary of Copper Mounds, and where the distant hills rise sheer beside the Great River is Mount Copper Factory. It was this to which Li Bo was referring in his lines:

> I love the pleasures of Copper Factory,
> I don't plan to leave for a thousand years.

I'm sorry I've never been there.

Finally I reached the Attracting Blessings Abbey at Phoenix Hill. The abbey was ravaged by fire and sword more than forty years ago, and has only recently been restored. It has five or six devotees of Daoism, and the abbot, Chen Tingrui, comes from Yiwu county in Wu prefecture. He says that this foundation is the ancient Blue Flower Abbey. There was once a Mr Zhao from Reed Port Town whose father was a tea merchant. Mr Zhao had had the given name King Nine when he was a child. At the age of thirteen he'd became seriously ill and his father had carried him off to the Blue Flower Abbey, and made a vow to put him into the religious life. That night Mr Zhao dreamed that an old man had been leading him up a high mountain, and had told him: 'I am the Patriarch of Hades.' The old man took out some cedar twigs for him to eat. He awoke, and didn't eat cooked food from then on. Later he dreamed again of the old man who taught him several hundred characters of a celestial Seal Script. On waking he remembered every one of them. Emperor Taizong summoned him to an audience, and ordained him as a Daoist priest. The cap and certificate were bestowed on him, his name was changed to Spontaneity, his travel costs were met and he was sent back home, and thereafter he became abbot. In the Dazhongxiangfu period [1008–16] he was once again summoned to the capital, the purple cassock was bestowed on him, and the horizontal tablet of the Blue Flower Abbey was changed to Attracting Blessings. Mr Zhao earnestly entreated to be allowed to return to his native hills to take care of his mother; but having got home he passed away the next day without ever being ill. His disciples were going to bury him in the hills, but half-way there the coffin suddenly became so heavy they couldn't carry it. His mother said: 'I'm sure there's something extraordinary happening to my son.' She ordered them to open the coffin and it turned out that there was no corpse in it, just his sword and sandals; so they buried the coffin at that spot. The tomb is still there today, and is referred to as the Tomb of the Sword. There is a biography of Spontaneity in the National History, and it's pretty consistent with what Chen Tingrui says, omitting only the matter of the Tomb of the Sword.

Reed Port is a little local market-town of Fanchang.

It was night before I got back to the boat.

The 'five or six devotees of Daoism' is, in more literal translation, 'five or six feathered types'. As we have seen feathered costumes were associated with Daoists. The Song government attempted to

Carrying a coffin. Limestone, mid-twelfth century.

exercise a measure of control over religious activity which might otherwise slide off into the unaccountable, the uncontrollable, and the untaxable. One method was to issue official ordination certificates which validated the Daoist priesthood, ensured government registration, and raised funds from the fees (though perhaps not in the case of Mr Zhao who appears to have been treated with signal honour; and on Day 8/4 we find Lu You meeting a Daoist priest who had been granted a Certificate of Ordination by General Yue Fei). Indeed, many potential clergy could not afford ordination certificates because of their inflated price. Another exercise in control and subordination was the granting of titles to gods, and grand and auspicious names to the temples which housed them. In some instances (as we saw on Days 6/26 and 7/7) this involved the bestowal of placards in the imperial calligraphy, or that of a distinguished local official.

Day 7/22 (4th September)

We crossed the Great River and entered the channel of the Ding Family Island before continuing once more on the Great River. Since leaving Dangtu the weather has been delightfully fresh, the ripples smooth as a mat. In the distance white clouds and ranges of green hills serve as a foil one to the other, and all day we seem to be journeying through a painting, quite forgetting the hardships of travel.

We passed Copper Mounds county without going in, and in the evening moored at the mouth of Water Narrows. People who live by rivers and lakes call the place where currents divide into separate channels a 'narrow', as in Wang Anshi's line:

In East River trees shed their leaves and the waters divide into narrows.

Day 7/23 (5th September)

As we passed Sunny Mount promontory the Nine Hua Mountains came into view for the first time. The Nine Hua were originally named the Nine Sons, and it was Li Bo who changed the name. Both Li and Liu Yuxi have poems about them, Liu going so far as to consider them as spectacular as the Taihua and Nüji mountains put together. When Song Qiqiu of the Southern Tang dynasty relinquished power he returned to a life of seclusion amongst these mountains, gave himself the soubriquet Master of the Nine Hua, and was enfeoffed as Duke of Qingyang. On account of this the Nine Hua became even better known. Those lines by Wang Anshi which read:

> Though the coiling base is mighty and sturdy,
> Their tips are slender and slight

is the most marvellous description, for all in all what is extraordinary about these mountains is precisely that they look slender and slight. But they're not imbued with a sense of grandeur, in this differing from Mount Lu or the Tiantai mountains.

Along the banks the reed-flowers were like snow. When I once met the Venerable Yanwei of the Heaven's Well Monastery he told me: 'The old monks of the Lu Mountains use this reed floss to line their clothes. In my youth, in the days when I was living in Hui, I did the same. The Zen Master Xun of the Buddha Lamp saw and got furious: "If you're trying to keep warm like this when you're young can you really be set on studying the True Way?" When I withdrew and asked my brother monks I found that only three or four out

Zen Priest, Liang Kai (c.1140–1210).
National Palace Museum, Taipei.

of a hundred in the community had floss-lining in their clothing, and they were all more than seventy years old. I felt mortified and hurriedly got rid of mine.'

We moored at Plum-root Port. There were more than ten huge pale-grey fish as large as ox calves appearing and disappearing in the water. Each time they emerged the water was churned into frothing white waves. It was a truly grand sight.

Song Qiqiu was, it will be recalled from Day 7/9, senior minister to the founding emperor of the Southern Tang.

The Lu Mountains (Lushan) are in Jiangxi province; Lu You had yet to reach them, seeing them first on Day 8/2. The temperature in the hills in summer is often ten degrees celsius cooler than a few miles away at river level. The Tiantai mountains in Zhejiang province lay south-east of Lu's home-town and were known for their associations with Buddhism. The Tendai sect derives from the Japanese pronunciation of the name.

Yanwei is not mentioned in the reference works. I believe Hui refers to Mount Hui monastery near Wuxi (No Tin) in Jiangsu province. Amongst its advantages was water of high quality, as Lu mentions on Day 8/10.[34]

Day 7/24 (6th September)

We reached Lake prefecture and moored at the Customs Post. The prefecture was established under the Tang dynasty and became the Transformed by Tranquillity Military Command in the Southern Tang. This has now been abolished. Furthermore Qingyang, which had been split off and made subordinate to Jiankang, has now been restored to its status quo ante. Only the two counties which had been established of Copper Mound and East Brook, and the change of Autumn Creek's name to Precious Pool, have been retained. When the Southern Tang had their capital at Jinling the eleven counties of Dangtu, Reed Lake, Copper Mound, Fanchang, Guangde, and Qingyang, together with Jiangning, Shangyuan, Li North, River Li and Jurong, were all brought under the jurisdiction of the capital territory. Nowadays Jiankang has the role of an auxiliary capital yet it consists of only the five towns of Jiangning, etc. This is something the authorities should deliberate.

When Li Bo was travelling back and forth in the lower Yangzi area he wrote an especially large number of poems about this prefecture; for instance his *Seventeen Songs of the Autumn Cove*, and his poems 'The Nine Hua Mountains', 'Clear Creek',[35] 'White Bamboo-shaft Mere' and 'Jade Looking Glass Pool'. The *Songs of the Autumn Cove* have the lines:

> Autumn Cove, as long as Autumn,
> Its desolation makes one sad.

He also said, in lines which illustrate the scenery of Lake prefecture:

> My brows, on entering Autumn Cove,
> In but a morn endured decay and loss;

> For gibbons' cries brought on my greying hair,
> Till in the end it turned to silken floss.

But when you see just how wonderful are these songs of Li Bo you realize that the 'Ten Paeans of Gushu' are definitely a fabrication. Du Mu's [803–52] poems from Lake prefecture are genuine, and they read with a delightfully sinuous purity. But read side by side with those of Li Bo they are as much a contrast in flavour as heavy or light wines.

When first our royal armies were conquering the Southern Tang dynasty, Cao Bin was given orders to divide his forces and go eastwards downstream from Jing prefecture. He made Fan Ruobing his local guide, but it was only first by capturing Lake prefecture that he was able to take Reed Lake and Dangtu, station his army at Coloured-Stone, and complete the pontoon bridge. So given Lake prefecture's current strategic importance it really is essential to defend it.

Lu You's interest in administrative history is not perhaps one that the modern reader will share; his point is that Nanjing, in the various guises in which it appears here (Jinling, Jiankang and so on), had boasted a large metropolitan district around it when serving as capital in the past. This it had now lost. Since in the Southern Song period Nanjing remained a subsidiary capital, and as we have seen Lu harboured hopes that with a more forward policy towards the northern invaders it might once again become the capital (Day 7/7), he argues here that Nanjing should have a larger constellation of directly administered counties around it.

Arguments over the fabrication of the 'Ten Paeans of Gushu' have already been disposed of to Lu You's satisfaction when he quoted Su Shi's views on Day 7/13. Du Mu was a leading poet of the Late Tang, but along with most traditional Chinese critics Lu gives pride of place to the High Tang (roughy the century following the accession of Emperor Xuanzong in 713) poets such as Du Fu and Li Bo. We find Lu quoting Du Mu again on Day 8/18 on the pleasures of having little work to do.

The story of Cao Bin and the pontoon bridge on which he crossed the Yangzi in 975, having been provided with the measurements by Fan Ruobing, has been recounted on Day 7/11. Here, two centuries later, in accordance with his anti-Jurchen posture, Lu You adds a contemporary gloss on the strategic importance of the area.

Day 7/25 (7th September)

Having called on Yang Shizhong, the Prefect and a junior Grand Master for Court Discussion and Auxiliary in the Imperial Archives; and Sun Dechu, Assistant Prefect and a junior Gentleman for Court Service, I visited the Glory to Filial Piety Monastery. The monastery possesses an iron flute left behind by the 'Sage of the Western Peak'. The Sage lived at the time of Yang Xingmi, Prince Wu [r.892–906] of the state of Wu. He feigned madness and behaved with abandon, and was fond of playing the flute with which he could command demons, spirits, serpents and dragons. He had lodged at the Regal Perspicuity Monastery in Lake prefecture (Regal Perspicuity being the Glorifying Filial Piety Monastery) and when he came to depart he left behind this flute which he consigned to the monk in charge of administration. The flute seems to be of copper and iron, though it isn't. It's green in colour, and lustrous as green jade, but I don't know what the material can be. The monks are terrified it will be appropriated by some busy-body, so when a Commandery official asks to examine it they always produce an ordinary iron flute in its place. I happen to be an old friend of the Procurator and exceptionally got a look at it.

There is a stone inscribed with the 'Commemoration of the Western Peak' written by Shen Liao. The language has an appealing antique elegance, but sad to say the calligraphy is not his.

The monks say that Precious Pool is twenty-seven miles from the town, and lies beneath Mount Xiu where a separate arm of the River converges to form the 'pool', with the rock of the mountain forming its banks on all sides. It produces carp with golden scales and scarlet tails that have a delicious flavour. This was originally why it got the designation 'Precious Pool'.

On Mount Xiu is the tomb of Crown Prince Zhaoming [501–31] of the Liang dynasty, dense with funereal trees. At the present day, to the west of the city wall of Lake prefecture, there is a highly efficacious deity called Nine Fellows. Some say that Nine Fellows is Zhaoming.

In the evening I climbed up to Toying with Water Pavilion about which Du Mu wrote poems. The pavilion is in exceptionally poor repair; but it directly faces Clear Creek and Mount Qi, and the view is most lovely.

Though the prefectural town lies on the banks of the River it's set on a hillock and water is fairly hard to obtain.

Xiao Tong, Prince Zhaoming of the Liang dynasty, was a literary patron under whose aegis the anthology *Wenxuan* (*Selections of Refined Literature*) was produced, a work that became a model for later makers of anthologies. The spirit, whosoever it might be, was performing the most important function of a deity: to respond effectively to the requests made of it. In addition to the offerings presented by the hopeful and the grateful, such deities would, on application by officials of the terrestrial civil service to the court, be given title and position in the celestial bureaucracy as reward for their assistance. Nine Fellows appears to have been one of those deities whose status had not yet been regularized despite his local reputation.

Day 7/26 (8th September)

We cast off and went past the Rākṣasa Rock at Long Wind Sands. In his poem 'On the River, Presented to Magistrate Dou' Li Bo says:

> Banished south three thousand miles to the country of Yelang;
> Three years till I travelled back past the Long Wind Sands.

And Mei Yaochen, in his poem 'Seeing off Graduate Fang on his Trip to the Lu Mountains' has the lines:

The waves at Long Wind Sands come as large as houses,
And Rākṣasa's rocky teeth are arrayed beneath the water.
But through this double jeopardy and having passed Pen Cove,[36]
At last you'll see the waterfalls suspended from green cliffs.

This is the place they mean. There is also Li Bo's 'Ballad of Changgan' in which he says:

One of these days you'll descend the Three Ba,
But write us a line so we know in advance.
I'll come out to meet you no matter the distance;
Even as far as the Long Wind Sands.

It's two hundred and thirty miles from Jinling to here, so it certainly would be a long way for a wife to come and meet her husband!

This area comes under the jurisdiction of Shu prefecture. In the past it was well known for the danger of its rapids, but in the reign of Emperor Renzong [r.1023–63] the Supply Commissioner Zhou Zhan employed three hundred thousand men to clear a three mile channel to avoid them, and to this day it's of benefit to navigation. The Rākṣasa Rock stands in the middle of the Great River and is just like Falcon Peak at Jingkou, but rather larger. White boulders loom round it, and at the top are clumps of bamboo and tall trees. There were also poles for streamers at a little spirit shrine, but I don't know to which deity.

Looking west, ranges of mountains stretch faint into the distance, their crags and cliffs muted and delicate, just as at home when one gazes south to the mountains by Looking Glass Lake. It made me heave many a sigh.

We are lodging at the Huai Family Wharf. Huai is a surname. There was a Secretarial Court Gentleman in the Wu dynasty [222–80] called Huai Xu (see the biography of Gu Yong [168–243]).

Rākṣasa are malignant spirits or demons, so we may infer the passage was not an easy one. Yelang was an ancient state to the south-west of the Han empire in what is now Sichuan, Yunnan and Guilin; Li Bo is bemoaning his distant exile. Mei Yaochen is offering the prospect of future delights to a young man off on a difficult journey to remote parts; whereas in the second of the Li Bo poems that Lu quotes Li is speaking in the person of a young wife whose husband has gone far up the Yangzi and whose return downstream to Nanjing she longs for.

Lu had passed Falcon Peak, or Hill as he previously refers to it, on Day 6/28.

Looking Glass Lake is near Lu You's home town of Shanyin (the modern Shaoxing) in Zhejiang Province, from which he had set out two months previously. (See illustratrations on page 20 and 21.) It was Lu himself who made the lake famous through his poetry.

Most Chinese surnames are common to large numbers of people, but the name Huai is unusual enough to be worthy of comment and a display of Lu's erudition; Gu Yong's biography is given in the Sanguo Zhi (Record of the Three Kingdoms) which was completed in 297.

Day 7/27 (9th September)

At the fifth watch [3–5 a.m.] a strong north-easterly blew up, and without telling us the boatmen cast off to take advantage of the favourable wind. We passed Goose Wing channel where there's a customs station, with two hundred or so households living there and a great many boats moored beneath the bank. We then went by the mouth of the Wan River and reached Zhao Village, and had already travelled fifty miles before we'd eaten our morning meal, but the wind was growing ever stronger so we moored in the channel. The mouth of the Wan River is the place where our royal forces destroyed the fleet of Zhu Lingbin, the Jiangnan Commander-in-Chief. Zhao Village has a garrison, and is also a small township.

Today's strong winds are still blowing this evening. I went up onto the embankment and walked to the mouth of the channel to watch the terrifying waves and breakers out on the River. Not even the tidal bore on the Qiantang River in the eighth lunar month surpasses this. There was a boat pitching and tossing in the waves. Two or three times it tried to enter the channel and failed, and almost capsized and sank. They were shouting and yelling for help, and it was a long time before they were able to get in.

Looking north you can see straight to Mount Wan. Li Bo in his poem 'On the River, Gazing at Mount Wangong' has the line:

> Precipitous, abrupt, it fulfils my expectations.

The two words 'precipitous, abrupt' have an inexpungeable brilliance. When Emperor Yuanzong of the Southern Tang dynasty was transferring to Yuzhang he saw Mount Wan from his boat, loved it and said to his attendants: 'What are those steep green peaks called?'. They replied: 'Mount Wan in Xu prefecture.' At this time the Southern Tang had just lost the area south of the Huai River. A court musician, Li Jiaming, was in attendance on the emperor and presented the following poem:

> Your dragon boat a thousand miles wafts on the eastern breeze:
> Wu of Han's Xunyang trip was just such an affair.
> You turn towards the lovely colours of the Wangong hills:
> Those setting rays will never reach your goblet of long life.

It made Emperor Yuanzong sob in misery and frustration. That's why Wang Anshi's poem says:

> South he 'hunted' at Mount Wan, not the old familiar country:
> A northern army on the Huai, for now he'd lost the name of king.

By my calculation the place can't have been far from here.

It's raining tonight.

Zhu Lingbin, the Southern Tang general, was defeated in 975. Lu You gives an account of the naval battle in his *History of the Southern Tang Dynasty*, which he completed in 1184: '. . . Zhu Lingbin couldn't stick to his earlier advice, so together with Wang Hui . . . he advanced with the current. At Lake Xunyang he tied trees together to make large rafts of over three hundred feet long, and his large ships could hold up to a thousand men. He was about to rush down and break through the pontoon at Coloured-Stone, but at the time the River's waters were low and his boats and rafts were running aground so our royal forces were able to make preparations, and when he reached Tiger Squat Island battle was joined. The ship on which Zhu Lingbin travelled was especially large and he had set up his admiral's pennants and drums on it. Though the ships belonging to our royal forces were small they attacked him en masse. Zhu set fire to them with burning oil and our royal forces couldn't withstand it. But then a north wind rose and turned the flames so the enemy were burned themselves, and they lost 150,000 land and naval troops without even engaging. Zhu was terrified, plunged into the fire and died. Grain, rice, weapons and armour were all consumed in the fire and not a jot remained, nor did the fire stop for ten days' (From Lu You's *Nan Tang Shu* juan 8).

The tidal bore on the Qiantang River is the world's largest, with a front of about twelve feet, and sometimes generates standing waves of thirty feet where two wave fronts intersect. The eighth lunar month would equate to the autumnal equinox.

Once again Lu You's associations of place are with historical events from the Southern Tang dynasty, the period he knew so well. Emperor Yuanzong (r.943–61) was the second of the three Southern Tang emperors. Though a competent ruler who had absorbed some smaller states into his dominions and had built a capital on the site of the present-day Nanjing, he was coming under pressure by 958. The area south of the Huai River was lost, but a polite fiction maintained that the emperor was on a tour of inspection like the one to Xunyang made in 107 BC by the great Han dynasty emperor Wu (r.140–87 BC), or a hunting trip, rather than in retreat, his kingdom's existence under threat.

Day 7/28 (10th September)

We passed East Brook county without going in. Since the mouth of the Thunder River we've been travelling on the Great River. The ranges of mountains south of the River, with their myriad folds of grey-green, are like rows of screens running on unbroken for tens of miles. There has been nothing like this west of Jinling.

Today the wind has been set fair, the sail hoisted, and the boat has moved forward at great speed. But the surface of the River is so vast and the white waves so mountainous that the one hundred and fifty ton boat in which we are travelling yawed and sheered as though it were a mere leaf.

We passed Lion Promontory, which is also called Buddha's Finger Promontory. Its mossy cliffs of a hundred foot, with their green woods and verdant bamboos growing upside down on the cliff face, could not be equalled in a painting. I'm still regretting that our boat went along the northern shore and we didn't manage to pass beneath it. By the side of it were several promontories with amazing crags, but none of them compares with the Lion.

We reached Madang, which is referred to as the Downstream Water Palace of the River God. The contours of the mountain are exceptionally elegant and elevated,

Hanging temple near Datong in Shanxi province, north China.

the base of its near side projecting right out into the River. The temple clings to a precipitous cliff, with a gallery built out on stilts. Those who make the ascent or descent all go by a little stone path to the west of the gallery half-way up the cliff, climbing by hanging onto the creeper and putting their feet sideways just as though they were mounting a ladder. With the sweep of its rafters, its winding balustrades, and the faint gleam of its paintwork in the distance, this is the finest of all the deity shrines along the River.

When our boat went under the rocky cliff the day suddenly went dark and the wind became very blustery. The boatmen were terrified and turned pale, frantically lowering the sail and dashing for the little harbour, tugging with all their might. We were only just able to make port and secure the hawsers, four or five other boats moored there all coming to help haul us in.

During the morning we had been travelling with another boat, also a 'Sichuan craft', when suddenly a huge bright green fish with an underbelly as red as cinnabar leaped up three feet or more out of the water beside its rudder. Everyone had been astonished at it. But this evening it turned out that their mast has been broken and sails torn, and they had barely escaped in one piece, which makes one wonder.

As night came on the wind grew ever more violent and an extra ten or more hawsers were attached. It's only with the dawn that the wind is dying down a bit.

As Chang and Smythe point out, the Downstream Water Palace of the River God is a mistake. The text should read Upstream Water Palace of the River God. Lu You had passed the Downstream Water Palace on Day 6/25.

Natural portents, such as brightly coloured fish, and the understanding of their import were part of the scholarly as well as popular mental furniture. Amongst educated Chinese such as Lu You and his like this lived alongside a rational interpretation of natural and historical facts.

Day 7/29 (11th September)

We were held up by the wind in the harbour at Madang. The wind and rain were bitterly cold, and for the first time we wore our padded coats, though little boats braved the wind-tossed waves to come and sell us firewood, vegetables and pork. One of them was also selling wild boar which they said they'd caught while hunting in the reed-beds. When our meal was over we climbed up onto the southern bank and looked across to the temple at Madang. The north wind was blowing so hard we couldn't speak. By dusk the wind was dying down a bit but the angry waves had still not subsided, buffeting the boat noisily all through the night.

The Storm Breaks, unsigned, Southern Song, c. twelfth century.

Day 8/1 (12th September)

We passed Brazier Promontory. In the Southern Dynasties [420–89] they established a string of beacon fires from Wuchang to Jingkou, and this mountain must have been one of them. Looked at from the boat the mountain simply towers above one; but having tacked along the River and passed beneath it there were caves and caverns in the sheer cliff in a myriad bizarre and strange shapes, glinting and gleaming with lustrous colours, utterly different from other rocks. There was also a rock detached from the mountain and rising all on its own to over a hundred feet high. It had scarlet vines and blue-green creeper draped over the top like a bejewelled screen.

Today the wind had dropped, the boat was moving quite slowly and, what's more, being well into autumn the rain-waters have receded. So one could fully see what old Du Fu [712–70] meant by:

> Luckily our vessel is moving slowly;
> Every marvel we pass I can fully absorb.

We passed Billowing Waves Promontory and the Lesser Lone Hill, the two hills facing each other east and west. The Lesser Lone Hill belongs to Susong county in Shu prefecture, and has a garrison. All the solitary hills in the midst of the River, such as Golden Mount, Jiao's Hill, Fallen Star and the like, are famed throughout the world, but for dizzy heights and elegant beauty none can match the Lesser Lone Hill. Seen from a dozen or so miles away, its bluish peak rising abruptly all alone, its top touching the high heavens, it already seems beyond compare with other hills; and the nearer you approach the more elegant it is. In winter or summer, in clear skies or rain, it presents a myriad different moods. It is truly a marvel of Creation. But the buildings of the shrine are extremely dilapidated. If it were somewhat embellished with towers and buildings, pavilions and belvederes, with the River and mountains to set them off, it would be even better than Golden Mount.

A temple lies on the western slopes of the mountain with a horizontal tablet giving its name as 'Salvation through Grace', the deity being called Lady Peace and Salvation. At the beginning of the Shaoxing period [1131–62], when Zhang Jun [1097–1164] was returning from the Hu and Xiang area, he carried out construction and repairs, and there's a stele recording the event.

There's also a separate shrine on the Billowing Waves Promontory, within Pengze county in Jiang prefecture, looking out over the River on three sides, its reflection inverted in the water. It dominates the whole mountain's scenery. As our boat passed the promontory, though it was windless, there was a swell of waves so presumably this is how it got the name. A poet of the past wrote the lines:

> Merchants in your boats, please behave well;
> It's years since the Little Maiden married Master Swell.

That's why tradition has it there is an image of Master Peng in the Lesser Lone temple, and an image of the Maiden in the Billowing Waves temple, though actually it's not so.

At evening we moored at Sandy Channel, which is a third of a mile from the Lesser Lone Hill. It was raining lightly but I took a small punt and revisited the temple. Gazing south to the Pengze and Duchang mountains, the sky was a haze of mist and rain in which gulls and egrets appeared and then were lost to sight. It was the very finest of panoramic views, and I lingered there for a long time before returning. Just as I was standing in the gateway of the temple a magnificent falcon seized a waterfowl and swept away over the River with it to the south-east. It was a really impressive sight. The sacristan told me there are a great many falcons nesting in these hills.

We have already had occasion to mention Du Fu (commentary to Day 7/17), generally considered the greatest of Chinese poets, and certainly one of the most difficult to translate. Day 8/1 is the first diary entry in which Lu You mentions Du, but the quotation is apposite rather than geographically relevant. It is not until the mid-ninth month that Lu's route overlaps with Du Fu's travels, albeit in the opposite direction, downstream, just over four hundred years before. Thereafter there were Du Fu associations all the way to Lu's destination in Kui prefecture, and beyond into Sichuan where Lu was to spend the next seven years.

Zhang Jun was a general and Grand Councillor. In concert with Yue Fei he cleared the Dongting Lake area of rebels and held the line against the Jin invaders. He was returning along the Yangzi from these operations in the area that is now Hunan province in 1135 when he carried out the building works that Lu You mentions. Zhang fell out of favour shortly thereafter when Qin Gui (Day 7/6) came to power, but was brought back into central government during the crisis of Prince Hailing's invasion in 1161 (Days 6/25 and 7/17). He was never popular with the peace party, and for that reason all the more admired by Lu.

The poet of the past was Su Shi, with whom we are now familiar, though his humour has not previously been on display. At the risk of explaining away Su's joke: his couplet quoted here depends on a double pun: Peng is a surname, its homophone meaning 'to swell' or 'billow'; *lang* 'a young gentleman' or, another word of similar sound, 'waves'. Likewise, the Lesser Lone (*xiaogu*) Hill provides the opportunity for a further pun with a Little Maiden (*xiaogu*). From such a play on words the popular imagination had apparently created two fictional characters from a rock in the River and the promontory surrounded by its billowing current. Looking across the River at each other they were sure to fall in love, and Su Shi is teasing the merchants on their long journeys away from their wives; though Lu You debunks the story that images of the lovers were set up in the shrines that faced each other across the water. Blakiston sighted the 'Little Orphan Rock' (our Lesser Lone Hill) on 6th March 1861: 'Porpoises disported themselves in the still muddy current of the Ta-kiang [Great River], as the Yang-tsze is called at this part. The day was bright, with a warm sun and little or no wind; and we viewed the cliff and crags of this interesting pass in their best colours. The "Little Orphan Rock" is a great resort for cormorants, which we observed in immense numbers perched on its ledges, and much of the cliff was whitened with the dung of these birds'. Isabella Bird, who estimated the height of the Greater and Lesser 'Orphan' rocks at 300 feet, found that they had been appropriated, 'as all picturesque sites are', by the Buddhists for religious purposes.

Day 8/2 (13th September)

In the morning we hadn't gone seven miles when suddenly wind and cloud roiled and boiled. There was a frantic tying of hawsers, but after a short while the sky cleared again. We then proceeded, sailing past the mouth of Lake Pengli. It was a boundless expanse wherever you looked, and I then realized the brilliance of Li Bo's line:

> With sail unfurled we enter a celestial looking glass.

For the first time I saw the Lu Mountains and the Greater Lone Hill. The Greater Lone Hill resembles West Ridge in shape; and though it can hardly be compared with the refined beauty of the Lesser Lone Hill this latter has a lot of sandy islets with reeds and rushes around it, whereas the Greater Lone Hill has the vast expanse of the Great River in every direction. It looks as though it were floating on the surface of the water, and is itself a wonder.

From the mouth of the lake the River divides, one branch forming the South River, and this is the route to Jiangxi. The River's water is turbid, and whenever we draw it for use we always filter it through apricot pits[37] overnight before it's fit to drink. But the South River is absolutely limpid, and at the place where they meet it's as if a string had been drawn between them, for they do not mingle.

By evening we had reached River prefecture. The prefectural administration is in Virtue-Transformed county, that's to say the Xunyang county of Tang dynasty times. Both Brushwood-Mulberry and Chestnut Village belong to this area. Under the Southern Tang

Near the mouth of Lake Boyang (Lake Pengli).

dynasty it was the Military Command of Fenghua, and is now the military prefecture of Dingjiang. The soil of the banks is red and perpendicular, as referred to by Su Shi in:

> The boatmen point out where the banks seem to blush.

We moored at Pen Cove. The water is very clear here as well, and doesn't mingle with the River's water.

From the twenty-sixth of the seventh month until now, a mere six days in all (and on one of those days we didn't travel because of contrary winds so it's actually four and a half days), we have travelled upstream some 230 miles.

Lake Pengli is the modern Lake Boyang lying to the south of the Yangzi which it serves as an overflow basin. The Jiangxi referred to here by Lu You, which was broadly equivalent to the modern province of the same name, was actually a contraction of Jiangnan Xilu meaning the Western Circuit of River South, a large administrative unit south of the Yangzi and to the west of the lake. Circuits were the administrative orbit of various senior officials sent out from the capital; they were charged with specific functions such as tax revenue, though not all such areas of geographic responsibility were contiguous with others having different functions: the modern system of provinces was still in its early stages of development during the Song dynasty. Lu You is drawing attention to the route from the south which joins the Yangzi at this point, the main River flowing in from the north-west, the direction in which he was heading. River prefecture, the modern Jiujiang, stands not far from the intersection of the ways. It was to suffer almost total destruction in 1858–9 during the

The Lute Pavilion, Jiujiang. Buddhists believe evil acts in one life lead to rebirth in a lower form in the next. This seems to be the fate of traditional Chinese buildings which are successively incarnated in ever more garish style, often reaching their modern apotheosis in painted concrete.

Taiping Rebellion but had been rebuilt and was prosperous once more when Isabella Bird visited it some thirty years later.

With regard to apricot pits for filtration, I note (to adopt Lu You's tone when about to deliver some arcane piece of knowledge) that Bird used condensed water for photographic printing on board her boat which, she says, was 'free both from Yangtsze mud and the alum used to precipitate it'.

Pen Cove was referred to on Day 7/26 in Mei Yaochen's poem which held out the prospect to a friend of good scenery after some difficult passages along the Yangzi.

Day 8/3 (14th September)

We transferred our mooring to Lute Pavilion and I called on Zhou Bian, whose courtesy name is Qiangzhong, the Prefect and a senior Gentleman for Court Audiences; Hu Kuo, the Assistant Prefect and a senior Gentleman for Closing Court; Shi Zhengzhi, whose courtesy name is Zhidao, the Supply Commissioner and Vice-director in the Ministry of Revenue; Cheng Tan, whose courtesy name is Lüdao, Administrator in the Supply Commission; and Cai Kan, whose courtesy name is Dingfu, Surveillance Circuit Judge and a senior Gentleman-litterateur.

I received for the first time official despatches from Kui prefecture.

Lu You, it will be recalled, was travelling to his new appointment in Kui prefecture.

Day 8/4 (15th September)

I visited the Celestial Blessings Abbey, which is referred to in Li Bo's poetry as the Priory of the Polar Constellation of Xunyang. Its engravings of the poetry of Su Shi and Huang Tingjian [1045–1105] no longer exist, but there is a stone with a poem of Li Bo's, though in commonplace calligraphy of recent vintage. I met the abbot, Li Shouzhi, and asked him about the Mushrooms of Immortality but he could give no answer. All the abbey's buildings are ancient, never having suffered the depredations of war, but its relics have been entirely destroyed. Only a statue of Lord Lao in the Hall of Supreme Purity, fashioned in the Tang dynasty, can be considered exceptional and ancient, with its two figures each of transcendents both male and female, immortals of the celestial officialdom, strongmen, and boy servitors. There is also a gilt-bronze image of Emperor Minghuang [r.712–56] of the Tang dynasty, dressed in gown and hat as a Daoist priest, his bearing one of simple dignity. It conveys an atmosphere of fifty years' secure enjoyment of peace and prosperity.

Li Shouzhi, who comes from Laian in Chu prefecture, described himself as coming from a family that used to be affluent, but during the troubles he left home to become a Daoist. It was when General Yue Fei [1103–42] presented him with his Certificate of Ordination that he first became a Daoist priest, and to the present day he reverences paintings of the Yues, father and son.

Shi Zhengzhi invited me for a drink in the Supply Commission offices, and we climbed up to the High and Far Pavilion to see the Lu Mountains. The weather was crystal clear and one could see each and every peak. Shi showed me some of the newly minted iron coins.

We shall make Huang Tingjian's acquaintance at various points hereon in the Diary. He was one of the leading poets of the eleventh century, a follower of Su Shi who experimented to establish an individual style known as the Jiangxi School, much imitated in the twelfth century. Huang's own poetry is more intense than Su's. He paid great care in the selection of words, and outdid even Wang Anshi and Su Shi in his respect for the eighth-century poet Du Fu whom he admired for his polished diction, introspective nature, and careful observation of the changes in nature. Huang is said to have avoided expression of passion as childish and primitive and this can make him seem cold and dry. Above all he was an intellectual, whereas poetry by the time of Lu You had returned to the world of feeling. Like Su, Huang opposed Wang Anshi's New Policies and like Su was exiled to distant provincial posts. This took him to Sichuan and, as Lu You's own journey proceeds, he notes a number of traces of Huang's travels of over seventy years before along some of the same route.

Mushrooms of Immortality, or Solomon's Seal, are known in Chinese as Jade Mushroom or, as Lu You tells us elsewhere, Goblin's Crucible, a plant which he says was common to houses in the mountains. It was believed to have

Iron coins were minted in the Hunan, Hubei area in 1166, as illustrated in F. Schjöth's *Chinese Currency*. They were circular with a square hole in the centre and stated the year of issue.

alchemical properties which commended it to the Daoists, so Lu must have hoped the abbot would have been able to shed some light on this plant.

During the first half of the eighth century Emperor Minghuang, also known as Xuanzong, presided over one of China's most prosperous eras both economically and culturally, a period in which literature flourished and when Chinese armies asserted control over Central Asia along the Silk Road and the Chinese were open to a range of ideas, products and fashions from beyond their borders. The reign ended in disaster, however. A revolt in 755 by a general of barbarian origin forced the emperor to flee his capital at Chang'an, the modern Xian, and make his way to Sichuan in the west. He was effectively deposed by his son who declared himself Emperor Suzong, relegating his father to a position of powerlessness on return to the capital after the rebels' star had waned. The Tang emperors, who shared the same Li surname as the purported founder of Daoism, Laozi or Lord Lao, favoured the Daoists and it is not surprising to find Minghuang's image associated with a Daoist abbey.

Yue Fei was the young general who fought with success against the Jurchen invaders but was recalled by Qin Gui in 1141 and executed the following year when a peace treaty between north and south was signed (see the commentary on Day 7/6). Yue had associations with this area; his mother's and his wife's tombs are near by. By 1170 his reputation was once more rising. That autumn the government gave agreement to build a shrine to Yue, the placard of which read 'Loyal and Valourous Temple'.[38]

Day 8/5 (16th September)

There was an official reception at Yu's Building. The building directly faces the Twin Swords Peak of the Lu Mountains and to the north it looks out over the Great River; its atmosphere is grand and beautiful. Westward of Jingkou are many places with panoramic views, but none better than Yu's Building. The building is not particularly tall yet one has the sense that River, mountains, mist and clouds all lie within one's grasp. It is truly an outstanding view. When Yu Liang [289–340] was serving as Prefect of River, Jing and Yu prefectures his administration was actually based in Wuchang, so it would be logical to call the South Building at Wuchang 'Yu's Building'. The present administrative seat of River prefecture is situated in what was in Jin dynasty times merely the Penkou Pass of Brushwood-Mulberry county. Very obviously the connection with this tower is a forced one. Yet Bai Juyi had certainly already referred to it in a poem:

> On the point of reaching Xunyang my thoughts run on and on,
> South of Yu Liang's Building, eastwards from Penkou.

So the misconception is a long-standing one. And when Zhang Shunmin [c.1034–c.1110] says in his *Record of a Transfer South* that 'when Yu Liang was stationed at Xunyang he began construction of this tower' he is compounding the error.

Yu Liang served the Jin dynasty in the period of division, governing the area in which Lu You now found himself from 334–40. River prefecture, the modern Jiujiang, stands on the south bank of the Yangzi at the point where its direction turns from south-easterly to north-easterly, near the mouth of Lake Boyang to its east, and with the Lu Mountains (Lushan as they are more commonly known nowadays) to the south. Only the haze of industrial pollution now detracts from the view Lu You saw.

Jiujiang (River prefecture) frontage along the Yangzi, from near the modern Yu's Building.

Day 8/6 (17th September)

Around 8 p.m. several hundred large spherical lanterns came downstream from Pen Cove, covering the River. On reaching the wide open river they dispersed as they gradually went further off, glowing like a multitude of stars in a beautiful sky. The locals say this will be a family that's releasing five hundred lantern-bowls to avert disaster and pray for blessings. It's said to be an old custom of these riparian districts.

Day 8/7 (18th September)

We went off to the Lu Mountains, resting briefly at Newbridge Market which is on the main highway between Wu and Shu. Lots of people from Shu have written their names on the walls of the market shops. Alongside the creek there are some handsome trees, many of them two or three hundred years old. The place lies on the lower slopes of the mountain; it's ten miles from River prefecture to the Ascendant Nation in Grand Tranquillity Priory, and at this point we were just half way.

Today there has been an uninterrupted bustle of carriages, horses and pedestrians. They speak of being 'off to the abbey'; that is, they are going to Grand Tranquillity Priory to burn incense, which they do from the first until the seventh of the eighth lunar month. This is referred to as the White Lotus Festival. The Lotus Society is based on the testament of Master of the Law Huiyuan [334–416] which, according to an old tradition, Huiyuan lent to the Daoists for a day, so down to the present the Grand Tranquillity Priory has made this a regular event. The East Forest Monastery also celebrates the festival, but by contrast the numbers that attend are nowhere near those that come to the Grand Tranquillity Priory. How droll!

In the evening I went to the Clear Void Retreat, which lies beneath the Cloud-Disperser Peak, where the Daoist Huangfu lives. Huangfu has the personal name Tan and comes from Jia prefecture. He was out visiting a neighbouring commandery and I only met his follower, Cao Mishen. We climbed to the Gallery of the Shaoxing Period's Literary Glories, in which is preserved the imperial calligraphy of Emperor Gaozong. In addition there were the Holy Spring and the Clear Void Halls, for both of which the imperial brush had inscribed placards.

We slept the night in the Western Chamber at Clear Void Retreat, and Mr Cao served wine in the hall, and grilled some delicious venison. The wine was a fine vintage. It was a cold night and we had to keep close to the fire.

Lu You had arrived at River prefecture on Day 8/2 and spent some ten days in this area before proceeding with his journey. Blakiston had reached River prefecture, which he called by its modern name in an old spelling Kiu-kiang, on 8th March 1861 in the wake of the Second Opium War which opened some of the Yangzi ports to British shipping: 'This was the place selected for the second open port on the river, but first appearances were anything but encouraging. It is one of those towns which have been in the hands of the Rebels, but retaken by the Imperialists, and it has not yet had time to recover from the plague. It is situated on the right bank of the river, backed by Lieu-shan mountain (the Lu Mountains) to the southward, between which and the city walls lies an undulating and picturesque country'. This was the country over which Lu You was now travelling to reach the Ascendant Nation in Grand Tranquillity Priory, stopping briefly at Newbridge Market. The main highway between Wu and Shu is to say the road between eastern China, the area of Lu You's home, and the west of China. Shu was the name usually chosen by kingdoms which established themselves in Sichuan, a prosperous plateau isolated from the rest of China by mountain ranges on all sides; it lay above the Yangzi gorges which served both as obstacle and access in communication with the rest of the country.

Lu's amusement at the activities of the pilgrims may need some explanation. The founding of the White Lotus movement was ascribed by later tradition to the fourth-century Buddhist monk Huiyuan; it was a confraternity of monks and laymen who worshipped the Buddha Amitabha and hoped to be reborn in his Western Paradise, but its traditions were populist and it seems that 'almost any religious group could claim to be pursuing the ideal of his White Lotus Society'.[39] In fact there is a dearth of material on the society from the early Southern Song to the early Yuan dynasty, and Lu's diary provides a rare insight into its continued popularity. Though Huiyuan was a Buddhist the celebration of his teachings had by some quirk become better attended at the Daoist priory than at the nearby Buddhist monastery where the tradition had begun. This irony, explained locally (with what authority I cannot say) by means of the story that Huiyuan had lent his teachings to the Daoists, was not lost on Lu You. Though it was common for lay people, including educated officials, to adopt an eclectic and inclusive view of the principal religions, those religions nevertheless had their separate and distinctive sets of beliefs and practices. There would, in other words, have been nothing to draw to the reader's attention had a devotee gone to both Daoist and Buddhist, and indeed Confucian, establishments; Lu does as much in the course of his journey up the Yangzi. But the popular pilgrimage to a Daoist temple to celebrate the teachings of a famous Buddhist is, in Lu You's view, amusing.

Buildings were often given name plaques. The main hall of the Buddhist Huayan Monastery in Datong, Shanxi province, was rebuilt under the Jin dynasty (for which Lu You felt such hostility) in 1140. The plaques read: 'Hall of Mahavira' and 'Puruṣa-damya-sārathi' or 'Tamer [of the passions of men]'.

We have seen something of how the Chinese calendar worked (commentary on the first day's entry of the Diary). The Shaoxing period was established when the emperor Gaozong, who had taken the throne in 1127, had begun to stabilize the Song's precarious situation following the Jurchen invasion of 1127. Shaoxing may be interpreted as 'perpetuating and prospering', and was intended to convey the sense that Gaozong had maintained the legitimacy of the Northern Song state. The Shaoxing period ran until his abdication in 1162 in favour of his adopted son who became Emperor Xiaozong. Gaozong, who continued at first to exercise some influence over political decisions, did not die until 1187, so the name of the gallery in which were preserved examples of his calligraphy expressed deference to a living man.

Day 8/8 (19th September)

In the morning we followed the mountain road to the Ascendant Nation in Grand Tranquillity Priory. Gateway and courtyard are very grand and imposing in aspect. In the Principal Hall is an image of the Investigation Commissioner of the Nine-fold Heavens, robed and crowned like an emperor. At the Numinous Immortal Abbey on Mount Qian in Shu prefecture they offer sacrifices to the True Lord of Destiny of the Nine-fold Heavens, and the Investigation Commissioner serves at his side. That's why in the Southern Tang dynasty the Numinous Immortal Abbey was called the Palace of Cinnabar Clouds, and the Ascendant Nation in Grand Tranquillity Priory was the Palace of the Comprehension of Mysteries. There is some background to this honour and esteem. In the time of Emperor Taizong a Palace emissary was sent to present a cape of crimson silk with gold leaf in a cloud and crane design, with instructions that it be changed once every three years. And in the time of Emperor Shenzong [r.1068–85] a further title was added, that of True Lord Who Responds to the Origin While Protecting What is in Flux, and a horizontal tablet for the Hall in gold lettering was bestowed.

On two walls are paintings of the Ten Transcendants, originally from the brush of Wu Daozi [c.689–c.758]. But in the Jianyan period [1127–30] two brigands, Li Cheng and He Shiqing, made their lair in the Lu Mountains, and the priory's buildings were burnt to a cinder. A copy had earlier been made of Wu's brushwork in the corridor of the main hall at the Great Unity Priory in these same mountains; so when the Ascendant Nation in Grand Tranquillity Priory was restored they made another copy from the version at the Great Unity Priory, but the craftsmen entrusted with the work were not skilful and it's no longer a good likeness.

We rested at the Hall of the Heartless Cloud which is on the former site of the Cold Azure Pavilion. The sound of the stream was so like a heavy rainstorm it made one's very hair and bones shudder with cold. It's the most picturesque place in the whole priory. In front of the Hall to the Investigation Commissioner stands a bell-tower a hundred or more feet in height. Its three storeys are made of courses of brick without the use of a single piece of wood, yet even the best carpenters couldn't improve on the sweeping and soaring of its eaves and rafters. But the bell is muffled by the brickwork and the sound doesn't carry very well, which is a fault. Hu Siqi, who is in charge of the abbey, tells me that this tower alone cost thirty-thousand strings of cash and the bell weighs over fourteen tons.

There's also a fine repository for sutras whose name board states: 'Treasure House of Illustrious Writings'. The lay-out of the Ascendant Nation in Grand Tranquillity Priory is roughly similar to that of the Jade Mound in Nanchang, but Jade Mound hasn't suffered a fire and still possesses its antique ambience, and so it's superior.

The Star God's Procession (detail), Wu Zongyuan (d.1035).

We then went to the Monastery of the Ascendant Dragon in Grand Tranquillity at East Forest. The monastery directly faces the Incense Brazier Peak. From the peak a spur comes off east and runs round westwards to its north, thus encircling it on all sides like a city wall, with East Forest lying in the centre. Geomancers call it the 'pattern of a dragon hanging upside down'. Outside the gateway of the monastery is Tiger Creek. It was origin-ally a little torrent, but in recent years it's been bricked in like a mere drain and has none of its antique ambience[40] any more. I urged the abbot Facai to remove the brickwork and make it a bit more natural. I wonder if he'll take my advice.

After we'd eaten we brewed [water from] the Goddess of Mercy spring and sipped tea. I climbed to the Avatamsa Arhat Gallery. This gallery, together with the Rocana Gallery and the bell tower, stand like the legs of a tripod and are amongst the most magnificent sights in the world. Even the famous Buddhist houses of Fujian and Zhejiang can't match them.

I then went on to the Five Firs Gallery, the Pagoda of Buddha's Relics, and Bai Juyi's Thatched Hall, all at the Uplands Vihara. To reach the Uplands Vihara you take a side path behind the monastery and penetrate the shade of pines, clambering by stone-flagged steps to no great height. In front of the Five Firs Gallery there used to be five old fir trees which by tradition were considered to date from the Jin dynasty [265–420]. Tutor to the

Spirit Way to the tomb of Emperor Zhenzong (d.1022). He had ordered the preservation of Bai Juyi's literary works.

Heir Apparent Bai Juyi referred to them as being ten feet in girth and now, several hundred years on, one can imagine how old they would have been. But in recent years the abbot, Liaoran, took it upon himself to cut them down, which is a huge shame. Inside the pagoda is an image of the Tathāgata Indicating the Way to Nirvāna. Originally Buddhabhadra [359–429] during the [Liu] Song dynasty [420–79] carried five grains of the Buddha's relics from the Western Regions to inter them here.

The Thatched Hall, when one looks into Bai Juyi's Record of it,[41] seems to be in roughly the right place. It has three rooms and two pillars, as he says in his description of it. And everything else, such as the waterfall and the lotus pond, are there too. One can still picture the refined elegance of the scene. Bai had left his Collected Works in the Thatched Hall, but later on pieces were repeatedly lost or dispersed. Emperor Zhenzong [r.997–1022] ordered the Imperial Library to copy them out and collate them, had them bound in wrappers of mottled bamboo, and presented to the monastery. But in the Jianyan period [1127–30] soldiers caused further damage, and there now remains only the single Gusu edition to provide continuity of evidence.

At the side of the Thatched Hall is another ancient site, said to be the foundations of the Retreat of Wang Shao [1030–81] of the Bureau of Military Affairs. It seems that it was with Wang that East Forest first became a Garden of Meditation, though Changzong [1025–91], the Zen Master Zhaojue, was in fact its first patriarch. There is a statue of Changzong who looks a solemn and distinguished man.

I spent the night at East Forest.

The court painter Wu Daozi was reputed the greatest of Tang artists, executing many wall-paintings in the Buddhist monasteries and Daoist temples of the capital Chang'an, and subsidiary capital of Luoyang, as well as secular figure painting and landscapes. None of his work survives and his achievement can only be dimly sensed from copies, rubbings of stone engravings, and descriptions; though some recent archeological discoveries of contemporary paintings may give a more vivid idea of his style. Very few of Wu's paintings were in existence even in the eleventh century, as the poet Su Shi and the painter Mi Fei attested. But Lu You in the twelfth century was sufficiently aware of Wu Daozi's style to feel disappointment at a remote copy such as he saw on this day. Wu is said to have 'split and scattered the dots and strokes' rather than giving the complete outline, and another writer spoke of Wu Daozi's 'figures reminding one of sculpture. One can see them sideways and all round.'[42] Amongst Wu's characteristic compositions are emperors attended by their suite in energetic progress conveyed by vigorous brushwork, and Buddhist saints. As Michael Sullivan says,[43] Wu probably represented the fusion of Indian metaphysical ideals and the traditional Chinese language of the brush.

Fan Chengda paints a depressing picture of the condition of the Ascendant Nation in Grand Tranquillity priory when he was there in 1177. 'In the Shaoxing period (1131–62) the brigand Li Cheng destroyed River prefecture, letting his soldiers pillage, and burned the priory to the ground. Just a few of the outer gateways were left. Later on Daoist priests rebuilt it, but only the True Lord's hall bears any resemblance to the proper style and the rest is all mean and sparse. The houses at the foot of the hill and beyond the ravine are now all overgrown with vegetation. . . . Moreover, the Daoist priests have each established their own quarters and the desolation of the scene is palpable'.[44] Li Cheng had stationed his forces at East Forest which accounted for the loss of many of its treasures, though the old inscriptions were unscathed, including calligraphy by Yan Zhenqing.

The bell that Lu saw weighed 24,000 catties or fourteen tons. Its cost is more difficult to equate. To gain an idea of what 30,000 strings of cash (the Chinese traditionally strung one thousand copper coins together through a hole in the middle, though at some periods inflationary pressures led to a reduction in the nominal thousand coins on a string) meant in the latter twelfth century we should attempt through some random examples to give comparisons: a county magistrate received a monthly salary of 30 strings of cash, which was enough to support a household of several dozen people. The average annual income of commoners at the end of the Song, a century after Lu's journey, was 50–70 strings of cash per annum, based on military income. A century before Lu's time Wen Tong, the painter of bamboos and brother-in-law to Su Shi, paid rent of 4 strings of cash a month for a house in the capital with ten small rooms where 10 people lived. And Su Shi himself, when living in reduced circumstances, was able to get by on 150 cash a day, or the equivalent of fifty-five strings per annum, and had enough spare to invite guests. In 1179 captains of ships who had no official rank were paid 250 copper cash (in other words a quarter of the nominal value of a string of cash) per day plus 2¼ pints of rice; their helmsmen 150 cash and the same quantity of rice. A basket of oranges weighing about 135 lbs. varied from 600 cash to one and a half strings, though such prices were of course influenced both by season and locality. The daily allowance for food for clerks to Song diplomatic missions was 200 cash, and for junior secretaries 150 cash, while kitchen boys and rank-and-file soldiers on such privileged duties received 30 cash per day. Perhaps more suggestive of the cost of the bell is the fact that in 1077 the entire circuit of Fujian's quota for tax on foreign trade stood at 240,000 strings of cash; a *mou* of land (10 *mou* was 1.4 acres) was worth 14 strings of cash in the late Song; a woman in 1179 gave 20 strings of cash to purchase stones to pave a road in Su prefecture (but how long was the road?); in 1157 porterage charges per picul (approximately 72 kg or 160 lb) carried were 300 cash (a third of a string) for a distance of about 1000 miles. The bell was, by any reckoning, expensive.

The abbot at East Forest must have got used to scholar officials advising him on aesthetic matters. He was still in post in 1177 when Fan Chengda told him to build a pavilion and what to call it. The area in which Lu You now found himself had rich Buddhist associations, notably because of the Buddha's relics brought by Buddhabhadra. Lu speaks of a Vihara: this is a pleasure garden, and by extension a Buddhist monastery; a Garden of Meditation is much the same.

Seated Luohan, glazed earthenware, c.1000. Produced under the Liao dynasty in north China. Metropolitan Museum of Art.

We were introduced to the Tang poet Bai Juyi on Day 6/19. Bai had lived in River prefecture and had first visited the two Forest Monasteries, the West founded in 379 and the East built for Huiyuan in 386, in the autumn of 816. Bai Juyi was delighted with the area and had completed the Thatched Hall by the following Spring, recording his love of the place in his Record of the Thatched Hall. Bai's friend Yuan Zhen, and later Bai himself, gathered his writings together and he had had one copy sent to the East Forest Monastery on Mount Lu. Two years before Bai died he had five copies made of his updated *Collected Works* to ensure their preservation; but even so, Lu You tells us, the *Works* survived only in the edition kept at Gusu, the modern Suzhou. But Fan Chengda is clear that the Thatched Hall, which he saw a few years after Lu's visit, was neither original nor was it on the original site.

Wang Shao, mentioned in the last paragraph of this day's entry, had advocated a forward policy against the Western Xia state which during the eleventh century controlled the north-western corridor out of China on the Silk Road. He had some success in the 1070s, while he held military appointments, in gaining the submission of the Qiang tribes on the western border and was made Deputy Commissioner for Military Affairs. Dismissed in 1077, he received a provincial appointment to Hong prefecture (which lay about 70 miles due south of the place Lu had now reached), and shortly before his death in 1081 he turned to Buddhism and created a Garden of Meditation (alternatively translatable as a Zen Garden). Changzong, who was from Sichuan, had been invited by Wang Shao to become abbot at East Forest in 1080. Changzong later received imperial recognition, including the award of the title Zen Master Zhaojue.

Day 8/9 (20th September)

We reached the shrine hall of the Jin dynasty Master of the Law Huiyuan, and I went up to the Spirit-Transported Basilica to burn incense, and had a rest in the hall at the government agency. There were eighteen images of the Reverend Buddhayaśas [fl. early fifth century], Liu Chengzhi [352–410] and others which are known as the Eighteen Wise Men. At Huiyuan's side there was another figure holding a *kundika* standing in attendance and called the Snake Charmer Boy. The tradition is that there were a lot of snakes at East Forest in times past and this boy gathered them all up and cast them away at Qi prefecture. The Spirit-Transported Basilica was originally a Dragon Pool of unfathomable depth. One night goblins and spirits filled it in and transported fine timbers here to build this basilica. I don't know if any of this is true or not, but the three words 'Spirit-Transported Basilica' are written in the calligraphy of the Tang dynasty Grand Councillor Pei Xiu [fl.823–61] so the story has been around for a long time. The government agency is fully equipped with a double hall, spacious side-buildings, kitchens and stables, and on the walls are written up poems by Zhang Lei. The monastery is extremely large and if you wandered through it for several days you wouldn't be able to cover it all. There are a great number of Tang dynasty steles, the inscription by Yan, Duke of Lu [709–85], being the most celebrated in our own time. There are also the Intellect Spring to the west of the abbot's lodgings and the Coenobium Spring behind Huiyuan's Shrine Hall. Both have long since fallen into decay and their waters are no longer drawn so I couldn't try them, for which I heaved a heavy sigh.

After we'd eaten I visited the Monastery of Enlightened Rule in West Forest. West Forest lies west of East Forest, and between the two of them is a small market town called Goose Gate Market. Tradition has it that Huiyuan was from Goose Gate and when he grew old he felt home-sick. So in imitation of the town of Goose Gate he built this market town. There's a parallel here with the building of New Feng in the Han dynasty. Originally it was Tao Fan [late fourth century], a prefect of River prefecture in the Jin dynasty, who gave the land to build the monastery at West Forest. Only in the fifteenth or sixteenth year of the Shaoxing period [1145 or 1146] did it become a Zen house, but it's cramped and doesn't compare with East Forest. It's also extremely dilapidated though the abbot, Rencong from Fujian, is just now making gradual repairs and restoration. But as the stream water burbles round the perimeter of the courtyard it gives a very rustic feel to the place. In the principal hall is an image of Shakyamuni Buddha wearing bejewelled headgear such as I have never seen elsewhere. The monks say that it was sculpted in the Tang dynasty. To the side of this hall is the shrine hall to Master of the Law Huiyong [332–414] who was the elder brother of Huiyuan. Beneath his image is a crouching tiger together with a lay acolyte standing in attendance, though I don't know whom this represents.

Behind the abbot's lodgings is a brick pagoda, not very tall and in a style of antique simplicity. I climbed up as far as the second storey. The eastern wing has a small gallery called 'Waiting On the Wise', which in times past was the guesthouse. It's now falling in. The old horizontal tablets of both the East and the West Forest monasteries are in Eight Part calligraphy by Niu Sengru [778–847]. The brushwork is very forthright. In the West Forest there is another inscription by Yan, Duke of Lu, and calligraphers consider these 'Two Forests' inscriptions to be the crowning glory of Yan's calligraphy.

Tang stone bodhisattva showing a bejewelled headdress such as Lu You might have seen worn by Shakyamuni Buddha.

I'd previously heard that when the brick pagoda at Celestial Lake in the Lu Mountains had just been completed a monk donated two boxes of sutras to it. Shortly thereafter one corner of the pagoda juddered and the sutras were nowhere to be found. Today, since I'd climbed up here to see the view, I asked the monks about this story and they said it was true. Some of them said the sutras had been written in blood and that was why this strange event had occurred. They also told me that this year the Celestial Lake pagoda had burned down and not so much as a foot of beam was left. It must have caught alight from a nearby wild-fire.

In the evening we once more took the road to the Ascendant Nation in Grand Tranquillity Priory to return to River prefecture, resting briefly at the New Pavilion which is eight miles from the prefectural town. We passed the well where the Transcendent Dong refined cinnabar, and drew some water to drink. It had an excellent taste. The Transcendent Dong's given name was Feng.

Northern Song pottery *kundika*.

Fan Chengda has what one may think a more credible version of the origins of the Spirit-transported Basilica: 'There is a tradition that when the temple was built in the Tang dynasty the timbers all drifted there on the River and so it was called 'Spirit-transported'. Lu clearly liked the rustic air which the monastery had acquired in its dilapidated state. Conditions must have deteriorated. Seven years later Fan found there was no abbot, the side-buildings were in a ruinous state with weeds growing in them; only the main hall was preserved. And the solitary monk who remained hid himself away when Fan arrived.

The founding emperor of the Han dynasty, the redoutable peasant leader Liu Bang, when he gained the dragon throne in 206 BC persuaded his father to move to the capital by building a simu-lacrum, called New Feng, of the town from which the family came. The Buddhist monk Huiyuan, whom we have referred to in the commentary to Day 8/7, seems to have been able to command similar resources! Huiyuan's brother (he was a relative rather than a brother in the strict sense) Huiyong was, like his kinsman, represented in this monastery but occupied a lesser position. The imagery makes reference to the story that a tiger visited Huiyong in his room; if others were fright-ened by it he would tell it to go off into the hills, but it would come back after the visitor had left and once more lie down tamely. The lay acolyte who attends Huiyong would have been a *kulapati*, one who takes Buddhist vows but continues to live a lay life with their family. He was represented

Tang calligraphy by Chu Suiliang (596–658).

holding a *kundika*, a vessel to carry water used by Buddhist priests when travelling. Buddhayaśas was a foreign monk from Kashmir or Kabul who arrived in the Chinese capital of Chang'an in 408. He translated a number of works into Chinese.

Lu goes on to mention a number of literary or political figures who would have been well known to his contemporary readers. Pei Xiu was Prime Minister under the Tang from 852–6. Zhang Lei, the Northern Song historian who criticized Fan Ruobing's disloyalty to his ruler (Day 7/11), was also a poet much quoted by Lu. Yan, Duke of Lu, was Yan Zhenqing, a Tang poet and influential calligrapher who was in addition a military commander, later ennobled as a duke. Niu Sengru, a major figure of the ninth century who held various posts up to Chief Minister, is remembered as leader of one of the cliques in the factional struggles of the late Tang. The example of his callig-raphy which Lu You saw on this day was in Eight Part, which we encountered on Day 6/16. Niu's forthright calligraphy suggests a strong character.

The practice of alchemy was associated with Daoists but many scholars, who in carrying out their official duties and in the home practiced Confucian precepts, were attracted to the theories which underlay proto-science. The manipulation and ingesting of chemicals known as External Alchemy, with its attendant dangers, was in the Song dynasty paralleled by Internal Alchemy which relied on dietary and breathing regimes, using the symbolism of the alchemist's laboratory, the transmuting of cinnabar and so on, to describe mental conditions. But physical experiments continued, though ofen difficult to disen-tangle from metaphorical description; on Day 8/12 Lu You refers to a cinnabar potion in a literal sense. The physician Dong Feng lived in the Later Han dynasty (25–220). In addition to his alchem-ical interests Lu You was always keen to pronounce on the quality of the waters, as we see on several occasions throughout the Diary; for instance in his next entry.

Day 8/10 (21st September)

Shi Zhidao presented us with several flasks of Valley Curtain water which really is of outstanding quality, sweet and full, clear and cold, possessing all the best characteris-tics. In earlier generations some people rejected the 'Classification of Waters' as untrustworthy, and certainly that work is not necessarily entirely dependable. But the Valley Curtain water is exceptional; Mount Hui's doesn't match it. So the book should not be disparaged. The water comes from the Jingde Abbey in the Lu Mountains.

In the evening I said goodbye to the others. It has been very cold these several nights in the mountains and we have had to press up to the stove. But back at the boat the autumn heat has not in the least abated and one spends all one's time fanning oneself.

Mount Hui was near the city of Suzhou on the Grand Canal, by which Lu You had passed on Day 6/10.

Day 8/11 (22nd September)

The boat cast off. Wu, Administrator in the Supply Commission, had requested that I wait for letters from Kui prefecture so we lingered for a while at the entrance to the River, gazing at the Lu Mountains. Up till now it has been ten days in all since our arrival in River prefecture, and every one of them has been clear, a crisp autumn with limpid atmosphere, the broad heavens without a speck of cloud. It's just right for climbing mountains to see the view; a happy circumstance indeed for a traveller.

We moored at the entrance to Red Sands Lake, and looking from the north-east still have the Lu Mountains in sight. Du Fu says in his poem 'The Daolin Monastery at Tan Prefecture':

Its hall's base intrudes upon Red Sands Lake.

His lake must have been in the area 'South of the Lakes'; but Huarong county of Yue prefecture and this place both have Red Sands Lakes. In this region of rivers and lakes there are many place-names which are the same; for instance, Red Cliff.

Lu You discusses the site of the famous battle of Red Cliff in his entry for Day 8/19.

Day 8/12 (23rd September)

I saw something in the middle of the River with a pair of horns which looked from a distance just like a baby ox-calf. It made a noise as it appeared and disappeared in the water.

In the evening we moored at Luqi Wharf. In the great mountains across the River were two dots of flame like lamps which went on and off for a long time. When I asked the boatmen about it none of them had a clue. Some said they were the eyes of a serpent or dragon, others that they were the efflorescence of the magic mushroom or a cinnabar potion, but I couldn't get to the bottom of it.

Blakiston, like Lu, had an encounter hereabouts with a strange fish 'just above the ruined temple and village of Lo-gi-kow (Luqi Wharf?) . . . When we anchored, numbers of boats came off from the shore offering fish for sale at a low price, some of which we found very good eating. We only bought one, however, out of curiosity, as being of a very singular appearance. . . . It was three feet in length, with a large bell-shaped projecting mouth, and a snout or horn sticking out over twelve inches beyond the head. From these particulars naturalists may perhaps be able to recognise the species; it had somewhat the appearance of a dog-fish or shark.'

Cinnabar was intimately connected with alchemy as we saw on Day 8/9; magic mushrooms likewise (Day 8/4), so we have here the suggestion of arcane Daoist practices.

Day 8/13 (24th September)

We reached the Temple of Glory and Gallantry at Lake Rich. With a flask of wine and a sacrificial pig I paid my respects to the deity, the King Gloriously Brave, Martially Compassionate, Much Beloved and Quick to Heed. The deity is Gan Ning [fl.180–220], the 'Storming General' at the time of the Great Emperor [r.222–52] of the Wu dynasty. Gan was once Governor of West Tumulus so his cult is celebrated here. In the Kaibao period [968–76], with south China pacified, the titles of the spirit shrines along the Yangzi and Huai Rivers were upgraded, and it was then that he was enfeoffed as Duke of the State of Bao. In the Xuanhe period [1119–25] he was advanced in title to King. During the Jianyan period [1127–30] the brigand leader Zhang Yu, nicknamed 'the hornet', led soldiers past the temple where one after another they carried out prognostications with moonblocks. One piece would float up in the air and not come down, the other leapt out through the doorway. The brigand band was so terrified they cleared off, and not long afterwards they were defeated. When General Liu Guangshi [1089–1142] reported this incident additional titles were granted by imperial decree.

While Yue Fei was serving as Pacification Commissioner he carried out a major restoration of the shrine buildings, and no other spirit shrine along the River matches them. Above the gateway he raised a great tower called Snow-swirler. Nail Island directly faces the temple so that, though the temple looks out over the Great River, it has a mooring for boats. Nail Island gets its name from its sharp extremity downstream.

The deity's consort has been given the title Lady Compliant Protector. His two sons were given the titles Marquis of Perpetuated Awe and Marquis of Perpetuated Spiritual Efficacy, and the deity's daughter was made the Lady Mild and Virtuous. There are images of all of them, and in the rear hall is a further statue of the deity and his consort seated together. Sumptuous sacrificial offerings are being made day and night, and since the sacristan pays over to the government one thousand two hundred strings of cash per annum you can tell how efficacious is the deity! The boatmen say that if prayers are offered with absolute sincerity the deity can separate the winds to suit the boats that are coming up-river and the boats that are going down. In the side-aisle is an image of Guan Yu [160–219]; but sacrifices should not be made to Guan Yu at Gan Ning's temple. Each was loyal to the man he served, so how could their spirits share these offerings without a sense of awkwardness?

When the ceremony was over I walked from the rear of the shrine to the Monastery of Education Extolled. The monastery has been turned into the Wine Bureau and its administrative offices, the images and altar furnishings gathered together and placed in a single room, and all the monks driven away. Things have come to a pretty pass!

Lake Rich is administratively subject to Ascendant Nation Military Prefecture.

We have seen (Day 7/7) how the Southern Song was a period in which local gods were beginning to acquire regional responsibilities in response to the greater mobility of merchants and

A moonblock, the kidney-shaped piece of wood used in temples for divination.

others who took their deities with them as they travelled. It was a time in which we often see the family members of the metamorphosed heroes included as subsidiary cults at their shrines. From the late eleventh century, and particularly in the twelfth century, the Song government awarded accolades and noble titles to gods in response to petitions from devotees; a sort of canonization procedure took place in which the gods' record of performing miracles was investigated and reported by the earthly bureaucracy to the emperor who was petitioned for government titles. The 'Storming General' Gan Ning, who had helped Sun Quan, the ruler of Wu referred to here as the Great Emperor and to whom we were introduced on Day 6/23, in the struggles of the Three Kingdoms, was clearly efficacious. He has the full panoply of eight Chinese characters in his title, the maximum that was bestowed in the laudation granted by the government, including specific reference to his responsiveness to the prayers of worshippers.

Guan Yu, himself a historical character who was deified and became a national cult, often known as the Chinese God of War, had been a bean-curd seller who assisted the founder of another of the Three Kingdoms states, that of Shu with its capital in Sichuan, in the period of division after the collapse of the Han dynasty in 220. He was therefore an opponent of the state of Wu which was based on the middle and lower reaches of the Yangzi. Lu You not unreasonably points out that since in life they were faithful to different and opposing rulers it is an odd conjunction to worship their images in the same temple.

Valerie Hansen[45] has addressed the question of popular demand for the recognition and authentication of deities by the government, but it appears that the government had motive enough, in addition to the wish to regulate religious establishments and to enlist the allegiance of local elites, for supporting some popular cults and suppressing others: there was a good income to be derived from prosperous temples and monasteries that were officially sanctioned.

Moonblocks are the kidney-shaped pieces of wood, often painted an auspicious red, which were used in one form of divination. One side was flat, the other curved, and devotees' questions received answer according to the fall of the blocks. Hong Mai (1123–1202), a scholar and contemporary of Lu You who collected anecdotes and miscellaneous information, reports a strikingly similar occurrence from the same area and the identical period when the bandit leader Ma Jin tossed moonblocks to obtain a deity's permission to conquer Ascendant Nation.[46] Ma was similarly confounded by the odd behaviour of the moonblocks.

The boatmen's belief in the ability of deities to satisfy both the travellers going up-river and those coming downstream reminds one that not all Chinese were so credulous. Su Shi, Confucian scholar and Buddhist believer, wrote a dry comment on such incongruities:

> We plough the fields and hope for rain, we reap and want clear skies;
> The wind behind us as we go those coming will dismay.
> Were everyone who says a prayer always to get their way
> Lord God would needs be changing things a thousand times a day.

Yue Fei has been referred to in the commentaries to Days 7/6 and 8/4. He was appointed Pacification Commissioner in 1137 at the age of thirty-four (thirty-five *sui* in Chinese calculation).

Day 8/14 (25th September)

It rained in the morning. We passed a small rocky hill of which half had been sliced away from the summit down; it was absolutely identical with Mount Shu on the banks of the Yuyao River. As we tacked along the Great River we came across a wooden raft of one hundred feet or more in breadth and over five hundred feet long. There were thirty or forty households on it, with a full complement of wives and children, chickens and dogs, pestles and mortars. It was criss-crossed with paths and alleys, and even had a shrine to a deity. I've never set eyes on such a thing before, but the boatmen said that this was still one of the small ones. The large ones have soil spread on the raft for vegetables allotments, and some have wine shops built on them, though they can't go through the channels; they only travel on the main River.

Today we had the wind against us so the boat was hauled, and from the crack of dawn till dusk we have made only five or six miles. We've moored beside the Liu Guan Promontory which is the demarcation line with Qi prefecture. My sons went ashore, and when they got back said they had found a little path which led behind the hills. There had been pools and lakes stretching far away, rich with lotus and water-chestnuts, and the sides of the lakes were full of hibiscus blooms. The few houses in the evening sunlight, with their wattle fences and thatched buildings, felt secluded and deserted, with not a voice to be heard. There were huge pears which they'd tried unsuccessfully to buy. People in a small punt in the middle of the lake were plucking water chestnuts, but though the boys called out they got no response. They had intended to go right on to the end, but when they saw traps set up by the side of the road they suspected there might be tigers and wolves, so hadn't dared proceed.

As to the Liu Guan Promontory, tradition has it that when Emperor Zhaolie of the Han dynasty was on his way into Wu he berthed his boat here.

In the evening we watched giant turtles swimming and diving in the water.

The rocky hill sliced away must, I think, have been the one Blakiston saw half a day out from Jiujiang (River prefecture) as he travelled comparatively fast up-river by steamer: 'A little before noon we passed 'Split Rock', a peculiar feature which occurs at a narrow pass where the river alters its course from S.S.E. to an easterly direction, and we entered the province of Hoo-peh [Hubei]'. The Yuyao River, which came to mind when Lu You saw this small rocky hill, is in eastern Zhejiang province not far from his home town.

Raft on the Yangzi.

Cooper saw rafts being broken up and others in process of building. They took from six to eight months to drift with the current some six hundred miles to the sea. 'When seen floating down-river they resemble large islands, some having as many as twenty small cabins built of them, nearly every one with its piggery attached, while numerous children, dogs, and fowls running about complete their village-like appearance'. Blakiston too recorded his sighting of rafts on the River: 'They were usually some two to three hundred yards long, but being formed in sections they could be easily divided. Small huts or shanties were erected on them where those engaged in their navigation lived; as we swept past, and the waves set in motion by the paddles washed up among the logs, the lumberers and their families came out and gazed in mute admiration and wonder.' The rafters' admiration of the British steam-powered gunboats and the wash they created was, perhaps, not unalloyed.

The bucolic scene which Lu You's children described to him is a common theme of Chinese poetry and prose, the unspoilt rural idyll; but interestingly it is here tempered by the reality of untamed nature.

This sector of the Yangzi had a further association with the Three Kingdoms period, in addition to Gan Ning of the previous day. Zhaolie was leader, and later emperor, of one of the three kingdoms into which China split at the fall of the Han dynasty in 220. He has been mentioned by Lu on Day 6/23, and will be met with again on Days 8/18 and 9/14.

Day 8/15 (26th September)

It was a bit overcast, but the west wind increased in strength and the boat became exceedingly awkward to haul.

Westwards from Lake Rich all along the southern shore of the River large mountains rise and fall like billows. There were people living here and there on the slopes of the hills, and every so often they'd built shelters and were lying in ambush up them with bows and arrows, waiting for tigers.

We passed Dragon's Eye Promontory which is just a fist of rock in the River. On the hill beside the promontory there's a Shrine to the Dragon.

In the late afternoon we picked up a favourable wind. We made a stop at Qi Mouth market town, with its large and varied local population. A great many Sichuan craft were moored below the bank. Gao Shidong, the Supervisor of Taxes and subaltern, came to call on me. I used to know him in Jingkou. He tells me that this market town contributes an annual tax revenue of 150,000 strings of cash, and that Goose Wing contributes 260,000 strings of cash annually.

At night I went ashore with all my children and we gazed at the moon as we looked out over the Great River. The surface of the River stretched far away to meet the sky, and the moon's reflection in the water quivered and quavered unsteadily just like a golden dragon. It was a sight to stir the heart and astound the eye.

Today I bought some medical preparations at Qi Mouth market. The packets of medicine all contain the necessary materials for heating and decocting them, such as mint, smoked plum and the like. Such things are not to be found in a hurry when one is travelling, and it's laudable of the pharmacist to take such trouble.

It may be recalled that Lu had passed Goose Wing channel, where there was a customs station, on Day 7/27.

Day 8/16 (27th September)

We passed New Wilds Channel, amongst whose thick woods and rocky rapids I heard my first autumn orioles. On the sandy margin were great numbers of water buffalo, often forming herds of several dozen, which doesn't happen in Wu. The area is within the jurisdiction of Daye county in Ascendant Nation military prefecure, and it must simply be that it's well-suited to producing them.

In the evening we passed Daoist Priest Promontory with its rock face hundreds of feet high. It's deep black in colour and absolutely without a nook or cranny, yet roots of bamboos and trees protrude, swathing the top in delightful shades of green. There has been no better peak or cliff looming over the River since we passed the Lesser Lone Hill. The Promontory's other name is Western Frontier Mountain, and it is as this that the Mystic True Man [c.730–c.810] refers to it in his 'Fisherman's Lyric':

Water buffalo.

Before Western Frontier Mountain the white egrets fly.

Li Bo says in his poem 'Seeing my Younger Brother off to Jiangdong':

> Western Frontier marks your journey's half-way point,
> Whence winds of the south will bear your boat on.

This must have been written in the Jing-Chu area, which was why he describes it as being half-way. And Zhang Lei spoke of:

> Promontories soaring, intrude on the River;
> Colour of rock: black jade prised apart,

which gives a pretty vivid depiction of this mountain. He also wrote:

> Having come upon the comeliness of Scattered Flowers Gorge,
> We'll not moor amidst the jeopardies of Daoist Priest Promontory.

In travelling on the River, it's Madang and Western Frontier which are the hardest to get past when going upstream on account of their dangerous cataracts.

We tacked along the River and moored at Scattered Flowers Island which is in a direct line from Western Frontier.

Yesterday evening the moon was still not completely full, for the mid-point of the month is actually tonight. Thousands of acres of empty river and the moon, like a dish of purple gold, welling forth from within the waters: I've never known such a mid-Autumn moon as this in my life.

There was an illegal trade in water-buffalo. Shi Zhengzhi (a governor of what is now north-east Jiangxi and southern Anhui and an admiral on the Yangzi who, amongst other matters, mentions construction of an economical 100-ton warship propelled by twelve-bladed wheels[47]) states in a report of 1168, just two years before Lu You made his own observation: 'Numerous merchants drive herds of oxen through Hezhou (on the North bank of the Yangzi), the smallest of them containing more than ten animals. They are en route from Jiangxi to sell them in Haozhou, Shouzhou, and Guangzhou (Canton), especially the last mentioned, all of these being places on the frontier.' Wu, where Lu says such herds were not to be seen, was his home region of the lower Yangzi and Zhejiang province.

The Mystic True Man was the soubriquet of a minor eighth/ninth-century official called Zhang Zhihe who retired to a New Age lifestyle. He painted, played the drums, drank, composed songs, and went fishing without using bait because 'his mind wasn't set on fish'. He lived in a thatched house whose beams had not been worked with the axe, and when asked about his way of living was given to saying 'the universe is my house, the moon my candle'.[48]

The Jing-Chu area refers to the central Yangzi valley. In the pre-imperial period, before the Qin dynasty united the country, there were two important states based in what was then southern China and has subsequently become central China as its civilization has spread southwards: Chu and Jing.

These were different in character from the states based around the Yellow River in the north. Chu, the traditional dates for which are 790–223 BC, absorbed Jing; but the names persisted in some toponyms, and were sometimes used in a historical or literary context to describe areas which no longer had administrative validity, rather as modern Englishmen might refer to Wessex, Mercia or Northumbria. For instance Chu was understood to cover the central Yangzi, Ba what is now eastern Sichuan province, Wu the coastal region south of the Yangzi. We shall meet these names again. At one point Lu You describes his travels over one thousand eight hundred miles as 'a journey from Wu into Chu', which any educated Chinese reader would have understood as the route from the eastern seaboard up the Yangzi into central and western China.

Day 8/17 (28th September)

We passed Whirlwind Promontory, which is no great mountain but a mere pile of boulders at the River's edge; yet the waters surge and the waves churn so it's very dangerous for boats to get by. And we passed Orchid Creek, referred to by Su Shi in the line:

> Beneath the mountain, orchid shoots so short the creek has drenched them.

We bought some venison for our provisions, and this evening have moored at the mouth of the Ba River, which is seven miles from Huang prefecture and where there's a fair. It has the Monastery of Equine Supplication, with the altar where the Great Emperor of the Wu dynasty slaughtered his horse, for tradition has it that when Wu was attacking Shouchun it was here that he slaughtered a white horse as an offering to the deity of the River.

Westwards from Orchid Creek the River's surface is particularly wide and the hills recede into the level distance.

We've had two days of contrary winds, but because our food supplies were used up the boatmen wanted to reach Ba River to purchase rice so they've hauled the boat with might and main, and we've made twenty-five or thirty miles on both days.

When Palace Gateman Su Che [1039–1112] was banished to Gaoan Mr Su Shi came as far as the Ba River to see him off; this is the very place. Zhang Lei also wrote a poem called 'On the Road to Ba River' which contains the lines:

> South-east where the land recedes sky and waters merge;
> Spring and summer winds are churning mountains out of waves.

Sun Quan, the Great Emperor of the Wu dynasty, appeared on Days 6/23 and 8/13 of the Diary. He was one of the heroes of the period of division that began on the collapse of the Han dynasty in 220.

'Level distance' was discussed in the commentary to Day 7/3.

Su Che was the brother of the poet Su Shi and himself one of the most distinguished prose writers of the period. In fact Chinese, ever attracted to the enumeration of qualities, elements, artists and so on, have traditionally referred to the 'Eight Great Writers of the Tang and Song Dynasties'; and amongst those eight have included Su Xun and two of his sons, Su Shi and Su Che, not a bad score for a single family considering the Tang and Song cover nearly seven hundred years.

Day 8/18 (29th September)

We only got under way at breakfast-time, but by late afternoon had arrived at Huang prefecture. The prefectural town is a backwater and there's not much business to conduct. As Du Mu put it:

> In all my life the only place I had sufficient sleep
> Was that prefecture south of the Cloud-dream Marsh.

But since the time Du Mu and Wang Yucheng [954–1001] served as governors here, and then Mr Su Shi and Zhang Lei lived here in banishment, it's become a well-known district.

We moored at the Lin'gao Pavilion where Mr Su Shi once lodged and which he referred to in a letter to Qin Guan [1049–1100], saying that 'A few paces beyond my gate lies the Great River'. Misty waves stretch far away through the vast open atmosphere.

I called on Yang Youyi, the Prefect, a junior Gentleman for Court Service and an Auxiliary in the Imperial Archives; and on Chen Shaofu, Assistant Prefect and junior Court Gentleman Consultant. The prefectural offices are very shoddy and the Residence can only accommodate a few guests, though the Assistant Prefect's digs are a little better.

In the evening the boat was moved to Bamboo Garden Jetty since Lin'gao is windy and rough and one can't moor there at night.

Huang prefecture and Fankou are directly opposite each other. Su Shi referred to it when he said:

> Wuchang and Fankou, obscure, remote places.

When Emperor Zhaolie of the Han dynasty made use of Lu Su [172–217] of Wu's strategy and advanced from Dangyang to occupy Fankou in E county, this was the place in question.

Huang prefecture had had some distinguished denizens: the late Tang poet Du Mu; Wang Yucheng, statesman and writer, was prefect in 998; and the eleventh-century poet officials Su Shi, who was in Huang prefecture from 1080–4, and Zhang Lei, prefect there in 1101. Du, Su and Zhang have been quoted by Lu You has earlier in his diary. And Qin Guan, himself a distinguished poet, was a follower and friend of Su Shi.

Emperor Zhaolie of the Han dynasty, the dynasty based in Sichuan during the Three Kingdoms period rather than the genuine article in power from 206 BC–AD 220, occupied Fankou in 208. We have encountered him on Days 6/23 and 8/14.

An official, Song dynasty, Henan province, in sandalwood. The iconography is similar to that of the Daoist deity on page 91.

Day 8/19 (30th September)

In the morning I visited the Eastern Slope. Eastwards from the gates of the prefectural town hillocks and mounds rise and fall, but as you approach the Eastern Slope the land levels off and opens out. To the east a rather higher mound rises with a three-roomed house on it and a [stone] tortoise [to support a stele] announcing 'The Pavilion of the Retired Scholar'. Below the pavilion and facing south is a very imposing hall with paintings of snow scenes[49] on all four walls. Inside the hall is an image of Su Shi in black cap and purple robes leaning on a bamboo staff. This is the Snow Hall. The large willow tree to the east of the hall is said to have been planted by Su with his own hands. Due south is a bridge with a notice board stating that it is the 'Little Bridge', which derives its name from the line:

> Don't forget the little bridge with its flowing water.

There never had been a brook beneath, and when it rained only a trickle of water would flow down; it used just to have a slab of stone placed across it. But recently they went and made it wider, turning it into a wooden bridge with a roof to cover it, which rather disappoints one's expectations.

To the east there's a well called the 'Hidden Well', taken from the line in Su's poetry:

> Runs over to report a hidden well has come to light.

The spring-water is cold enough to set one's teeth on edge, but not very sweet.

There's also the Pavilion of the Four Views directly opposite the Snow Hall and set on a high hillock. It's regarded as the finest place in the commandery from which to survey the River and mountains. The pavilion's name may be found in the collected works of Su Shi and of Zhang Lei. The bamboo grove to the west of the slope was formerly the property of the Gu family and was called the Southern Slope, but nowadays it has been almost entirely cut down. Nor does the land belong to the Gus any more.

Remote View of Hills and Streams (detail), Xia Gui (fl.1190–1225). National Palace Museum, Taipei.

A couple of miles outside the town you reach Peace to the Nation Monastery where Su Shi also once lodged, though after the ravages of war not a trace of this remains. Only the singing of birds in the dense woods around the monastery still possesses something of the atmosphere of his day.

There was an official reception at the Clouds' Nest Building. This was originally built by the governor, Lǚqiu Xiaozhong, whose courtesy name was Gongxian. In his ballad Su Shi says:

> My little boat lies athwart the springtime river.
> Reclining, I see on verdant cliffs a red building rise.

It was precisely to this tower that he was referring. One looks down on the Great River, with misty trees faint in the distance and a few specks of far off hills. It's a charming place; and the building is most beautifully decorated. Previously the commandery possessed a Hall of Good Auguries which was said to be the birthplace of a former Grand Councillor, but this was later demolished and replaced with the present building.

The wine has a foul taste, and Su Shi's quip about pickle water and honey was no idle one. A poem by a native of this commandery, He Xiezhi, goes:

> All through the year we drink this filthy wine;
> Dare we abhor the epithet Inspector?

And yet Zhang Lei highly praised the wine in the prefecture of Huang, considering it unsurpassed outside the capital. That's why his poem states:

> When first I was sent to this far off position,
> God questioned the Deity managing Wines:
> 'This fellow', he said, 'is a serious drinker;
> Can't you give him some grog to improve his condition?'
> In the hundreds of miles that I've travelled abroad,
> The wines of Qi'an have proved the best vintage.
> When it's starting to rain in a conflagration
> One reveres the indulgence of Heaven's High Lord.

Could it be that when Zhang Lei was banished to Huang prefecture there happened to be a skilled vintner here?

I pursued a little path that wound around behind the prefectural offices and came to the Bamboo Building, which is of very crude design. I wonder whether it was as simple as this at the time of Wang Yucheng. Below the Building and slightly to the east is the Red Cliff Promontory, which is just a knoll covered in mallows and pretty well devoid of other plants or trees. This is why Edict Attendant Han Ju's [c.1086–1136] poem states:

No lofty nests are hereabouts, nor any roosting falcons.
The past has left no vestiges, just the flying gulls.

This promontory is held, both by the illustrated gazetteer and by tradition, to be the site of Zhou Yu's defeat of Cao Cao. But there are many places with this name along the River and the statement can't be verified. In Li Bo's 'Song of Red Cliff' he says:

Raging fires filled the sky, lit up the sea of cloud;
Here it was that Zhou Yu overcame Cao Cao,

but he doesn't specifically say that it was at Huang prefecture. And Su Shi was even more sceptical. His prose-poem says:

Might this not be where Cao Cao was beset by Master Zhou?

And his ballad states:

The western side of the ancient ramparts was, so people say,
The Red Cliff of the days of Master Zhou.

Such was his scrupulousness with language. Whereas when Han Ju says:

Here it was that he was able to put Cao Cao on the run,

he is definitely indicating that he considered it to be Zhou Yu's Red Cliff. What's more, the people of Huang prefecture actually refer to the Red Cliff [Chibi] as the Red Nose [Chibi], which make the matter even more doubtful.

In the evening the boat was moved again to the Market Garden Jetty which is a mile or mile and a half further on from the Bamboo Garden Jetty; for though Huang prefecture is beside the Great River it possesses not a harbour nor anchorage in which one can moor. Someone told me that there used to be an anchorage but the local officials got sick of passing travellers so they filled it in!

The eleventh-century poet and painter, whom we have met as Su Shi, is also known both in Chinese and to Western readers of his poetry in translation as Su Dongpo (or Su Tung-p'o in an alternative orthography); indeed Lu You refers to Su in the Diary by variations of this name, for instance Mr Dongpo, which for reasons of consistency and comprehensibility are all given here as Su Shi. Dongpo was the soubriquet which Su chose when he came to live near Huang prefecture from 1080–4. It is in fact a place-name meaning Eastern Slope, and consisted of a few acres of land that a local official had allowed him the use of. It lay a little distance from where Su was living at Lin'gao (mentioned by Lu You the previous day) and just outside Huang prefectural township. Su was proclaiming himself to be Su of the Eastern Slope, suggesting a scholar in quiet retirement. He was

Su Shi Leaning on a Bamboo Staff, unknown artist. National Palace Museum, Taipei.

in fact in political disfavour. As we have seen, reforms introduced by Wang Anshi in the 1070s under the name of the New Policies had sharply divided the political class. Su had languished in a number of provincial posts through most of the 1070s, becoming increasingly critical of the operation of the New Policies until in 1079 he was arrested and accused of slandering the emperor, the evidence being statements in his own poetry. Though released after 130 days at the beginning of 1080 he was banished to Huang prefecture. As Lu You tells us this was an obscure town, despite being on the Yangzi. But because of Su Shi's fame and the fact that he adopted the Dongpo soubriquet the Eastern Slope has acquired an enduring fame in literary culture. Amongst the poems that Su wrote in his banishment is a series of eight (six have been translated by Burton Watson[50]) composed in 1081 and entitled 'Eastern Slope'. From one of these comes the line about the well which was found as Su cleared the derelict land at Eastern Slope. At the Eastern Slope he built the Snow Hall, so-called because it was finished in the February snows of 1082, and had painted snow scenes on the walls. He used to stay there sometimes, though his wife and family went on living at Lin'gao. It sounds as if the edifices which Lu saw at the Eastern Slope ninety years later had suffered 'improvement', no doubt a consequence of Su Shi's fame. The Gu family is a reference to Gu Gengdao, a farmer friend of Su Shi's during his exile in Huang prefecture; Gu's obscurity other than in relation to Su Shi is suggestive of the limited audience to which Lu You was addressing his diary, an audience he clearly expected to be as familiar as he was with the works of literary figures and the anecdotes connected with them. Lüqiu Xiaozhong was another friend of Su Shi's at this period of his life.

The 'epithet Inspector' comes from a story in *A New Account of Tales of the World (Shishuo Xinyu)*, a collection of anecdotes by Liu Yiqing (403–44), and was applied, for reasons that need not detain us, to bad wine.

Lu You had now reached the place which by some accounts was the site of one of the most famous battles in Chinese history. Even before the formal ending of the Han dynasty in 220 and the division of China into three kingdoms, a complicated game of shifting alliances had begun between the leaders: Cao Cao based in the north, Liu Bei and his adviser Zhuge Liang in Sichuan to the west, and Sun Quan (whom we have met several times already as the Great Emperor of Wu) in the lower Yangzi and the south. In 208 Cao Cao, faced by the combined forces of Liu Bei and Sun Quan, launched an attack south with the intention of expanding his control from the north China plain, and attempted to cross the Yangzi at Red Cliff. This campaign came to an end when the fleet intended to transport his army across the river was destroyed by fire-ships under the command of Zhou Yu, the Wu commander. (This was why fires lit up the cloud in Li Bo's poem). But, as Lu You tells us, there were other possible places with the name red cliff where the engagement might have taken place; Wuchang, for instance, a few miles downstream from Huang prefecture. Lu was right to be mistrustful of the claims of Red Cliff near the Eastern Slope, for as his contemporary poet and fellow diarist Fan Chengda, whom we met as an ambassador on Day 6/28, remarked in his *Record of a Boat from Wu* (written in 1177) which covered some of the same route as Lu: 'At around 8 a.m. we passed Red Cliff and moored below the Lin'gao pavilion at Huang prefecture. Red Cliff is a little hill of red earth and I never saw the place where there are supposed to be "piles of rocks piercing the sky and a confusion of peaks". Su Shi's prose-poem is a bit exaggerated.' The prose-poem from which Lu quotes Su Shi's cautious wording is one of two Su wrote in late 1082 when he went out on a little boat with a friend below Red Cliff. In fact the words are put into the friend's mouth, further distancing Su from the assertion that this was indeed the site of the famous battle. The second quotation is from a lyric Su wrote earlier that year in which, though he cautiously mentions that 'people say' that this is the Red Cliff battle site, he goes on to imagine the romantic hero Zhou Yu and the destruction of Cao Cao's fleet.

The illustrated gazetteer mentioned on this day, Chang and Smythe believe, was the one compiled under imperial auspices and completed in January 1011.

The Red Cliff, Wu Yuanzhi (late twelfth, early thirteenth century). Wu lived under the Jurchen Jin state, demonstrating a sophistication Lu You would have been loath to concede. National Palace Museum, Taipei.

Day 8/20 (1st October)

At daybreak we left Huang prefecture. The River was smooth, there was no wind, and the boat was hauled directly beneath Red Cliff Promontory with its many extraordinary rocks in a multi-coloured jumble, glinting delightfully. It was these that Su Shi described in his 'Offering of Strange Stones'. After we'd been hauled some five miles the River started to get a bit narrower and we were separated from the main river by an extended line of hills and mounds on which the luxuriant greens of bamboos and trees set off the fishermen's houses in their delightful seclusion. When we re-emerged onto the Great River we passed Three Rivers Mouth where the view was boundless.

We've moored at Qi Promontory Harbour.

Day 8/21 (2nd October)

We passed Twin Willows Channel and looked back over the River at the distant mountains rising one upon another, profoundly beautiful. Since leaving Huang prefecture we have been travelling along channels, but they've all been broad and stretched far away into the distance. The lie of the land has been gradually rising, and it's mostly planted with crops such as pulses, millet and buckwheat.

In the evening we moored at Yangluo Wharf. There are high embankments with tall willows, and a dense population. Fish are dirt cheap, and you can feed twenty people for a hundred cash. What's more, they're all huge fish, and when I tried to look for some small fish to feed the cats I couldn't find any.

Day 8/22 (3rd October)

At dawn there was light rain. We passed Green Mountain Promontory where there were many loose boulders and shallow rapids. In the evening we moored at the mouth of White Willow Channel which is ten miles from E prefecture, though it's only three miles or so by the overland route. There are a great many inhabitants and moored boats, though for the most part these are military.

Hibiscus and Rock, Li Di (fl. mid-twelfth century). National Palace Museum, Taipei.

Day 8/23 (4th October)

With the wind set fair the sail was hoisted. This has been the first wind we've had from the 14th until today, and by breakfast-time we had reached E prefecture and moored at the Customs Post. Countless traders' boats and travellers' craft ran on bow to stern without a break for several miles. There's been nothing to match this west of Jingkou. In his poem 'Presented to Governor Wei of Jiangxia' Li Bo says:

> A myriad vessels converging on this place,
> A line of sails past the prefecture of Yang.

So this commandery has been a major crossroads since Tang times.

We were joined by the escort detachment from Kui prefecture. I called on Zhang Tan, whose courtesy name is Zhiyan, the Prefect and a junior Gentleman for Court Service; and Xie Shiji, Assistant in the Tax Transport Bureau and a junior Grand Master for Court Audiences. The market town is highly prosperous and the shops are many and varied; the South Market outside the town walls also runs on for a mile or two. Not even Qiantang and Jiankang surpass it. In effect it's a metropolis. The Wuchang which the Wu dynasty made its capital is nowadays Wuchang county, while under the Wu this prefectural town was called Xiakou, and was a place of strategic importance. That was why Zhou Yu sought to advance and occupy Xiakou with crack troops; and why Emperor Wu [r.265–89] of the Jin dynasty issued an imperial command that 'Wang Jun and Tang Bin [235–94], having gained control of Baqiu, are to combine with Hu Fen [third century] and Wang Rong [234–305] to take Xiakou and Wuchang in a long-range sortie downstream'.[51]

It is two hundred and thirty miles from River prefecture to here and if you are going upstream, even with a favourable wind every day, it will still take you three or four days. So when Han Yu [768–824] said

> Pen City from the prefecture of E,
> If the wind's in your favour, it's just a day,

he was exaggerating. Han had probably never travelled this route.

The prefecture of E was on the southern bank of the Yangzi; it was later known as Wuchang (though confusingly the county town Lu knew as Wuchang was downstream from Huang prefecture). In our own time the combined cities of Wuchang, Hanyang and Hankou (at the mouth of the Han river, a tributary of the Yangzi) are known as Wuhan, a major central Chinese city which remains an entrepot, communications centre and civil and military headquarters. Even in the third century, when generals of the Three Kingdoms were charged with capturing them in a campaign which brought an end to a period of division and led to a brief and approximate re-unification of China, these cities were of strategic importance.

By the Southern Song many cities were bursting forth from their medieval walls into the surrounding areas. One writer[52] notes in the context of Suzhou that prosperous suburbs had

Wuhan waterfront.

developed substantially, especially to the west in the direction of the city's main commercial trade route, the Grand Canal. By 1084 Suzhou had grown so rapidly that 'it spilled out of its walls' and even 'the narrow alleys in the near suburbs were paved with bricks'. This was happening in E too, which according to Lu You rivalled the capital at Hangzhou (which he refers to as Qiantang after the river on which it stood) and Jiankang (which it may be recalled was another name for the modern Nanjing). Shiba Yoshinobu[53] remarks that 'These new extensions often made it necessary to establish extra officials for the maintenance of public order. E prefecture had both a satellite town to its south, handling an influx of goods from all parts of the country, and a built up area along the bank of the Yangzi containing several tens of thousands of houses, shops and taverns, and constituting in itself an important city.' Some of the boats at E prefecture had a capacity of 10,000 piculs or more, which would equate to about 700 tons. Lu You's contemporary Fan Chengda moored below the dyke at South Market. This suburb was 'outside the city wall, with tens of thousands of houses along the River and a busy bazaar, the rows of shops like the teeth of a comb' with a huge turnover of every type of merchandise. And just as Lu's escort from Kui had come ahead to join him here, so at this point Fan sent back half the Sichuanese soldiery who had been accompanying him down-river.

As in modern China the army found this city a convenient base: the Huguang military command had its headquarters at E prefecture and in the Southern Song period distributed 1,307,000 piculs of rice (or roughly 90,000 tons) annually, all bought from merchants. Even at the nadir of China's decline in the second half of the nineteenth century the area was vibrant. Isabella Bird describes the activities along the Yangzi hereabouts in these terms: 'So ceaseless are the industries by land and water, that it is hardly a surprise to find them culminating 600 miles from the ocean in the "million-peopled" city of Hankow (Han Mouth), the greatest distributing centre for goods in China, with miles of craft moored in triple rows along the Han, itself navigable for 1,200 miles.' And Blakiston describes the scene at Han Mouth in 1861 thus: 'The immense number of river junks crowded together at the mouth of the Han, and lining its shores for a considerable distance up, and the fleet of white sails seen in the distance as one looked up the main river, at once convinced us of the commercial value of this port which the next few months were to prove. A walk in the crowded streets of Hankow . . . was a bright contrast to the wretchedness and misery which had almost invariably met our gaze on the lower portion of the river.' The bustling prosperity of this section of the Yangzi has struck visitors in much the same way through the centuries.

Han Yu was a Tang forerunner of the Confucian revival known as Neo-Confucianism which came to maturity in the succeeding Song dynasty. He was a fierce critic of Buddhism, though the dissolution of their monasteries did not take place until some years after his death. Han was also a considerable poet, and is particularly significant as a prose stylist who advocated a return to the Ancient Style of classical Chinese which took as its model the historical and philosophical writings of the fourth and third centuries BC. Lu You greatly admired him, and speaks of his role in the reform of prose writing in the entry for Day 8/26 of the Diary; but he cannot resist putting Han right when necessary.

Day 8/24 (5th October)

In the morning Fiscal Commissioner Xie invited me to a meal at the Hall of Shimmering Light in the Fiscal Authority Gardens. The ten or more pavilions and other structures along the hillside are not in very good repair.

In the evening there was an official reception at the Qizhang Hall, so named because Niu Sengru of the Tang dynasty was once Military Commissioner of Wuchang.

Niu Sengru, the Tang dynasty Grand Councillor to whom Lu You introduced us on Day 8/9, was made Duke of the Commandery of Qizhang, hence the name of the hall in which Lu dined. A nearby pavilion with the same name was in ruins (Day 8/26).

Day 8/25 (6th October)

We watched the Grand Fleet on naval exercises. There were seven hundred great ships, all of two or three hundred feet in length. They were fitted on top with bulwarks and observation turrets, decked in bright flags and pennants, with their gongs and drums booming as back and forth they breasted the huge waves, as swift as swooping birds. There were tens of thousands of spectators. It was truly one of the great sights of the world.

Shiba Yoshinobu says warships with a lake boat's hull were 83 feet long, 20 feet wide, had a crew of 200 and a capacity of 800 bushels (some 26 tons), so those Lu You saw were much bigger.

Day 8/26 (7th October)

I visited the Dhūta Monastery together with Tong and Shu. The monastery is situated on Stonewall Hill at the eastern corner of the prefectural town's wall. The hill winds around like a snake, stretching from west to east, and the wall is built along the top of it, but there remain only gaps and damaged sections. Both the prefectural offices and the Fiscal Commission abut this hill. The monastery was destroyed in the war, but a monk from Kaifeng, Shunguang, has presided here for thirty years, and his rebuilding and restoration work are almost completed.

From north-west of the prior's lodgings we clambered up a side path to the summit. A Pavilion of the Duke of Qizhang used to stand there, but is now in ruins. As one looks out in every direction at the rivers, mountains, hamlets and villages, it lacks for nothing. Li Bo said in his poem 'In Jiangxia, Presented to Wei of Nanling':[54]

> Dhūta Monastery, beyond the clouds, imbued with monastic aura,

and it exactly describes this temple. And Huang Tingjian said:

> When Dhūta Monastery was in its heyday,
> Its palaces and halls formed a stairway to the sky.

Behind the Repository of the Sutras is a stele written by Wang Che [d.505] of the Southern Qi [479–502] dynasty. It was erected in the sixth year of the Kaiyuan period of the Tang dynasty [718]. The calligraphy is by the Prefect of Su prefecture, Zhang Tinggui [c.664–734], whose courtesy name was Wenyu. The obverse side of the stele was composed by Han Xizai [902–70], and Xu Kai [920–74] wrote the horizontal inscription. The final passage reads: 'Set up again in the jisi year of the [Southern] Tang dynasty [969] by Yang Shouzhong, Deputy Military and Surveillance Commissioner for Wuchang and Administrator of Military and Prefectural Affairs. Calligraphy written by Han Kui, former Registrar of Tangnian county in E prefecture and Proof-reader in the Imperial Library.' The obverse of the stele states: 'and then I ordered my nephew Kui to correct the old text and to have it inscribed.' From this we can tell that Kui was the son of a brother of Han Xizai. The writing on the stele is in the same hand throughout. Furthermore, the character 'wen' is incomplete, for the Southern Tang revered Xu Wen [d.927] as its 'Honorary Ancestor' and therefore eschewed the use of his personal name. So this stele must have been rewritten in Han Kui's hand. On the obverse of the stele it also says: 'Our august emperor has refounded our culture for the instruction of both Chinese and barbarians; the wonderful teachings of Tathāgata have been comprehensively grasped; the writings of all ages have been thoroughly understood. There was no question but that the stele at this monastery should be raised.' I note that the stele was set up in the jisi year, which equates to the second year of the Kaibao period of our own dynasty, when the situation of the Southern Tang was becoming more critical by the day and a mere six years before its downfall. That a senior minister,

Han Xizai, was not fearful of its overthrow, but on the contrary said that his ruler had 'refounded our culture for the instruction of both Chinese and barbarians' really is rather extraordinary. And furthermore to regard the grasping of the teachings of Buddha and a command of the literary canon, together with the raising of this stele, as such splendid achievements was vainglorious and absurd. It really should make later generations laugh. But when Han Xizai died the Last Ruler of the Southern Tang dynasty regretted that he hadn't had time to make Han a Grand Councillor. With a ruler and minister as deluded as this, could they have lasted for long even had they tried to?

Under Tang dynasty regulations, if Military Commissioners were not based in their commands a Vice-Commissioner or Deputy resided *en poste*, and was spoken of as 'the Administrator of the Military Commission's affairs'. The reference here to an 'Administrator of Military and Prefectural Affairs' represents a gradual adaptation. Tangnian county was originally the old name under the Tang which was changed under the Liang dynasty to Linxia. The Later Tang reverted to the old name, and the Jin dynasty changed it once more to Linjiang. But throughout the Five Dynasties period E prefecture never came under the [northern authorities in the] Central Plain; these changes were simply made at a distance.[55] That is why this stele, though erected in the Kaibao period [963–75], still speaks of 'Tangnian'. It is said that it was only with our conquest of southern China that the name was changed to Chongyang.

Wang Che wrote the inscription on this stele in a mean and weak Parallel Prose. He had never been better than anyone else, and the world valued him solely because he was included in the *Selections of Refined Literature*. During the period of the Han and Wei dynasties this style of writing burgeoned. It reached its apogee in the Qi and Liang dynasties, and the Tang valued it highly. The empire was as one in this until Han Yu and Liu Zongyuan [773–819] made their great reform of prose style which was emulated by scholars with one accord. Yet throughout this the writing of Parallel Prose did not die away. So, as we see, Han Xizai and Han Kai, who were nicknamed the Patriarchs of Literature in the Lower Yangzi, stuck tenaciously to the style of Wang Che's stele. In our own dynasty the writings of Yang Yi [974–1020] and Liu Yun [971–1031], which so dominated the world and were transmitted to the eastern and northern barbarians, were also in Parallel Prose. It was only with the rise of Ouyang Xiu that it was swept away without a trace. Gentlemen of later generations, regardless of the level of their ability, in general all model themselves on the Ancient Style. As for this stele, modern people wouldn't be able to read to the end of it without falling asleep, much less imitate it. So Ouyang Xiu's achievement was great indeed! As for Huang Tingjian saying:

> This stele of Wang Che,
> What a towering piece of writing,

he must have been joking!

Tong was one of Lu You's sons, and I assume Shu was an affectionate name for another. The Dhūta Monastery (Dhūta means the throwing off of the trials of life so as to attain nirvāna) which they visited with their father had suffered in the Jurchen attacks which brought down the Northern Song, but the following thirty or so years to 1170, though not without incursions (we have seen on Days 6/25 and 7/17 that the Jin under Wanyan Liang, Prince Hailing, reached the Yangzi area in 1161), had been ones of reconstruction and increasing prosperity. The abbot Shunguang's rebuilding was part of this process. The fact that he was a refugee from the Northern Song capital of Kaifeng, now lost to the Jin, indicates where his political sympathies lay. By the time Lu You came past again in 1178 Shunguang had recently died and a stupa to him had just been completed.

When we come to the inscription on the stele behind the Repository of the Sutras, in other words the monastery library, the reader may welcome an escort through the forest of Chinese names, titles and dates. The story appears to be this: the stele had been erected in 718 under the great Tang dynasty at one of the heights of China's prosperity and power by Zhang Tinggui, a famous calligrapher and statesman who at the time had been serving as a local official. It was inscribed with a text by a late-fifth-century author, Wang Che. It must have collapsed, and over two hundred years later a senior adviser to one of the minor dynasties (which referred to itself as the Tang in deference to its illustrious predecessor, though known to us and to Lu You as the Southern Tang in order to distinguish it) during the period of division in the tenth century had written a piece for the rear side of the stele to commemorate its re-erection by the local military commander in 969. This senior adviser happens to be more familiar to us than might otherwise be the case because of a contemporary painting, now held in the National Palace Museum, Taipei, called *The Night Revels of Han Xizai*. Han had asked his nephew to do the calligraphy which would have been inscribed on the obverse of the stele to accompany the fifth-century text on the front. Lu You notes, however, that the calligraphy is all in the same hand, and that one of the characters is written in incomplete form, an important clue for dating since it points to a taboo in force under the Southern Tang. Lu therefore surmises that the whole stele was rewritten in the nephew Han's hand.

Lu goes on to mock the pretensions of the Southern Tang, which finally fell to the Song in 975. The ambitious claims for cultural influence and devotion to the teachings of Buddha were made a

The Night Revels of Han Xizai (detail), Gu Hongzhong (tenth century).

mere six years before the overthrow of the dynasty by the Song, and quite failed to address the parlous condition in which Han Xizai and his ruler found themselves.

Lu then animadverts on administrative and toponymical history, a subject which he rightly recognises as another tool for dating of the stele. Though the Song dynasty marked its foundation as 960 some other minor dynasties, including the Southern Tang, continued for a while thereafter; place-names were not changed until the new regime had taken control of an area.

Having dealt with the Southern Tang Lu You turns his attention to literary history. Wang Che, the author of the inscription on the front of the stele, wasn't much of a writer and his reputation had been based solely on the lucky chance that he had been included in the influential *Selections of Refined Literature (Wenxuan)* compiled by the sixth-century Crown Prince Zhaoming of the Liang dynasty; Lu passed Prince Zhaoming's tomb on Day 7/25. The Parallel Prose in which Wang had written was a formal, ornamental and allusive style which, as its name suggests, tended to pairs of sentences that balanced each other with consequently predictable rhythm and limited room for individual expression. It was a form much used in official writing throughout the first Christian millennium, and indeed continued in certain genres of writing, such as odes to the deities, thereafter. Lu You describes in this passage the reform of prose style in the early ninth century by Han Yu (see the commentary to Day 8/23) and Liu Zongyuan, who advocated a return to the models of classic works of the third and fourth centuries BC with their more natural rhythms and diversity of sentence length and structure; and the renewed impetus given to the movement in the eleventh century under Ouyang Xiu. It is striking how closely this account would be accepted by most later critics. Though Lu was not to know it, the Ancient Style which from the eleventh century replaced Parallel Prose became the dominant literary form both for civil service examinations and other types of scholarly writing for the following thousand years until the triumph of the colloquial movement in the twentieth century.

The eastern and northern barbarians to whom Lu refers as the beneficiaries of early-eleventh-century Parallel Prose were the Koreans and the Khitan people whose state of Liao occupied much of Inner Mongolia and Manchuria with its capital near modern-day Beijing.

Day 8/27 (8th October)

There was an official reception at South Building which is south of Yi Gate on Stonewall Mountain, otherwise known as Yellow Crane Mountain. It's built on a grand scale, and the view when one climbs it is spectacular. There are many buildings and observation points in E prefecture, but only this one commands a strategic panorama of the River and the mountains. This is what Huang Tingjian was referring to in his couplet:

East of the River, north of the Lake, you travel through a painting;
But South Building in E prefecture has no equal in the world.

As one gazes down on South Lake the lotus leaves stretch away as far you can see, and in their midst is a bridge called Broad and Flat lined with shops, and on either side very beautiful galleries over the water, but I couldn't go there because wine was being sold. Huang's line:

Leaning on the balustrade, scent of water caltrop and lotus for three miles

refers to South Lake.
Today we had light rain in the morning, but by evening it had cleared.

Wine was sold under government licence during the Song dynasty and I assume Lu You means that since official sales of wine were taking place when he visited the public was therefore excluded; but this is a guess. Blakiston climbed to pagoda Hill where 'a spectator looks down on almost as much water as land, even when the rivers are low. At his feet sweeps the magnificent Yang-tsze, nearly a mile in width; from the west, and skirting the northern edge of the range of hills already mentioned, comes the river Han, narrow and canal-like, to add its quota, and serving as one of the highways of the country; and to the north-west and north is an extensive treeless flat, so little elevated above the river, that the scattered hamlets which dot its surface are without exception raised on mounds, probably artificial works of a now distant age. This flat is completely covered during summer . . . so that a view at that season from this position presents an almost unbroken expanse of water.'

Day 8/28 (9th October)
Together with candidate scholar Zhang Fu, whose courtesy name is Guanzhi, I climbed to Stone Looking Glass Pavilion and paid a visit to the site of the Yellow Crane Building. Stone Looking Glass Pavilion stands at one corner of Stonewall Mountain, hard by the Great River. Towards the west it faces Hanyang, separated only by a stretch of water; you can make out people, animals, plants and trees. In the Tang dynasty Mian prefecture was the prefectural seat for Hanyang county. This is why Li Bo says in the preface to his poem 'In Mian Prefecture, Taking a Boat on Langguan Lake South of the City Walls': 'When I was transferred to Yelang I met my old friend the Secretarial Court Gentleman Zhang Wei who was setting out on an assignment to Xiakou, the Governor of Mian prefecture Mr Du, and Mr Wang the Prefect of Hanyang, and we drank together at South Lake by the city walls along the River.' Later Mian prefecture was abolished and Hanyang was made subordinate to E prefecture as a county. When Emperor Shizong of the Zhou dynasty conquered the land south of the Huai River he gained control of this area and restored it to the status of a military prefecture. As Li Bo's poem puts it:

> Who claims this river's broad?
> It's slim as a bolt of silk.
> At Jiangxia stands Yellow Crane Building,
> Those green hills are Hanyang county.
> Their booming tones still audible
> Though friends are lost to sight.

It's a marvellous description. Huang Tingjian had the same sense in his:

> By night we journeyed through Jiangxia county,
> And woke to rise at Hanyang Town.

And Du Fu wrote poems entitled 'At Gongan Seeing off Li Jinsu on his Way to Sichuan, and Myself Going Down to Mian and E Prefectures', and 'Boarding a Boat about to Set off for Hanyang'. How tragic that he died in the Lei River.

Hanyang is built against the mountain and girdled by the River. There are Buddhist monasteries on the little hill to its south, this being the Greater Bie Hill. There's also a Lesser Bie Hill, so they are known as the Two Bie. According to an old tradition it was at Yellow Crane Building that Fei Yi [d.253] flew off into the sky. Later he suddenly came back riding on a crane; hence the name of the building. It was reputed as having one of the world's outstanding views. Cui Hao's [d.754] poem about it is widely known, and Li Bo had very many brilliant lines come to him here. The building is now destroyed; nor does its former site any longer exist. But I asked an old clerk about it and he told me that between Stone Looking Glass Pavilion and South Building, directly opposite Parrot Island, there still seem to be signs of where it was. Only the stone inscription of the Building's placard in Seal Script calligraphy by Li Yangbing [mid-eighth century] remains. Li Bo climbed this building to see off Meng Haoran [689–740], and his poem reads:

> Your lonely sail a distant gleam that fades amidst blue hills;
> The River's course to far horizons all that I can see.

That gleam of sail and mast against distant hills is particularly admirable, and not something you can understand if you haven't travelled for a long time on the River.

I went out of the Hanyang Gate again with Zhang Fu to visit the Immortal's Grotto. It's just a rock face several feet high with vertical fissures, but no grotto or cave. There's a hoary tradition that immortals secluded themselves inside and would open up the grotto to emerge and go about. An old soldier encountered them and was given several ingots of gold which later turned to stone. Su Shi has a poem which records the story. At first he doesn't say what sort of people [the old soldier] had encountered, though Li Bo had already made this abundantly clear.

> Much have I heard of eminent immortals,
> How hereabouts they learned the art of flight;
> Then parting for the Islands of the Blessed,
> Here left a thousand years their empty cell.

Nowadays the people of E prefecture call it the Grotto of Mr Lü, but this is probably a forced association of popular folklore. There's a Daoist who comes from Chan prefecture and who's constructed a shelter beside the grotto in which he has set up an image of Mr Lü [755–805]. A little to the south of the grotto, the lower slopes of Stone Looking Glass Mountain are of coarse irregular rocks, umber in colour, rough and totally unreflective; it's rather a misnomer.

I returned to the boat along the top of the riverside embankment. There were miles of houses and shops without a break, amongst which were lanes and alleys with a

Hanyang, photograph by Isabella Bird.

bustle of people shuttling to and fro. Merchants and traders from all over have congregated here, with Sichuanese forming the majority.

Zhang Fu was said to have been what the Chinese call 'untrammelled', a non-conformist, bohemian character. Lu You gives him the designation *xiucai*, which is sometimes translated 'cultivated talent'; but in the Song dynasty it served as an unofficial label for all candidates in the Metropolitan Examinations and 'candidate scholar' seems more clearly to convey this sense. Zhang wrote a poem when he came to say goodbye to Lu You, and Lu sent one to Zhang in return after their encounter.

The Lei River is a tributary of the River Xiang which itself flows northwards into the Yangzi. Du Fu died in the winter of 770, as it happens exactly 400 years before Lu You was writing his diary, but the precise circumstances have long been debated. Lu here espouses one of several versions of how Du Fu died.

Hanyang, which appears in the title of the second of Du's poems, was on the northern bank of the Yangzi where it is joined by the River Han, and looked across to E prefecture on the south side of the Yangzi (these, together with Hankou, now forming the combined city of Wuhan, as we saw in the commentary to Day 8/23).

Fei Yi, otherwise known as Fei Wei, was a high official of the state of (Shu) Han. He was murdered by a defector from the state of Wei while drunk at a party.

We are thoroughly familiar with Li Bo by this point; two other of the great Tang poets are now mentioned by Lu, though these fleeting references point up the comparatively small number of poets he draws on in his diary despite his wide reading. And some opportunities to quote admired poets are missed. For instance Bai Juyi wrote his famous 'Lute Song' near Parrot Island which Lu passes a couple of days later without mentioning it. This may in part reflect contemporary taste, but Lu certainly thought highly of Bai. Meng Haoran was an early representative of the so-called High Tang period, the artistic flourishing which took place in the early and mid-eighth century. Unusually for that period he served for only a year as an official. His verse is varied but uneven in quality; unlike his more famous contemporary Wang Wei (699–761) his nature poetry is more specific and personal. In the words of William Nienhauser

Meng is 'a warm poet, who does not often lose himself totally in his scenes. Meng is, however, an extremely moody and erratic poet'. Cui Hao was known for his bohemian lifestyle and his many marriages, a freedom from restraint carried into his poetry which sometimes broke the rules of Chinese prosody. Cui's quatrains are his best known pieces, of which the one referred to here by Lu, 'Yellow Crane Building' (or Tower in some translations) is amongst the most famous of the High Tang period.

We shall meet Mr Lü, variously known as Lü Dongbin or Lü Yan, once more on Day 10/5.

Day 8/29 (10th October)

In the morning the Buddhist monks Shiquan from Guanghan and Liaozheng from Zuomian came to join one of our following boats.

At dusk our boat was moved to the mouth of the River. Looking back towards the embankment, from the jumble of buildings and galleries came the light of lanterns and the sound of singing which went on until midnight.

We called Doctor Zhao Sui to examine Lingzhao.

Lu You does not tell us the purpose of the two monks' journey, but both were from Sichuan and so presumably were returning to their native places. He was in effect giving them a lift. Judging by the expeditions which Lu and they took together over the next month and a half he seems to have got on well with them.

Lingzhao was one of Lu You's daughters.

Day 8/30 (11th October)

At first light we left E prefecture. There was a favourable wind, the sail was hoisted and we proceeded along the south side of Parrot Island. The island is thickly wooded and there are spirit shrines, so from a distance it looks like Little Hill Islet. It's the spot where Mi Heng [c.173–98] is said to have been killed. That's why Li Bo's poem says:

> To this very day on that island of scents,
> The fragrant orchid dares not grow.

When Wang Sengbian [d.555] of the Liang dynasty attacked the army of Lun, Prince of Shaoling [d.551], he reached Parrot Island, that's to say this place. From here on south is the Han River, to which the Tribute of Yu refers: 'From Bozhong Mountain he made a passage for the Yang, which flowing eastwards becomes the Han.'[56] The colour of the water is limpid and reflective. Li Bo speaks of this when he says:

> The rivers of Chu are clear as the sky.

We passed the Xie Family Promontory and the Golden Cockerel Wharf. The promontory isn't very high but the rocks are all split horizontally like repeated courses of bricks. We caught a short-necked fresh water bream which weighed thirteen pounds. Beside the wharf is a hamlet, rather like a small county town, which produces sturgeon. For the most part the inhabitants make their living by selling preserved fish.

In the evening we moored at Tongji Mouth. From here one goes into the Narrows, the word being pronounced like the word for 'seal'. The dictionary states that it is 'the name of a river in Jiangxia'. After the ninth lunar month the Narrows dry up and become impassable, and you have to reach Jingzhu via Baling.

Mi Heng was a brilliant, eccentric and arrogant young poet of the period of division at the end of the second and beginning of the third centuries. He was shunted between one or other of the leading figures of the day, managing to insult them all while remaining an arbiter of literary taste; his best known extant work is a prose-poem on a parrot. Eventually he overstepped the mark and was executed.

Lun, Prince of Shaoling was Xiao Lun, the sixth son of Emperor Wu of the Liang dynasty; he and Wang Sengbian were engaged in a dynastic struggle for power towards the end of the Liang dynasty. The events Lu You describes took place in 550. Xiao Lun was killed the following year.

The Tribute of Yu was an early geographical work describing the provinces of China and their products. The statement that south of Parrot Island is the Han River is curious; the Han River joins the Yangzi from the north-west. It seems that in Lu You's time the next sector of the Yangzi going up-river was known locally at the Han, just as still further upstream it was called the Shu River. This would explain why a little later on (Days 9/12 and 9/15) he speaks of the county towns of Stone Head and Gongan as abutting the Han River.

In the final paragraph above Lu You signals a diversion from the Yangzi route. A few miles south-west of E prefecture (the modern Wuhan) he takes a side channel to the north of the main river and proceeds west across country, to re-emerge onto the Yangzi on Day 9/8. As he remarks, this was a summer route because as the water level fell in autumn the channel became too shallow for boats such as his. In fact the region lies below the summer level of its rivers but in winter the waters recede. Lu was fortunate that he was just in time to use the channel, or rather not so much a channel as a series of lakes connected by waterways, for by so doing he cut off the long south-westerly course up-river past the modern Yueyang (called Baling in his day) near the top of Lake Dongting, and the turn to the north-west as it zigzagged up to Stone Head (Shishou), the point at which Lu once again rejoined the Yangzi. Cooper calculated that the River makes a bend of 366 miles, while the distance by the lakes and their connecting natural and artificial canals was only 100. Lu also avoided the Yangzi current against which he was travelling. Even travelling with the current was difficult. Fan Chengda describes the route via the Yangzi: 'Where Yueyang connects with Lake Dongting the waves reach the sky, and if there's a wind it's impassable, so most passenger boats avoid it.'

Day 9/1 (12th October)

We started into the Narrows, which is actually a small channel of the River proper, and passed Newpool where there's a most beautifully decorated shrine to a dragon. From this point on there were no more inhabitants, and on either bank reeds and rushes stretch as far as the eye can see. It's known as the 'thirty mile wasteland'. Nor is there a tow-path, so the boatmen use little boats to pull the thousand-foot tow-rope. As night came on we had travelled barely fifteen miles, and moored amongst the clumps of reeds. It's all too common for boats travelling hereabouts to encounter brigands, but the Tongji police inspector provided an armed patrol. I lay awake till dawn.

Yangzi reed beds, and channels off the main river.

With the introduction of Buddhism into China the native concept of dragons merged with that of *nagas* – creatures with a dragon's body and a man's head – who occupied underwater kingdoms.[57] Worshippers wrote prayers to the reigning dragon on metal or stone tablets and threw them into the water where the dragon was supposed to reside.

Fan Chengda explains the Narrows (*zhuan*) in his *Record of a Boat from Wu* which, as we saw in the commentary to Day 8/19, covers some of the same ground Lu was travelling. They are, he says, 'side-channels of the River, like inlets of the sea, and only as broad as the Grand Canal'. In confirmation of Lu's account he adds that with reeds on either bank and only a scattering of habitations, and a complex of waterways connecting with little lakes, it was an area of brigands. Fan was fortunate enough to meet a detachment of two hundred soldiers on rotation to a new assignment who came aboard his boats. The moonlight was bright as day and they travelled on through the night to the creak of the stern oar, the drum sounding and the soldiers with their bows at the ready.

Day 9/2 (13th October)

Where the reeds on the eastern bank became sparser, from time to time we could see the vast expanse of the Great River. That is the route to Baling. In the late afternoon we made a stop at Xiajun where at last there were some twenty or more households, all engaged in fishing. Their rush fences and thatched houses had a feeling of seclusion. Fish cost practically nothing.

From this point on the tow-path begins again. I climbed up at the stern of the boat and gazed at the distant hills of Jingling. We moored at White Mortar which has a few farmsteads; outside all their gates were ancient willows reaching skywards.

> Cooper noticed the evidence of drift stuff clinging to the trees on a level with the eaves of the houses he passed in this area. 'A strange existence is that of the inhabitants of this reed-growing country; they alternately dwell in houses and boats, one moiety of the year tilling the ground and reed cutting, and the other fishing over their fields . . . in the dyke lands much care is bestowed upon the planting and pruning of willows, which here also serve as a breakwater in the summer floods, while the roots bind the soil of the dykes together.'
>
> The Jingling hills were more than fifty miles away to the north-west, but the area through which Lu was now travelling was very flat and open.

Day 9/3 (14th October)

Since entering the Narrows we've had no vegetables with our food. Today at last we obtained some cabbages and turnips, but they wouldn't agree to dig them up by the roots, and simply cut off the leaves. Past the mouth of Eight-fold Wharf it was all inhabited.

In the evening we moored at Guizi Fort where there were another ten or more households. It was full of mulberry trees, mountain mulberry, elm and willow.

Day 9/4 (15th October)

Only at dawn did the boat cast off. The boatmen say that from here on the marshlands are very dangerous, with tigers and wolves about. If you travel before daylight the trackers are often attacked by them.

This morning I saw the boatmen burning incense and praying to deities. They were appealing to the skipper Red-Whiskered Scullion:[58] don't make us give the wrong orders. I asked what 'skipper' meant and they told me it was a helmsmen. (The character *zhang* in the phrase is pronounced as in the expression for young and old.) So then I realized the import of Du Fu's 'Ballad of the Skipper' with the words:

> In broad daylight tossing their coins into the lofty waves.

Given that, I asked what 'tossing coins' referred to, and they replied that it was 'wagering'. I note that Liang Ji [d.159] was skilled at the game of 'guessing coins', and the commentary says that this was 'tossing coins', so it's plausible that 'tossing coins' means making a wager.

We passed Convoy Jetty where there are more than twenty households. In the evening sunlight amidst the tall willows, with their nets drying on low fences and little punts going back and forth, it really was a scene such as one sees in a painting and is the loveliest place on the Narrows. We moored at Bi Family Pool. It's in a well-aired and dry situation, and there are a lot of people living here. One or two of the houses, though they are of wattle and thatch, have proper windows and doorways, sturdy fences, and flourishing orchards alongside the buildings. These must be the leading families of the community.

I went up onto the bank on foot with my sons and the two monks, and we visited the Monastery of Universal Blessings Ever Sure. It was absolutely silent and deserted. In front of the White Cloud Balcony on the eastern side were orange trees that had just fruited, and though the oranges were small they were strongly scented. Together we brewed tea and peeled oranges, and only when the sun set did we return to the boat.

Bi Family Pool comes under the jurisdiction of Wide Waves township in Jade Sands county of Fu prefecture.

> Liang Ji was a mighty subject, a maker and unmaker of emperors during the middle years of the second century. He is said to have amassed an immense fortune; over three hundred of his dependants suffered in his fall.

Day 9/5 (16th October)
We moored at Purple Banks.

Day 9/6 (17th October)
We passed Eastern Arena. All along the water's edge were dense bamboo and tall trees, and the embankments were as pristine as if they'd been swept. Chickens and dogs dawdled in idleness, wild ducks bobbed on the water, and people were going back and forth in the shade of the trees. There was even someone calling for a boat at the ferry crossing! It made one as happy as if one had stumbled upon an enchanted land. The boatmen said this was all property belonging to village bigwigs.

We moored at Cock Crow town.

Day 9/7 (18th October)
We moored at the Zhan River.

Day 9/8 (19th October)
In the morning we made a stop at Concordia market town in Jiangling, which is at the mouth of the Narrows. In the Jin dynasty, when Wang Cheng [d.313] abandoned Jing prefecture, his Administrative Aide Guo Shu [late second/early third centuries] refused to follow Wang downstream to the east and stayed camped at the mouth of the Narrows. And Hou Andu [506–63] of the Chen dynasty harried Wang Lin [526–73] as far as the mouth of the Narrows. Both these incidents occurred here.

The winds were contrary; and in the water innumerable large fish went swimming by.

We've been travelling in the Narrows for seven days in all, but from here on we shall be sailing the Yangzi proper, entering the boundaries of Stone Head county.

At night we watched the burning reed-beds across the River. Smoke and flame stretched across the sky like a wall of flame and lit up the inside of the boat all red.

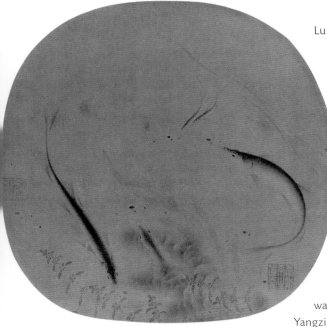

Spring Stream, Fish and Waterweed, Liu Cai (Northern Song).

Lu You had been travelling along the Narrows in a west-south-westerly direction, having left the Yangzi a few miles south-west of E prefecture. As we have seen, this was a short-cut which avoided the Yangzi route's long meander southwards to the Dongting Lake and north-west again. Blakiston describes the portion of the Yangzi from Lake Dongting to Stone Head thus: in 'a direct distance of 44 geographical miles, the river is so exceedingly tortuous that its course measures 120 miles'. In any case the Narrows were said to be safer because of the large waves to be met with on that sector of the Yangzi, though from Lu's account dangers human and animal lurked along the Narrows too. As we may recall (Day 9/1), Fan Chengda took this same Narrows diversion in the opposite direction, coming downstream, in 1177, and says it was the usual route for those going east and west rather than towards Yueyang, Lake Dongting and the Xiang River to south central China.

Concordia market town was on the Yangzi at the junction, Mouth of the Narrows, which logically but confusingly had the same name as the other end of the Narrows where it rejoins the Yangzi south of E prefecture. Whether Lu You was correct in ascribing these historical events to this rather than the other end of the Narrows I cannot say.

The term 'wall of flame' describes, not a city on fire nor a burning wall, but the official displays during the Tang dynasty of several hundred candles on the First Day of the year and the Winter Solstice. In other words Lu You is using the simile of a procession of torches to evoke the burning reed-beds on the opposite bank of the river.[59]

Day 9/9 (20th October)

In the morning I paid a visit to the Shrine to the God of the Earth. The houses of the common people along the side of the road were covered with reed thatch over a foot thick, all neat and tidy without so much as a twig out of place.

The sail was hoisted and we tacked along the River for ten miles, mooring at Pagoda Promontory, a large hill at the River's edge. This was the first hill we had seen since leaving E prefecture. We bought mutton and prepared a dinner since at the village jetty they were celebrating the Double Ninth festival. A sheep had been slaughtered and all the boats bought some; it was gone in a trice. I went in search of chrysanthemums at houses by the River, and found a few sprays with a delightful scent which immediately befuddled and intoxicated me.

It's raining tonight and is very cold, and for the first time we've put on the padded bed-covers.

The Double Ninth festival, which manifestly fell on the ninth day of the ninth lunar month, was celebrated by climbing up to high places and feasting. It was also closely associated with chrysanthemums: both appreciation of the blooms which are in flower at that time, and the drinking of chrysanthemum wine.

Day 9/10 (21st October)
We were held up by wind and rain. I sent someone in a small boat across the River to the other shore to buy some meat. He obtained half a large fish and also got a black cockerel which we hadn't the heart

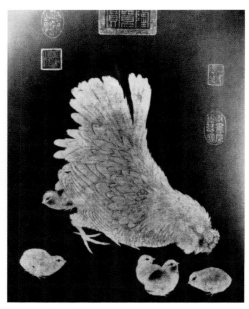

Hen and Brood, anonymous Song artist. National Palace Museum, Taipei.

to kill, so we're keeping it on board. A while later an old man from the village came bearing a bunch of shoots of aquatic vetch as a present. He wouldn't take reimbursement.

I've sent someone on ahead to Kui.

There's a clear sky this evening and we've opened the windows of the boat to gaze at the moon.

Kui, it may be recalled, was Lu's destination, the prefecture to which he had been appointed Assistant Prefect.

Day 9/11 (22nd October)
As the boat proceeded you could see a point to the south-west where the River and sky met which the boatmen said was Ambuscade Harbour, since in ancient times military forces would lie in ambush here waiting for the enemy. From far off I could see there were two jet black dots in the harbour which I thought were distant trees, except that they weren't connected with the ground. After a long while I could make out as we gradually grew closer that they were in fact large ships of eighty tons capacity.[60] There were also pairs of water birds floating on the River, white in colour and like geese, but larger. The people of Chu call them celestial geese [swans]. They soar up to a great height. One had been speared and had a delicious taste; some people say they are snow-geese.

We moored at the mouth of Three Rivers. The water was shallow and the boat had great difficulty in proceeding. It's from here on that there are no more hills. The lines by Li Bo:

> Hills reach their end in the level plain
> And the River flows into wilderness,

must have been written here in Jingzhu.

As Fan Chengda points out in his travel journal Three Rivers is for obvious reasons fairly common as a name. Lu had passed another Three Rivers on Day 8/20. The featureless land around Shi-show (Stone Head) was noted by Blakiston: 'At every point is an extensive flat; and, the whole plain being of an alluvial nature, the river seems to be continually gouging out the land on one side and forming these flat points on the other, so that embankments have frequently to be renewed and dwellings shifted.'

Day 9/12 (23rd October)
We passed Stone Head county without calling in. Stone Head first became a county in the Tang dynasty. It lies on the lower slopes of the Dragon Canopy Hills looking out over to the Han River, so it occupies a marvellous position. Du Fu wrote a poem called 'Seeing off the Magistrate Xue, who Comes from Stone Head'. This is the town he was referring to.
We have moored at Lotus Root Pool.

Stone Head county was on the right bank of the Yangzi on a small eminence, the Dragon Canopy (Longgai or Yueshan hills). The Han River lies some fifty-five miles to the north at its nearest point, and I have perhaps strained the Chinese in translating 'xialin' as 'looking out over to' rather than 'looking down on' which Lu You literally writes. Perhaps (see the commentary to Day 8/30) the explanation is that this section of the Yangzi was known as the Han. Blakiston considered Stone Head (his Shi-show) 'a small walled town of little importance' which 'might almost be passed without notice, were it not for a small group of hills which attract the attention at a long distance, and are the only eminences for miles around'. These, presumably, were the Dragon Canopy Hills.

Day 9/13 (24th October)
We moored at Willows. At night I went over to visit the two monks, Shiquan and Liaozheng, in their boat and heard them chanting the Prajnaparamita Sutra in Sanskrit. Only monks from Sichuan can chant this sutra.

In other words, only Sichuanese monks could chant the Wisdom Sutra in its original Sanskrit.

Ânanda, a disciple of Buddha, Song dynasty, Shanghai Museum.

Remote View of Hills and Streams (detail), Xia Gui (fl.1190–1225).

Day 9/14 (25th October)

We made a stop at Gongan, which was anciently known as Oil [River] Mouth. It was when Emperor Zhaolie of the [Shu] Han dynasty stationed his troops here that the modern name was first used. In scale and atmosphere it's most imposing, but after the ravages of war the common people's dwellings are largely of thatch and bamboo. Nevertheless, these thatched houses are exquisite and delightful. The commercial area is pretty prosperous; rice costs sixty or seventy coppers a quart.

Zhou Qiansun, the Magistrate and a junior Gentleman-Confucian, came to call on me. He comes from Hu prefecture.

We visited the Zen monastery dedicated to the Two Sages of Requited Kindness and Glorification of Filial Piety. The Two Sages refers to the Qingyeji Tathāgata and the Louzhide Tathāgata. They are both represented in the form of demon strongmen, over twenty feet in height, and possessed of a chilling and awe-inspiring majesty. In the main hall is Sakyamuni Buddha in the centre with Qingyeji, known as the Great Sage, to the right; and on his left Louzhide, known as the Second Sage. All three images face south. I note that the ju section of the Tripitaka contains a reference to Śāla, the Extraordianary Kumara attaining enlightenment and becoming the Qingyeji Tathāgata, and when Qingyeji Tathāgata appeared in the world again he became the Louzhide Tathāgata. So the two Tathāgatas are essentially the same person. There was a stele stating that on the self-same night some local citizens dreamed of the two deities which said: 'We are the Tathāgatas Qingyeji and Louzhide. There are two huge logs on the foreshore which we transported there. Await the arrival of a person travelling from Shan (in Chinese Turkestan) and have him carve our images.' Later on someone who described himself as travelling from Shan did indeed arrive, and what's more he was skilled at fashioning images. The local citizens were delighted and asked him to do the job. When the images were completed they all said they were just as they had dreamed them to be. But the stele is undated so one can't tell what period this refers to.

The Venerable Zuzhu is from Nanping Military Prefecture.

At the rear of the monastery is an abandoned city wall which seems to be perfectly preserved. The local gazetteer refers to it as Lǚ Meng's [178–219] Wall. But Du Fu states:

> Where the land broadens out is Lǚ Meng's camp,
> Where the River lies deep stands Liu Bei's wall.

Probably both Liu Bei and Lǚ Meng camped here.

There's an annotation to Du Fu's poem 'Setting out at Daybreak from Gongan' which states: 'I rested in this county for several months'. And I note that his poem 'On moving to Gongan' has the couplet:

> The river's mist has permeated grass along your path,
> Autumn dews enveloping the sunflowers in your garden;[61]

while his piece 'A Poem on Parting from the Monk Taiyi of Gongan' says:

> At sandy village white of snow still retains its chill,
> In river county plum's red bloom is burgeoning with Spring.

This means that he arrived in this county in autumn and only left at the end of winter, which is why he speaks of resting here for several months.

We've moored at Halt Awhile Pavilion. Water-fowl have been flying low back and forth, quite tamely, and haven't left us all day.

Chang and Smythe have identified the Qingyeji Tathāgata and the Louzhide Tathāgata, which do not appear in the standard reference works of Buddhism, as coming from the Puṇḍarīka (White Lotus) Sutra. Louzhide, or Rucika, is the last of the thousand Buddhas of our present *kalpa*. Fan Chengda notes the popularity of these sages who, no doubt amongst other qualities, were able to check the erosion of the river bank which was common hereabouts. Tathāgata is the Buddha in his corporeal manifestation, and is one of the highest titles of a Buddha. A Kumara is a servitor of Buddha or of a bodhisattva. Shan, from which the traveller who carved the images came, was in the modern province of Qinghai in the west of China.

We have had occasion to speak of Liu Bei in the commentary to Day 8/19, for he was one of the heroes of the heroic age when China split into three kingdoms on the collapse of the Han dynasty in the early third century. Lü Meng, likewise, was a general of this era who, together with Zhou Yu, defeated Cao Cao.

Day 9/15 (26th October)

Magistrate Zhou says that originally the county seat was near by, abutting the Han River on its north side, but as the sands were worn away the bank was eroded and gradually shifted southwards. The present course of the river runs where the town once stood. He also says that the county has five townships, but that in total they amount to fewer than two thousand households. With such a large area and small population the common people have a particularly hard time cultivating the land. The dyke defences are often breached, and year by year without cease they must be added to.

In the evening I took my family back to the Two Sages Monastery. In the community's living-quarters there's a very beautiful image of Vimalakirti carved in wood. We were told that it was made by a craftsman of Sandy City. And to the west of the Abbot's Lodgings is a most lovely bamboo balcony. The Venerable Zuzhu says that when the Fifth Patriarch Zen Master Fayan [c.1022–1104] first lived on All Sides Mountain he spent a full two years entirely alone. It was only then that a Daoist priest came to seek the Way, and was asked to become Administrator. After a further three years the Buddhist monk Baoliang arrived, and together with the Daoist priest applied himself to devotional studies from morn till night till they both attained the Dharma. From then on the Way of Fayan became steadily better known, and a few scholars from every part started coming here. But though later on he had a reputation throughout the world for the legions of his disciples, in fact they never numbered more than a few dozen during his own lifetime. Zuzhu had heard this from his teacher, the Zen Master Yan of the Sauvastika Retreat.

Jing prefecture has not a single Zen 'Grove of Meditation' other than that of the Two Sages. When monks from Sichuan emerge through the passes [from their native province] they always head for the Yangzi and Zhe River areas, and on their return they claim they've already attained the Way so they're no longer applying themselves to devotional studies. Thus, as the saying has it, 'Those coming down-river, like smoke along they tear; while those who go up-river hold their noses in the air'. Though it would only put them to the trouble of making offerings to another two Buddhas, you don't see a single monk meditating here.

In such a flat area as this maintenance of the dykes was proving a problem even in a period of stability and good governance. The situation had deteriorated in the mid-nineteenth century. Blakiston wrote: 'This system of dyke-land is continuous for some distance farther up the river; but there does not seem to be the same attention paid to its security everywhere, for we

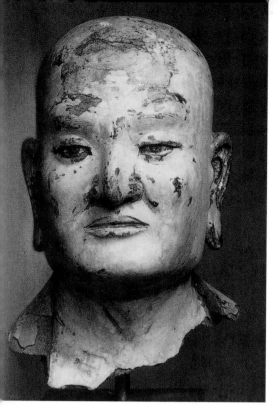

Buddhist monk, in lacquer (late eleventh or early twelfth century). Nelson-Atkins Museum of Art.

observed several places where the embankment was broken through; and in June, when we passed down, there was a great rush of water into such places, and the country was flooded far and wide. One would have thought that such works as these, the stability of which must affect thousands of industrious people, would have been under the supervision of the government, and such they may have been; but if so, their condition only proves the rotten state of that power'.

Fayan was not, as Chang and Smythe point out in an invaluable note, the Fifth Patriarch of Zen Buddhism but an eleventh-century monk from Fifth Patriarch Mountain where the real fifth patriarch, Hongren, had lived in the seventh century.

Lu once again seems to speak of this stretch of the Yangzi as the Han River (see the commentary to Days 8/30 and 9/12). The Sichuanese monks wanted, he says, to head for east China to pursue their studies and ignored the monasteries of Jiangling, which Lu You bookishly refers to by its Tang dynasty name of Jing prefecture.

Day 9/16 (27th October)

We passed White Lake which was a boundless expanse, and tacked along the River to Ladle Staging-post. There were several hundred celestial geese [swans] there, taking off or bobbing at the water's edge.

When the sun went down we moored at Sandy City. It had been twenty miles from Gongan to here, and from here on to Jingnan is three miles overland, for the boats can progress no further. Du Fu had a poem:

> When we bought firewood we were still in White Emperor City,
> A creak of the paddle and it's already Sandy Bank.

Liu Yuxi has another:

> At Sandy Bank when you stand by the mast,
> You first see how vast is the River in Spring.

Both of them were speaking of this place.

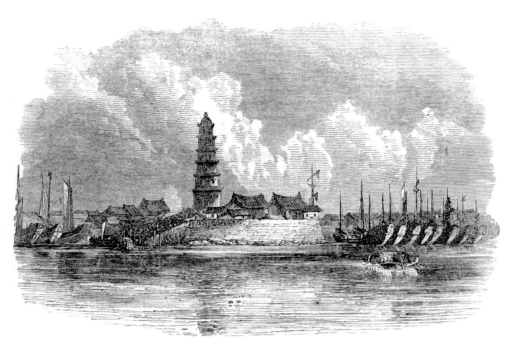

Sha-sze pagoda as depicted by Blakiston's illustrator.

Blakiston observed of Sandy City, or Sha-sze as he gives it in romanized form: 'It is a long unwalled straggling place on the left bank, with a fine stone pagoda on a point which juts into the river, and which may be seen at a very considerable distance. We were rather surprised at coming suddenly on a place where such a number of junks were collected, while we had met with so very few on the river between this place and the Tung-ting Lake; but this was accounted for when we learned that the 'Taiping Creek' or canal, which we had before heard of as connecting the Tung-ting Lake with the upper river, comes out only eight *li* (2½ miles) above, and that we were now at Kin-chow.'

Day 9/17 (28th October)

After the sun had gone down we transferred our baggage to a boat belonging to Zhao Qing of Jia prefecture. This is a boat that goes through the Gorges.

The population along the embankment at Sandy City is for the most part Sichuanese, and even those who aren't are married to Sichuanese.

Blakiston tells us, some seven hundred years on, that 'these Sz'chuan junks are of much the same form, with flat bottoms, square bows, and turned up sterns, and are strongly put together to resist the knocking about which they get in the rapid and rocky portions of the river'. He had been put in a passenger junk, not as commodious as his former craft and with the roof taken up with the bamboo ropes and lines that were being constantly coiled and uncoiled; the forward half of the boat was uncovered, and the cook had his fire and copper in the middle. At night the crew slept under waterproof mats in this forward part. But regular cargo junks were much larger, some more than a hundred feet in length, though of much the same lay-out.

Blakiston goes on to describe Sandy City: 'Sha-sze seems to be of considerable importance in a mercantile way, and the immense number of junks which we observed closely packed along the river bank, for nearly two miles, indicated a large trade on the river. It appears, however, that its importance is chiefly due to the transit business, the junks from Sz'chuan for the most part making this the end of their voyage in an easterly direction, and the cargoes for Hoo-nan [Hunan] and the south, as well as for Hankow and the lower Yang-tsze, being transported onward in boats of a different description. True, one sees Sz'chuan junks with their rounded sterns in the crowded waters of the Han, but their contents are but a very small proportion of the exports from that fertile province. Some transhipment is also done at I-chang, but it is not of the same amount as at Sha-sze. The reason of it appears to be that, as the Sz'chuan boats are built very strong, and suited especially for the rough navigation of the rapid river above, where sailing is a matter of secondary importance, they are too heavy and unsuited for the lake and tranquil river waters below; besides, the boatmen of Sz'chuan being a peculiar class, and bred up to one kind of occupation, and it requiring a far larger number to work each boat on the upper river than below, the discharged extra hands would be thrown out of work; in fact, we judged that that law which regulates such affairs in other places besides China, caused this particular division of labour, as any other would not pay.'

Day 9/18 (29th October)

I called on Liu Gongfu [1122–78], whose personal name is Gong, Prefect of the Superior Prefecture and an Academician of the Hall for Aid in Government; Quan Siyan, Assistant Prefect and a junior Court Gentleman Consultant; and Chen Ru, a senior Court Gentleman for Instruction. Jingnan is considered by the local gazetteer to be Ying, the capital city of the state of Chu. Emperor Yuan [r.552–5] of the Liang dynasty also once made his capital here. During the Tang dynasty it became the Jiangnan Military Commission under Jiangling Prefecture, and this has been perpetuated in our own day. But the Prefectural Governor's official title is merely Administrator of Jingnan Military Prefecture, exactly as are those of Yongxing and Heyang. This never had any particular significance; it's just following the old precedent.

In the commentary to Day 8/16 we saw that the pre-imperial state of Chu had dominated the central Yangzi valley for several hundred years before the Qin dynasty united China in 221 BC. Its capital from the early seventh century BC until 278 BC was Ying, though the name was also applied to other capitals to which the Chu kings were obliged to move as they came under pressure from contending states. The original Ying was indeed in Jiangling in what is now Hubei province, so it looks as though the identification with Jingnan in Lu's gazetteer was correct.

Day 9/19 (30th October)

There was an official reception at the State Corral at Newbridge. The Corral lies thirteen miles beyond the town's western gate. Once you emerge from the town

Hunting, Hu Gui (tenth century). This scene is set in the desert; the area Lu You was traversing was covered with reed beds. National Palace Museum, Taipei.

wall yellow reeds stretch as far as the eye can see, with hamlets of just a handful of households every three or four miles.

On the road we met a few dozen horsemen who had been ranging around on a hunt, the foxes and hares they'd caught tied to their saddles. They were skinning their catch, lying on the grass and drinking, and said they were soldiers from Xiangyang.

Today has been as bitterly cold as the depths of winter. The locals say they've already had snow at the beginning of this month.

The reed beds were a feature of the Yangzi valley. Archibald Little,[62] writing at a time when China was at the nadir of her modern economic history, described them in these terms: 'These reeds which cover the marshy banks and extensive flats bordering the Great River [the Yangzi] from its mouth to where it issues from the mountains below Ichang, a distance of 1000 miles, are a notable product of, and peculiar to, the Yang-tse valley. They grow to a height of fifteen to twenty feet and form the building material and fuel of a vast population. Nothing can be more wretched than the appearance of the few villages we passed – collections of ten to twenty reed-huts perched on the top of a steep mound, with occasionally a few willows planted on the slope, which is covered to the water's edge with buffalo dung, and straw, in which a few pigs wallow.' Blakiston too noted that in March the osiers 'were being cut and transported up the river; and reeds we saw in large quantities, which are mixed with mud in the manufacture of houses'.

Yangzi reeds.

Day 9/20 (31st October)

The mast has been dismantled and rowlocks for the stern-oars have been installed, since when you go up through the Gorges only oars and thousand foot tow-ropes are used; they don't hoist the sail any more. The thousand foot tow-ropes are made of huge bamboos split into four, as thick as a man's arm. Ships of fifty-five tons capacity such as I'm aboard all use six oars and have two windlasses for the thousand foot tow-ropes.

Lu You had now transferred to a boat designed to ascend the higher reaches of the Yangzi and go through the Gorges, and this entailed not only a different type of construction but another means of locomotion, the tow-rope, which he had mentioned on Day 9/1. These references to thousand-foot tow-ropes may sound far-fetched. European travellers in the nineteenth century were equally struck by their size. Unfortunately Lu does not directly describe the boats he used, but let us prepare ourselves for the navigation ahead with Little's late-nineteenth-century account of the tracking: 'A big junk of 150 tons carries a crew of over 100 men, viz. seventy or eighty trackers, whose movements are directed by beat of drum, the drummer remaining on board under the direction of the helmsman; a dozen or twenty men left on board to pole, and fend off the boulders and rocky points as she scrapes along, and also to work the gigantic bow sweep formed of a young fir-tree. Another half dozen of the crew are told off to skip over the rocks like cats, and free the tow-line from the rocky corners in which it is perpetually catching; besides a staff of three or four special swimmers called 'tai-wan-ti' or water-trackers, who run along, naked as Adam before the fall, and may be seen squatting on their haunches on rocks ahead, like so many vultures, prepared to jump into the water at a moment's notice and free the tow-line, should it catch on a rock inaccessible from the shore. These tow-lines are made of strips of bamboo plaited into a cable as thick as the arm, and which requires great skill in coiling and uncoiling, which is constantly being done, as the necessities of the route require a longer or shorter line. Notwithstanding its enormous toughness, owing to constant fraying on the rocks, a tow-line only lasts a single voyage, and when one sees deep scores cut by the tow-lines into the granite rocks along the tow-path, the fact is readily accounted for.' Isabella Bird corroborates and expands on this description: 'In small house-boats like mine the trackers are landed from the boat, but in junks from the attendant sampan. Except the *tai-wan-ti*, they wear short cotton drawers, and each man has a breast strap. The huge coil of plaited bamboo, frequently a quarter of a mile long, is landed after being passed over the mast-head, a man on board paying out or hauling in as is required. Small boats pass under the loftier tow-ropes of big ones, which often saves time, and often leads to noisy quarrels and entanglements. The trackers uncoil the rope, each man attaching it to his breast strap hitch, which can be cast off and rehitched in a moment.' She adds that 'the roof of the housed portion (of the boat) is used for the monstrous coils of bamboo rope, ofttimes three inches in diameter and 1200 feet in length, which are used in tracking, and are coiled and uncoiled continually. These ropes only last one voyage.' Van Slyke[63] explains how 'the tracking hawser – the lifeline of junk and tracker alike – was of woven bamboo strips, two to four inches in diameter, made in exactly the same way as larger suspension bridge cables . . . and drilling cables. . . . The core is woven of the inner part of the bamboo, and around this core are spiral-wrapped long strips of the bamboo's hard and friction-resistant outer surface layer which grip the core ever more tightly as the strain increases. The result is an extremely

Mast being lowered, detail from *Qingmingshanghetu*, Zhang Zeduan (fl.1111–26). Palace Museum, Beijing.

strong hawser of any needed length. A two-inch bamboo is three times as strong as hemp rope of the same dimension, and about half the strength of mild steel. Moreover, the tensile strength of the bamboo cable increases by 20 per cent when wet, as opposed to loss of strength in hemp rope.'

Day 9/21 (1st November)

Commander Liu went into mourning for his mother, so he divided the reception detachment into two halves, one of which will take him ahead by litter, returning to Kui prefecture on the mountain route.

Today we have been completely surrounded by dense fog.

Mourning was an elaborately prescribed procedure, and mourning for parents was of the highest importance in a society where filial piety was considered the foundation from which all morality sprang. Liu commanded the escort from Kui prefecture which had met Lu You on Day 8/23.

Day 9/22 (2nd November)

At the fifth watch [3–5 a.m.] I proceeded to the Sakyamuni Cloister and took part in a ceremony for the Festival of Congratulations.

After midnight the boatmen sacrificed to the deities of the Gorges, slaughtering a pig.

The Festival of Congratulations was in celebration of the birthday of the reigning monarch, Emperor Xiaozong (r.1162–89). By contrast the boatmen begin to prepare for the daunting passage up through the Gorges.

Day 9/2 (3rd November)

I paid my respects to the memory of Commander Liu's mother, Mme Zhuo, Grand Lady of Anding Commandery. The etiquette with which Commander Liu accepted my condolences is the same as that practised in Wu.

Wu, as we have seen (commentary on Day 8/16) is a loose term for central eastern China, Lu You's home area. Liu's mother had been granted a title of some seniority which probably indicated her husband or some other male relative was a man of distinction.

Day 9/24 (4th November)

I called on Niu Dake, a senior Gentleman for Court Service, and Superintendent in the office of the Hubei Military Commission; Tang Heng, a junior Court Gentleman Consultant and Administrator for the Military Commission; and Zhao Yun, a junior Gentleman for Court Service and Administrator for the Military Commission.

Day 9/25 (5th November)

Gao Qi, a junior Gentleman-litterateur and Magistrate of Mount Xing county in Gui prefecture, called on me.

Day 9/26 (6th November)

As soon as the refit was completed my kith and kin went on board the new boat, and I offered sacrifices of a pitcher of wine and a sacrificial pig at the Temple to the River Watercourses. The temple is a mile or so east of Sandy City, and the deity is called the King of the Boundless Source, Gloriously Efficacious, Sure in Response and of Overpowering Compassion. As one of the Four Watercourses these orthodox ceremonials are most properly regulated; nonetheless, in the annexes on either side are shrines to a great many heterodox cults which seem to be old customs of the Jing and Chu area.

Wang Shidian, the junior legal officer and a junior Gentleman for Meritorious Achievement, called on me with a copy of *Commentaries on the Hexagram Song* by his great-uncle Edict Attendant Wang Junyi. Wang Junyi, a native of Yan prefecture, was taught by my late grandfather and was an expert on *The Book of Changes* but his writings are no longer extant; only this single section of the *Commentaries* remains and it was, moreover, written in his youth.

As Valerie Hansen points out, deities were awarded titles of ever increasing length according to the veneration in which they were held. A title of eight descriptive characters such as this was the longest and highest honour. The Four Watercourses had in 747 been granted titles as Dukes of the Responsive Source, the Pure Source, the Boundless Source and the Far-distant Source, but by the twelfth century had been elevated to kingship. Heterodox cults, on the other hand, were proliferating without government sanction. Neo-Confucian critics (the re-assessment of Confucian thought in the light of Buddhist and other philosophical developments which we know as Neo-Confucianism was in full spate during Lu You's lifetime) deprecated the social background of many new gods that sprang from popular local beliefs. The deities were unknown commoners rather than rulers, generals and other great men; and there were moral grounds as well for seeking to stamp out these cults: the word 'heterodox' can equally be translated 'licentious'. It seems, though, that government inspectors could be persuaded to endorse the claims of certain heterodox cults for official status and respectability, to the chagrin of some officials.

Lu You's grandfather was Lu Dian (1042–1102). The reforming Prime Minister Wang Anshi, whose pupil Lu Dian had been, found his support less than fulsome and Lu senior's career never prospered, neither an opponent of Wang's nor sufficiently distanced from him; but despite a chequered administrative career he received academic posts including that of Lecturer in the National University, and was regarded as an expert on ritual as well as a historian entrusted with the redaction of the records of empeorors Shenzong and Zhezong. *The Book of Changes*, sometimes known to Western readers as the *I Ching* or *Yi Ching*, is made up of hexagrams consisting of broken and unbroken lines, the former representing yin and the latter yang, together with explanations of the hexagrams and commentaries on them. Modern scholars consider the work to have been composed between the sixth and fourth centuries BC.

Day 9/27 (7th November)

The boat cast off, and to the beating of drums and the creaking of oars the boatmen bellowed out as a phalanx of people crowded along the dyke to watch. We moored a mile or so from Sandy City at the mouth of the New River, which is where the Sichuanese repair their boats.

Isabella Bird took three days to reach Sandy City (Sha-shih or Sandy Market as she knew it) from Hankou (part of the modern Wuhan) and she was not much taken with it, though the dyke was impressive. 'At low water Wan-cheng Ti, the great dyke, averaging 150 feet in width at the bottom, and twenty-five at the top, twenty feet high on the river side, and forty on the land side, which follows the Yangtse for twenty-five miles to the west of Sha-shih and thirty to the east, effectually conceals the town from view, only a seven-storeyed pagoda and the curved roofs of temples and yamens appearing above the heads of the crowds which throng the roadway on the dyke-top. China must have been a greater country when this great public work was constructed than she is now, for this dyke where it protects Sha-shih is a noble, three-tiered, stone-faced construction, on the top of which are remnants of a stone balustrade; and broad, stately flights of stairs are let into the stonework at intervals, each tier of stairs being about twelve feet high. It must have been fully as impressive as the superb walls on the Chia-ling at Paoning Fu, which still remain a thing of grandeur and beauty.' But, though no stranger to rough conditions in her travels round the world, she goes on to describe Sandy City as 'pre-eminently and abominably dirty; and on this fine embankment dirt is in the ascendant, and dirt and bad smells assail the traveller on landing. Much of the refuse of the crowded city at the back is thrown over the river wall, accumulating in heaps which at low water conceal half of it. Steep steps lead up these vile mounds, and appear to be preferred to the stone stairs covered with slippery, black ooze. Below the heaps lie from one to two thousand junks with crews on average of ten men each, and frequently the junkman's wife and family in addition, giving an average floating population of 10,000. Beggars' huts encroach on the top of the embankment; and when I write that hosts of gaunt, sore-eyed, mangy dogs, and black pigs each with a row of bristles standing up along his lean, curved back, and beggars, one mass of dirt and sores, are always routing and delving in the heaps, the reader will not be surprised that I did not find Sha-shih prepossessing.'

Day 9/28 (8th November)

We moored at Square Town. There's a man from Jia prefecture called Wang Baiyi who had earlier been recruited as the 'engager' for our boat. 'Engagers' are in charge of the three helmsmen. Their wages are fairly generous, and whenever sacrifices are made to the deities they get double the quantity of meat offerings handed out to ordinary crew members. Later on the owner of the boat, Zhao Qing, employed his chum Cheng Xiaoba as 'engager' instead. Wang Baiyi felt resentful at losing his job but couldn't make up his mind to leave. Then he went crazy and threw himself into the water. I hurriedly sent people off to save him. He floated about half a mile, going under and resurfacing three times, and they only just pulled him out. If losing a job as 'engager' can push someone to death's door, won't that be even truer in cases of greater moment?

Blakiston had noticed Square Town, a mile up-river from Sandy City, which in his time was a garrison town for the Manchus. 'In form it seemed, from the view we got of it, to be nearly a square, enclosed with high walls in the usual manner.'

Lu You is no doubt thinking of the vicissitudes of official life when he mentions matters of greater moment; as a Confucian servant of the state he was concerned for the common people and, like many of his contemporaries, wrote about their daily lives and economic conditions, particularly those of farmers, with real sympathy. But he would have been too conscious of the responsibilities of members of the ruling élite to equate the dilemmas facing officials with those of mere boatmen. Little's boat nearly lost a man, though through accident: 'Suddenly I heard a great outcry, and could just distinguish the hair of a man in the water, ahead of our boat. I ran quickly down to go in after him, but before I reached the shore our boat came up with him, and dragged him on board half drowned. It was one of our trackers, who, in fording a shallow between two reefs of rocks, had got out of his depth and been saved just in time. I do not understand how he floated so long and quietly, with only just his hair above the surface.'

Lu was now heading due west from Sandy City to Jiangling; this, as we have seen, was the area where goods were transhipped between the craft from Sichuan and those that plied the middle and lower reaches of the Yangzi. It was also the point at which shipping that had taken the canal diversion to the west of the Yangzi from Lake Dongting (Lu had avoided Lake Dongting by going almost due west across from E prefecture to Stone Head – Days 9/1 to 9/8) re-emerged onto the Great River.

Day 9/29 (9th November)

There were adverse winds.

Day 10/1 (10th November)

We passed Melon Island Dyke, Villeins, and Thirty Mile Island and moored at Tuoyong. There are hamlets all along them amidst lush bamboo and trees, with the settlements in sight of each other. There were even village school-masters teaching their pupils, and when the lads saw boats passing they all came out clutching their books to watch, some even going on reciting their lessons.

Tuo ['channels' in the toponym Tuoyong] is another name for 'river'. The Book of Songs says 'the river has channels'. And the phrase in The Tribute of Yu 'From Mount Min he made a passage for the River, where eastwards it separates into channels' refers to this. As for yong, the dictionary Examples of Refined Usage defines this as a place where there is water in spring, summer, and autumn but not in winter.

The Book of Songs, or *Classic of Poetry* or *Shijing,* is the earliest collection of Chinese poetry. It was composed around 600 BC from various sources, both court poetry and popular songs, the material dating from about 1000–600 BC. *The Tribute of Yu* is the early geographical work we encountered on Day 8/30. *Examples of Refined Usage,* perhaps better known by the transliteration of its title as the *Erya Dictionary,* was written in the third century BC and is the earliest lexicographical work in China. Guo Pu, our old friend from Day 6/28 to whom Lu You makes further reference in this latter part of the Diary, wrote his commentary on it in the early fourth century. As Chang and Smythe point out, Lu

Dian was an authority on *The Examples of Refined Usage* dictionary and Lu You might therefore have seen amongst his grandfather's papers a different version of it from the extant recension, which does not contain the definition of *yong* which Lu provides.

Day 10/2 (11th November)

We moored at Cassia Forest Bay. The Buddhist monks Shiquan and Liaozheng came overland and said the people living along their route were mostly from other parts of the country, and that locals made up only one in ten of the population.

The boatmen killed more than ten pigs to sacrifice to the gods. They call this 'The Outset'.

Isabella Bird.

Seven hundred years later similar preparations were still being made. 'Before starting my boat's crew made offerings and vows at their favourite temples, and on the first evening they slew a fowl as an offering to the river god, and smeared its blood over the bow-sweep and fore part of the boat. My preparations', says Isabella Bird, 'were to pack my plates, films, and general photographic outfit, journals, a few necessaries, and a few things of fictitious value, in a waterproof bag, to be carried by my servant, along with my camera, at each rapid where we landed'.

Day 10/3 (12th November)

The boatmen were dividing up the sacrificial meat and we were to travel on a little later than usual, so I went up on the embankment with my sons to look at the Shu River. It was then that I realized how good a representation of the scene is the line by Li Bo in his poem 'At the Gates of Jing I Gaze at the Shu River', which runs:

> The river's colour, verdant, bright.

Here it is that for the first time since leaving Pagoda Promontory we have caught sight of the Ba Mountains. The mountains are in Pine-burgeon county.

We moored at Guanzi Mouth which lies between the two towns of Pine-burgeon and Branch River. Pine-burgeon was established as a county under the Jin dynasty; from here on one enters upon the Shu River. Branch River was set up as a county under the Tang dynasty, and was the ancient state of Luo. The ninety-nine islands of Jiangling lie within it. When, in the Jin dynasty, Liu Yuezhi, Luo Shu and Zhen Jizhi heard that Huan Xuan [369–404] had died they came down from White Emperor City to Branch River, this very place. Ouyang Xiu wrote a poem in verse of five characters to the line using twenty-four [different] rhymes entitled 'Travelling Through the Branch River Hills'. It seems Ouyang must have travelled overland from here as far as Xia prefecture when he was on his way to Yiling. That's why his poem called 'Prefectural-view Slopes' says:

Mountains and river.

> Days of rugged mountain travel wholly wear me out,
> Yet from these slopes I relish the prefecture of Xia.

Guanzi Mouth is also known as Pine-burgeon Crossing. Liu Yuxi had a poem which ran:

> People of Ba have shed their tears in response to the gibbons' cries;
> Travellers boats from Sichuan return in the wake of birds.

From the market town of Branch River the route up the Yangzi swings southwards to Pine-burgeon Crossing and then north-north-west to Xia prefecture. Traditionally the plateau of what is now Sichuan province was known as Shu, and the area to its east through the Yangzi Gorges and below was Ba. The Shu River which Lu You refers to here was simply the Yangzi by another name in the stretch leading from Pine-burgeon (Songzi) into Sichuan. It is worth alerting the reader to the fact that there was, for Chinese from the north or east, a palpable sense of strangeness and wildness to the topography, fauna and flora, as well as the local customs, as one approached Ba. The cries of gibbons were particularly maudlin and poignant for the stranger.

Liu, Luo, Zhen and Huan all died in 404. The first three were loyal to the Jin dynasty and brought their forces down-river on hearing that Huan Xuan, who had usurped the throne in the previous year, had died.

Day 10/4 (13th November)

We passed Willow Wood Palisade. Pine-burgeon has four palisades which they call Willow Wood, Carriage-goat, High Plane and Taxman.

We have moored at Dragon Bay.

Monkeys Playing in a Loquat Tree, anonymous (late eleventh, early twelfth century. National Palace Museum, Taipei.

Day 10/5 (14th November)

We passed White Goat Market which is on the boundary of Yidu county in Xia prefecture. Yidu was made a county under the Tang dynasty.

I paid my respects at the tomb of Zhang Shangying [1043–1122], whose posthumous name was The Cultured and Loyal Duke. Trees around the tomb, fallen or chopped down, straddle the path and make it almost impassable. Zhang's son Mao, who was an Auxiliary member of the Dragon Diagram Hall, is already dead. Of his two grandsons, one held office but was afflicted with a personality disorder,[64] and the other is a commoner. His tomb had at first been constructed on the banks of the river, but when it was finished he wasn't actually buried there. He was buried instead in the hills, which is where this present tomb is. However the old tomb wasn't destroyed, and its tunnel has been opened up to allow access to the inside which can seat several dozen people.[65] A Daoist has constructed a house alongside and looks after it.

The Daoist produced [a rubbing of] a stone inscription in Draft Script which read:

Seek not from external things the marvellous treasure; You should ask the True Teacher the proportions of mercury and lead.

Despatched to Zhang Zigao of the Eight Minerals Grotto.

When I, Zhongli Quan, first visited the capital from the King's House Mountains[66] my disciple, the Hermit of Mount Floating Jade, came to beg of me these words. Now that I am about to return to the west once more the Master of the Cinnabar Origin has asked for a second time that I should inscribe them at the end of this scroll.

Fifteenth day of the middle month of winter of the first year of the Shaosheng period.

Quan is known to the world as Master Zhongli, and Zigao was Zhang Shangying. The Master of the Cinnabar Origin was someone with whom Su Shi had an exchange of poems.

There follows a colophon by Wei Tai [c.1050–1110], whose courtesy name was Daofu, which states that:

Painted doorway to a Song dynasty tomb, Luoyang area.

When Zhang Shangying had successfully mastered the Yellow Signet liturgical methods the Hermit of Mount Floating Jade said to him: 'High Heaven has registered Your Excellency's achievement and made you Master of the Eight Minerals Grotto on Mount Sumeru. You should have a seal carved to thank God and wear it at your waist.' But Zhang Shangying did not believe him, so the Hermit of Mount Floating Jade also brought out this calligraphy of Master Zhongli's as evidence. Later on the Master of the Cinnabar Origin also requested [Zhongli] to write some calligraphy at the end of the scroll for Zhang Shangying's sake.'

A certain Xu Zhu has also written a colophon:

When Zhang Shangying was calling at Zhen prefecture by boat, just as he had gone to pay his duty calls someone in a plain gown and ordinary hat got straight into his boat, demanded a writing-brush and wrote ten characters in a large script: 'The idler Lü Yan has come to visit Zhang Shangying.' Then he cast the brush aside and left. When Zhang Shangying got back the ink was still not dry.

Xu Zhu was from Zhen prefecture and said he had seen the writing himself.

On a wall of the building housing the inscriptions in front of the tumulus there is a poem which runs:

> Ten leagues through autumn winds we gazed for the Tristar Lord,
> Longing to see that icy flask shine down and purify.
> Now rains benign are here again as Dan the Duke drives in;
> He strokes his beard and listens to the Yewang lutanists.
> The elder statesman of three reigns, his heart robust as ever,
> Has people of the whole wide world inclining of their ears.
> Your white-haired friend of old has come to bid you now farewell,
> Returning to the woods these times of concord to observe.

This must be a poem that Wei Tai presented to Zhang Shangying and which has been written out by some later person.

There is also a poem by the Drafter Tang Wenruo [1106–65] of which the last couplet reads:

> No monument where one might shed a tear;
> I write these lines to summon back his soul.

Lü Dabian, the County Magistrate of Yidu and a junior Gentleman-litterateur, came to call on me.
We moored at Red Precipice.

We have come to a passage of the Diary which needs more than the usual exegesis, but with patience we can unwrap its meaning and it will serve to illustrate the layered texture of a Song scholar's range of allusion.

Lu You has now arrived in Yidu county, which is administratively part of Xia prefecture. One of the better known officials who had been banished here was Zhang Shangying. Zhang was a statesman of the Northern Song, a literatus, Daoist scholar and lay Buddhist. He held office under emperors Shenzong and Zhezong in the late eleventh century, and had risen to senior rank by 1102/3 when Emperor Huizong came to the throne. At first he prospered in the new reign, being a close associate of the Prime Minister Cai Jing, the man whom we met on Day 6/2 of the Diary who had been criticized in connection with the lavish burial of his father. But Zhang fell out with Cai in 1106, and in 1107 was banished to minor posts in relatively remote areas such as Xia prefecture. Cai's administration was unsuccessful, not helped by severe drought, and Zhang was recalled to power, becoming Prime Minister on 26th June 1110. Rain fell the next day.

Zhang had written an account of a pilgrimage to Mount Wutai in Shansi in 1088, and while in office maintained his Daoist interests, encouraged by the emperor, himself a devotee of Daoism, who wrote to Zhang in 1110 about the commissioning of a book on Daoist ritual liturgy. Zhang chose for himself a soubriquet of Daoist significance, Layman of the Infinite (though by contrast he also wrote a book on military strategy and tactics). With these interests in mind it is not surprising to find that Zhang's excavated but unused tomb was being tended by a Daoist, and that memorabilia of a Daoist colouring were kept there. Zhang, who as Lu You tells us was also known as Zhang Zigao, had it appears been awarded the title Master of the Eight Minerals Grotto. The Eight Mineral Elixir was a term known to Chinese alchemy,[67] and indeed the inscriptions Lu quotes are redolent of terminology to do with alchemy and the prolongation of life – mercury and lead, the Cinnabar Origin (a Daoist term referring to the mind or state of mind, mood), and the Yellow Signet liturgical methods, purification rites in which sacrifices are offered, confession made, and pardon sought with the end of becoming an immortal.

Evidence of Zhang's proficiency in these occult pursuits does not end there. Zhongli Quan, who had written the first of the inscriptions quoted, lived under the Tang dynasty (618–907) but has dated his writing to the Western equivalent of 25th December 1094. He was one of the so-called Eight Immortals of Daoism. And the man who mysteriously appeared in Zhang's boat when he was out making official calls was Lü Yan, otherwise known as Lü Dongbin, a Tang contemporary of Zhongli Quan who became an immortal. His cult was popular in the twelfth century; he has cropped up already as Mr Lü on Day 8/28. In many of the stories told about him he shows a playfulness which is also caught in Lu You's account of his tantalizing manifestation in Zhang Shangying's boat. Lu You's interest in such stories may have been encouraged by family tradition. His great-great grandfather, Lu Zhen, who lived in the eleventh century, had met the immortal Shi Jianwu walking three feet above the ground and from him acquired the art of making elixirs and abstaining from cereals (the latter, as we have seen on Day 7/20, was associated with corporeal immortality). Shi Jianwu had lived in the early ninth century (the lapse of a couple of centuries was no bar to an encounter between Lu Zhen and an immortal) and was said to have been a disciple of Lü Dongbin himself.

We then come to the poem that Wei Tai presented to Zhang Shangying. Though far from straightforward in its references it is conventional in its sycophancy: a poem of congratulation to Zhang on his recent appointment as Prime Minister. The Tristar Lord refers to the three stars in the Big Dipper and is a deft allusion to the trinity of what were nominally the most senior posts in the Song government. An icy flask is a metaphor for the purest moral character, as well as the moon. The duke was the brother of the founder of the Zhou dynasty; when the founder's son, King Cheng (r.1025–05 BC), sent the Duke of Zhou, who had been serving as regent during Cheng's youth, into exile heavy rains fell until at last the duke was recalled and the rains ceased. The Duke of Zhou was a Confucian paragon of the loyal and selfless adviser; the poet has neatly inverted the story of constant rain to applaud the ending of the drought when Zhang Shangying was brought back to power. The lutanists of Yewang is probably an allusion to two wise hermits who gave the founder of the Eastern Han dynasty (25–220) enlightened advice. The elder statesman of three reigns is, of course, Zhang himself who served under emperors Shenzong, Zhezong and Huizong in the late eleventh and early twelfth centuries. Zhang's friend the poet has no ambitions but to retire to the simple life of a recluse now that the government is in safe hands.[68] (Wei Tai had no official career: he never got a degree because he nearly killed an examiner and was forbidden to retake the examinations. Instead he became a recluse, though also a friend of several leading officials of the late eleventh and early twelfth centuries).

The concluding couplet of Tang Wenruo's poem alludes to a famous third-century statesman associated with this area at whose stele people wept, and which was given the name 'Shed Tear Monument'. The summoning back of souls had a long tradition in China, and invocations to the souls of the dead or the sick by a shaman have a particular association with the area which Lu You is now describing. In the ancient anthology *Chu ci* (*Songs of Chu*) are two exemplars from the second half of the third century BC known to any educated reader in imperial China, 'The Summons of the Soul' ascribed to Song Yu, a fairly shadowy figure at the court of Chu in the third century BC whose supposed house Lu You visits on Day 10/19; and 'The Great Summons'. But in the hands of a twelfth-century poet such as Tang Wenruo 'I write these lines to summon back his soul' is little more than a figure of speech, but apt in the circumstances since Zhang Shangying had once served as an official hereabouts.

Day 10/6 (15th November)

We passed the Twelve Stacks of the Gates of Jing with their high precipices, sheer cliffs and towering rock faces, so one can tell how precipitous the Gorges are going to be. As we passed the Stacks I gazed towards the Five Dragons and Hen-coop Mountains, as high and rugged as the strange peaks of summer clouds. The Gates of Jing must have earned their name as a strong point. But on the Stacks is a cranny in the rock, quite square and high enough to let a man pass through, and this is popularly known as the 'Gates of Jing', which is ludicrous.

By evening we had reached Xia prefecture and moored below the Pavilion of Supreme Delight. In the Tang dynasty Xia prefecture 峽 [with the mountain radical and meaning 'straits'] 州 was known as Xia prefecture 硤 [with the stone radical and meaning 'gully'] 州. This was later changed to the current usage, though the wording on the official seal became [yet a third character pronunced Shan] 陝州. In the Yuanfeng period [1078–85] Director He Xunzhi recommended that because there was confusion between the characters Shan 陝 and Xia 陜 his official seal should be recast using the character with the mountain 山 radical [i.e. 峽]. The matter was referred down to the Directorate of Imperial Manufactories, but Vice-Director Ouyang Fa [1044–89] said that the character 陝 in Shan prefecture 陝州 in Hubei was composed of 阜 and 夾 (夾 containing two 入); whereas the 陜 of Xia prefecture 陜州 was composed of 阜 and 夾 (夾 containing two 人). Since the right-hand components in the characters were different no confusion existed, and he feared [that if the change were made] the whole world would say that officials in the Directorate of Imperial Manufactures were illiterate. At that time opinion amongst court officials was all in agreement with Ouyang Fa, but in the end it's said

Cliffs along the Yangzi.

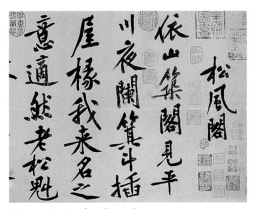

Huang Tingjian's calligraphy.

the official seal was recast as He Xunzhi had proposed.

The Dedication for the Pavilion of Supreme Delight was composed by Ouyang Xiu and the calligraphy is by Huang Tingjian.

Ouyang Fa was the son of the great eleventh-century prose stylist and statesman Ouyang Xiu; the department whose reputation the former was anxious to protect was responsible for supervising a number of government artisinal workshops including the agency for coinage. Ouyang Xiu spent the late 1030s in this area and Lu You is constantly reminded of his presence by inscriptions, lines of verse and other memorabilia.

Xia prefecture is the modern Yichang and is the last major city before the Gorges as one goes upstream. Blakiston approached it in early April. 'A nearly perfectly straight reach, which absorbs the last seventeen miles, tends to set off the beauties of this truly picturesque district. With us the weather was just such as one would wish for – a cloudless sky with clear and dry atmosphere – it was the first really warm weather of the year, and it seemed as if we had skipped the intervening season and jumped suddenly from winter into summer . . . I-chang [Yichang], or rather its smoke, and the pagoda about a couple of miles below the place, are within sight a long way down, and I thought at the time that I had never beheld a more beautiful river scene. On either hand the banks had become high and precipitous, bold cliffs of rock – a mixture of conglomerate and sandstone – rose immediately from deep water, allowing our boatmen no chance either of tracking or poling, and we were fain to make our way along with the skulls, assisted by a slight breeze. To our left hand, as we ascended – that is, beyond the river's right bank – was entirely a mountainous country, and we could observe it extended to the northward beyond the town, that lay on the other side in the river valley, behind which the country rose gently into plateaux and ridges, broken occasionally by a narrow, rice-planted valley . . . .' As Cooper noted, Xia prefecture 'derived its importance from its position as a border town of the plains, and the first customs' station at the entrance of Hoopeh from Sz-chuan'. A few miles above Yichang where the Yangzi narrows is the Gezhouba Dam which opened in the early 1980s.

Day 10/7 (16th November)

I made a call on Ye Anxing, whose courtesy name is Lǚdao, the Prefect and a junior Grand Master for Court Audiences, and we took a small boat to visit the Sweet Spring Monastery at West Hill. Its bamboo bridges and stone steps gave it a secluded air. There are two pavilions, Profound Erudition and Purified Mind, which look down over the River where the scattered mountains begin to open out. To the right of the Dharma Hall is a little path running a few dozen paces to a spring named the Spring of the Filial Daughter-in-law, a reference to Jiang Shi's [first century AD] wife Miss Pang, and above the spring there is even a shrine to Miss Pang. But Ouyang Xiu gave the story no credence, which is why in his poem he says:

> Ruined the earth-spirit's altar, though the Jiang shrine remains:
> The facts are hard to come by in Chu's distorting dialect.

The first stanza of that poem speaks of:

> Lone peak above the River, Green Creeper obscured.

When you first read this you think simply that the lone peak is covered by vines and creepers. It's only when you come here you realize that at the foot of the hill lies the Green Creeper Creek.

I also went to the Temple of Emperor Jing [r.156–41 BC] of the Han dynasty, and the East Hill Monastery. I'm not sure why there's a temple to Emperor Jing here. When Ouyang Xiu was serving as the Magistrate he wrote a Prayer for Rain which is in his Collected Works. The East Hill Monastery, which is a couple of miles from the Gazing to the Capital Gate, also appears in poems by Ouyang. Beyond the monastery is a pavilion overlooking a little pool and surrounded by a screen of hills. It's most lovely. The holly and cedars in front of the pavilion are all over a hundred years old.

We then reached Yiling and I called on the County Magistrate Hu Zhen, a senior Gentleman for Governmental Participation. The Hall of Supreme Happiness to the east of the administrative offices was built for Ouyang Xiu by Prefect Zhu of the Bureau of Forestry and Crafts. It has been burned down, though the stone bases of the pillars still remain and it would have been on a most grandiose scale. Further east is the shrine hall [to Ouyang Xiu] which is plain and humble, with an image which bears no resemblance to him. What a shame! The well in front of the administrative offices was, according to tradition, sunk by Ouyang. The water is very sweet and cold and is considered the best in the prefecture. The camphor tree beside the well is a full arm's girth in diameter, and it too is said to have been planted by Ouyang personally.

In the evening there was an official reception at the Passes of Chu Building and we went all over the Refined Usage Terrace and Brocade Hillocks Pavilion. The two crab-apple trees in front of the pavilion are a hundred years old. The Refined Usage Terrace is considered by the local gazetteer to be the place where Guo Pu wrote his commentary on the *Examples of Refined Usage* dictionary. There's also a Pavilion of Crimson Snow, a name taken from Ouyang Xiu's poem 'The Thousand-Leafed Red Pear'; but the red pear-tree exists no longer.

Jiang Shi and his wife, *née* Pang, were known for their filial devotion to his parents. But Lu You's friend and fellow poet Fan Chengda, who passed here in late August 1177, cast doubt on whether this place was really associated with Jiang and Miss Pang.

The age of the holly that Lu You saw is entirely credible. Peter Valder records in *The Garden Plants of China* (1999) an *Ilex rotunda* var. *microcarpa*, the small-fruited holly, which was 715 years old, in other words planted only a century after Lu was writing.

According to Chang and Smythe Prefect Zhu was Zhu Qingji who held office in Xia prefecture in 1035, so the dates fit for Ouyang Xiu's time in the area.

For Guo Pu see Day 6/28, and for the dictionary to which he wrote a commentary Day 10/1.

Day 10/8 (17th November)

Once the fifth watch was over [after 5 a.m.] the boat cast off and we went through the Xialao Pass. The River was flanked by a thousand peaks and ten thousand cliffs, some vying one with another, others soaring solitary; some crumbling close to collapse, others teetering as they towered; some split horizontally, others cleft vertically; some protruded, others were concave, yet others fissured. I cannot fully describe their wondrous strangeness. Though it's early winter the plants and trees were a deep green, not withered at all. To the west, where the ranges of mountains resemble portals with the River emerging between them, is the so-called Xialao Creek. Ouyang Xiu wrote a poem called 'The Xialao Ford' in which he says in reference to this place:

> Entering the Gorges, and the mountains start to wind;
> Twisting through the rapids, more mountains and yet more.

Our boat was secured, and with my sons and the monk Liaozheng I climbed to the Three Visitors Grotto, clambering up nearly a mile of stone steps which in places were so dangerous there was no foothold. The grotto is as big as a three-roomed house, and had a cavity large enough for one to get through, but so dark and steep it was really alarming. Then one winds round mid-way up the mountain, crouching under the rock-face, to make one's way back to the front of the grotto. It was just passable, but when we looked

down into streams and pools from a cliff-face of over a hundred feet the sound of the water was terrifying. There was another cavity behind which were walls such as to make it habitable. Age-old stalactites hang down to the ground like pillars, serving as a doorway to the gap. Above was an inscription: 'Huang Dalin and his younger brother Huang Tingjian, together with Xin Hong and his son Xin Dafang, visited on the xinhai day of the third month of the second year of the Shaosheng period [22nd April 1095].' On the rock face to the side there is inscribed: 'Tenth day of the seventh month of the fourth year of the Jingyou period [23rd August 1037], Ouyang Xiu of Yiling . . .' Below there is a word missing. It continues: 'Administrative Assistant Ding . . .' and then several more characters are missing below this. This Ding was Ding Baochen [1010–67], who

Yangzi rock strata.

had the courtesy name Yuanzhen. Now you can just about make out the two characters after Ding's surname, but they are nothing like the characters Yuanzhen. Furthermore, after Ouyang Xiu's given name it merely states that he was 'of Yiling' without adding the designation Magistrate. Outside the grotto there's also a boulder fallen flat across the stream, on which is carved: 'Huang Tingjian and his younger brother Shuxiang, his son Xiang, and his nephew Qing, together with the Daoist Tang Lü came to visit, and when we saw our old inscription with the *xinhai* date it seemed like something out of a dream. *Gengyin* day of the third month of the first year of the Jianzhongjingguo period [29th April 1101]'. I note that Huang Tingjian came past here in the second year of the Shaosheng period [1095] on first being banished to Qiannan, and that this was the *yihai* year. So when it now refers to the *xinhai* [year] it's wrong.

We moored at Stone Tablet Gorge. Within the rock cavity there's a stone shaped like an old man holding a fishing rod which is accurate in almost every detail.

Lu You had now reached the point at which the Yangzi, still a good half-mile across at Xia prefecture, suddenly rushes out of a cleft in the mountains from a gorge (in Blakiston's words) 'not above two hundred and fifty yards in width, and its sides mount up vertically to three and five hundred feet, broken into crevices and ledges, where ferns and creepers of the brightest green flourish on the scanty soil of the moss-covered rock by the sides of dripping waterfalls . . . a scene of wild grandeur which baffles description, and might test the skill of no mean artist'. Isabella Bird at the same spot felt 'we were then in what looked like a mountain lake.

No outlet was visible; mountains rose clear and grim against a grey sky. Snow-flakes fell sparsely and gently in a perfectly still atmosphere. We cast off from the shore; the oars were plied to a wild chorus; what looked like a cleft in the rock appeared, and making an abrupt turn round a high rocky point in all the thrill of novelty and expectation, we were in the Ichang [Yichang] Gorge, the first and one of the grandest of those gigantic clefts through which the Great River, at times a mile in breadth, there compressed into a limit of from 400 to 150 yards, has carved a passage through the mountains.' Cooper found 'the steep sides of the gorge seemd to be composed of the debris of shattered hills; huge masses of rock were everywhere piled in formless and chaotic disorder, some projecting hundreds of feet above us, as if poised, ready to roll from their resting place and crush the intruder. In mid-

Moraine beside the Yangzi.

First Rapids of the Yangzi, from Blakiston.

river similar masses, as though hurled from the cliffs, reared themselves from the water in fantastic confusion.' 'No house, tree, or vestige of cultivation spoke of man – all was bare, silent, and awful'. Man's work is now all too apparent: the site of the Three Gorges Dam lies near by.

The Three Visitors Grotto was first given the name after a visit by Bai Juyi, his brother who was also a writer, and Bai's friend Yuan Zhen in 819. We touched on the friendship between Bai and Yuan on Day 6/19. But in 1056 Su Shi, his father and his brother (for whom see Day 8/17) also came to the grotto so that occasion came to be known as the 'Latter Three Visitors'. Lu You mentions none of this, though he shares the Song scholars fascination with epigraphy and inscriptions, intimating that the inscription recording Huang's second visit may have been spurious since it confused day and year signs. Chang and Smythe have themselves been confused in converting some of these dates to the Western calendar. This and the immediately following passage have, however, been accurately translated by Richard E. Strassberg.

Ding Baochen was a literary and political figure who was a friend of Ouyang Xiu's.

Day 10/9 (18th November)

There was light snow[69] as we passed through Screen Gorge. The ranges of mountains overlap each other just like the leaves of a screen, and I suppose this is why the gorge was given the name. I climbed Toad Stack which is listed by the 'Classification of Waters' the fourth amongst springs. The Toad is at the foot of the mountain and looks down over the River. Its head, nose, lips and jaw are very like, and the warts over its back particularly realistic. Such are the wonders of Creation! From its back one finds one's way deep into a cavern of damp green stone. A spring issues from the grotto with a tinkling sound and, dropping straight down from the toad's mouth and nose, forms a curtain of water as it enter the River. Today has been extremely cold, with snow drifts on the summits and crags, yet within the grotto it was as mild as spring.

The Yangzi narrows.

The Stack and the grotto are opposite each other. A bit further west a solitary peak, called Pillar of Heaven Peak, rises to pierce the clouds. From here on the mountains begin to level out somewhat, but on either bank of the River are piles of large boulders, and into the furthest distance it looked just as though a canal had been dug and the spoil piled up.

This evening we have made a stop at the Yellow Ox Temple where the mountains are precipitous once more. A great throng of villagers came to sell us tea and vegetables, amongst whom were women who all had green stippled kerchiefs wrapped round their heads. Their complexions were fair and they had quite standard accents; but their tea was like twigs and grass-leaves, and so bitter it was undrinkable. The temple is dedicated to the Efficacious and Responsive One, and the deity has been ennobled as Marquis of Good Omens and Guarantor of Peace; both titles bestowed by imperial rescripts of the Shaoxing period [1131–62] onwards. Below the temple are the Rapids of Unrighteousness, a jumble of rocks blocking the central channel. Terrifying as they were to look at, our boat passed without my being much aware of them, which must have been due to brilliant navigation. Tradition has it that the deity won merit by helping Emperor Yu [2205–2198 BC] of the Xia dynasty to control the waters, and that's why it enjoys offerings here. On either side of the gateway is a stone horse, very commonplace and small, under cover of a little roof. The horse on the right is missing its left ear, and must be the one that Ouyang Xiu saw.[70] Behind the temple is a thicket of trees similar to holly, but not the same. No one knew their name. The leaves they shed have black markings on them resembling the sort of Seal Script used in magic charms, with no two leaves alike, and my sons collected several of them. A poem of Ouyang's is carved in stone within the temple. There's also an eulogy by Zhang Shangying, the words of which are:

> Mighty indeed, the Yellow Ox,
> Possessor of great spiritual power;
> Huge rocks he carried and gathered together
> In their hundreds and thousands and tens of thousands:
> Swords and halberds, jagged teeth,
> Piled in masses by the River's edge,
> Blocking and churning waves and billows,
> Incalculable danger
> Menacing the boatmen
> Who blench in fear and dread,
> Slaughtering sheep, making libations
> As temple offerings these thousand years.

Zhang seems to be suggesting that the deity gathered together the rocks to block the current in order to threaten people and solicit sacrificial offerings. If that were really the deity's intention it would surely not have been enjoying a thousand years of temple offerings on such a grand scale. It seems rather far-fetched!

Tonight the boatmen came to request that we shouldn't sound the drum for the watches of the night. They said there were many tigers in the mountains behind the temple and they come out when they hear drums.

Isabella Bird describes the river hereabouts as one approaches from downstream: 'The change from a lake-like stretch, with its light and movement, to a dark and narrow gorge black with the shadows of nearly perpendicular limestone cliffs broken up into buttresses and fantastic towers of curiously splintered and weathered rock, culminating in the "Pillar of Heaven", a limestone pinnacle rising sheer from the water to a height of 1800 feet, is so rapid as to bewilder the senses.' Blakiston, like Lu, observed the 'heaps of granite boulders, forming small islands and promontories, causing the river to narrow in some places to 150 yards . . . while the shores are still broken with boulders and solid rock'.

Valerie Hansen has noted that, with the exception of dragon temples, there were few cults to animals in the Southern Song. Lu had remarked on dragon shrines along his route; here he passes a well-known cult to an ox. The ox-like shape of the mountain-top is visible for miles, and many poems were written about it. The symbiotic relationship of gods and men is well illustrated here: man needs the god to make the passage through the gorges safe; gods need men to maintain the supply of offerings and to acknowledge their power through official titles. In Chinese mythology Emperor Yu, a minister to the Emperors Yao and Shun, laboured for nine years to drain the great floods. Having tamed the waters he became the founder of the first hereditary dynasty, the Xia.

It may be that the horse with the missing ear, which Ouyang Xiu had visited in 1037, is another example of an animal which has taken on magical properties. Fan Chengda says that people thought it possessed numinous qualities and they were much in dread of it. Fan had also passed the Toad and provides the information that gentlemen from Sichuan who were on their way to the examinations in the capital would scoop up some water from the spring running over the toad's back to use in their ink-stones when they ground ink.

The tigers, long extinct in this part of China, who responded to the boats' drums would have been perplexed by the sound of heavy earth-moving equipment at work hereabouts on the Three Gorges Dam project.

Day 10/10 (19th November)

In the morning we made offerings at the Efficacious and Responsive Temple with a sacrificial pig and a pitcher of wine. We then set out and passed the Antler, Tiger's Head and Governor's Rapids. The water has already gone down by two-thirds but the swift current was still terrifyingly dangerous. We moored at Underwall, which is on the boundary of Zigui county in Gui prefecture. I strolled along the sands with my boys and when we turned to look back we could see straight to Yellow Ox Gorge. Behind the temple the mountains were like the folds of a screen, jaggedly piercing the sky. On the fourth fold was the shape of an umber-coloured ox, with what looks like a man wearing a hat standing in front of it. Yesterday and this morning clouds have wreathed the mountain-tops, and it was only now that we saw them.

We continued to the Compassionate Salvation Cloister at White Sands town where I called on the abbot, Zhijian, and asked him the origin of the place-name Underwall. He told me that behind the Cloister there was an ancient city wall of the state of Chu which still existed to this day, so we went to visit it together. The wall is on a hillock, and is very small. There are gateways to north and south; at the front it looks out over the waters of the River and faces Yellow Ox Gorge. The hill to the north-west of the

Jagged mountain peaks beside the Yangzi.

city wall winds about to embrace it, and on it is a temple to Wu Yuan [late sixth, early fifth century BC]. Generally speaking, there are a great many temples to Wu Yuan westwards of Jing.

The many remarkable stones at Underwall are similar to those of Lingbi and Lake Mouth.

Gui prefecture, called by Blakiston Kwei, was in the nineteenth century 'a small walled town, with neither trade nor anything else to give it importance' thirty-nine miles above Xia prefecture (Yichang).

Wu Yuan was a citizen of the ancient state of Chu which, as we have seen, was based in this central reach of the Yangzi, and whose family was killed by the King of Chu. Wu Yuan then went to the eastern state of Wu to assist its king in attacking Chu, eventually falling foul of the king of Wu and committing suicide in 483 BC.

Connoisseurship of rocks held aesthetic interest for Song dynasty literati. Unusual rocks were collected for gardens, the fashion having been put on an almost industrial scale by Emperor Huizong in the early twelfth century with his Flower and Rock Network which gathered *objets trouvés* for the imperial palace at Kaifeng (its gardens were destroyed in the Jurchen invasion of 1127 and by neglect thereafter). Song literati also appreciated the quality of stones that could be turned into ink-stones on which to grind their ink sticks for painting and calligraphy. Stone chimes, often in the shape of fish, hung in Buddhist monasteries; the musical quality of stone was another facet of this aesthetic.

Day 10/11 (20th November)

When we went past the Traverse Grotto Rapids, which are atrocious, my kith and kin and I all travelled overland in sedan chairs to get by. At the edge of the rapids are many wonderful stones, multi-coloured and gleaming delightfully, some of them even having markings in the shape of objects or magic charms. We could still see the mountain behind the temple at Yellow Ox Gorge; Li Bo has a poem which goes:

> Three mornings up Yellow Ox Gorge,
> Three evenings of progress slow.
> Three mornings and then three evenings,
> Till I find my hair's turned to snow.[71]

And Ouyang Xiu has one:

> Morn after morn, eve after eve I see that Yellow Ox:
> All you ever do is make those who pass here sad!
> On mountain high still visible the further off one goes,
> Isn't it that Yellow Ox that's holding back our boat?

There's a popular saying that:

You see Yellow Ox in the morn,
you see Yellow Ox in the eve;
three mornings and three evenings,
Yellow Ox you still can't leave.

So both Li and Ouyang drew on this. When Ouyang Xiu was making his way from Jingzhu to Yiling he wrote poems on 'Xialao Creek', 'The Three Visitors Grotto', 'Toad Stack', and 'Yellow Ox Temple', so he probably came to visit these places while on official business. That's why his poem entitled 'Remembering the Yiling Mountains' has the lines:

Recalling how I carried out my duties;
Points large and small, I'd deal with every one.

And at the end of the poem he wrote:

In the wilds and mists of Xialao Fort
The freshet's blocked eight hundred feet;

Ten Thousand Li of the Long River, Xia Gui (fl.1180–1230), detail of handscroll, ink on silk. National Palace Museum, Taipei.

> The Toad spews forth its waterfall,
> Sweet liquid better than vintage wine.
> And I went to Yellow Ox as well,
> Mooring to hear the gibbons call.

In the evening we moored at the mouth of the Horse Liver Gorge where a pair of slender mountains stand opposite each other, soaring to touch the sky, and somewhat similar to the Lu Mountains. Along the bank of the River the thousand-foot tow-rope became entangled with the many rocks, and it was extremely difficult to get past.

There's a light rain tonight.

Cooper watched a large junk, carrying 80 tons, being pulled through the rapids in this sector of the River. 'Upwards of 100 men, who had been collected from many of the adjacent villages, laid hold of the long plaited bamboo rope attached to her mast-head, and dragged her up, moving her inch by inch, while a few hands on board worked steadily at the bow sweep, by which she was steered clear of rocks and the river bank. It was often necessary for the trackers to slacken the tow line or make a sudden stop, and in order to convey the orders from those on board, a man sat on the deck beating a monotonous tune on a tom-tom, using certain variations of the tune as signals to those on shore. In the crew of these large junks there are always several men called water-men, whose duty it is to clear the towing line from projecting and sunken rocks. This, as may be imagined, is a very arduous and dangerous occupation, for it often happens that the line gets foul of a sunken rock in the middle of the rapid, and then these water-men have to clear it. They are, however, very expert in swimming and diving, and appear quite at home in the midst of the fiercest rapid; but it occasionally happens that they get jammed among the rocks by the tow-line and lose their lives.' Blakiston at this point on the journey notes that 'all hands being ashore, except two or three men to manage the long sweep-oar . . . and two more to attend to the paying out and hauling in the tracking-line and to pole off rocks, and all else being ready, the strongest bamboo line being in use, the word is given and off the trackers start, sometimes eighty or a hundred on the line at once, and the boat stems the troubled waters and steadily ascends. Frequently there is a hitch in the performance, caused by the line getting foul of a rock out of the water, and then one or two of the most daring venture to swim out and clear it.'

Day 10/12 (21st November)

In the morning we passed East Bend Rapids and entered the Horse Liver Gorge. On a precipitously high part of the cliff-face is a rock hanging down like a liver, after which the gorge has been named. To one side of it there's also the Lion Crag, in the centre of which a small rock in a crouching attitude, jaw agape, and covered in verdant grass, really is like a green lion. A little burbling spring emerges from the crag. Our boat was going so fast, though, that I couldn't get any to taste, but it must be a fine spring. Above the creek another lone peak rises with something of the elegance of Lesser Lone Hill.

This evening we have reached New Rapids where we've come ashore and are staying at the New Peace Post-house. It's snowing tonight.

It is not always easy to equate Lu You's place-names with those current in the nineteenth century or today, and not only because of the vagaries of Western romanization of Chinese words, and changes in the names of gorges and rapids over the centuries. We should also remember that the River presents vastly different aspects in the course of the seasons, rising and falling dramatically to reveal or cover rocks so that the dangers were never constant. And in addition to seasonal variation this part of the Yangzi was subject over the years to fresh rock-falls which created new rapids, and to the efforts of man at clearing some of the obstructions, most notably in the past half century but also, as Lu amongst others attests, in earlier times. In short, travelling the Yangzi today is a different proposition from the one Lu You faced, quite apart from the use of modern ships.

Entrance of Lu-kan Gorge, Upper Yangzi, from Blakiston.

The Horse Liver Gorge, variously known as Ox Liver or Horse Lungs, is Blakiston's Lu-kan gorge; he describes how 'on rounding a point of the river, we suddenly opened to view a huge split in the mountain mass ahead of us. It was the second, or Lu-kan gorge, by which the river escapes, as though through a funnel. As we entered, the gloom was very impressive; huge walls of rock rise vertically on either hand to a prodigious height, with great table-shaped slabs standing out from the face of the cliff, for all the world like sounding-boards of pulpits, hanging from which are long pointed stalactites; and on the upper surfaces of some are trees, looking like diminutive bushes, whose roots droop in festoons from the edges.' Cooper, too, was impressed: 'it seemed as though we were about to enter some subterranean passage, so great was the gloom. The river, scarcely 100 yards wide, flowed between walls of rock rising perpendicularly several hundred feet, and then sloping at an angle of perhaps 80 degrees till they terminated in peaks at least 2000 feet high. This is the most striking of the Yang-tzu gorges in its solemn grandeur, and is well worth travelling a thousand miles to see.'

Day 10/13 (22nd November)

Our boat was going up the New Rapids, keeping to the southern shore, and we'd gone seven or eight tenths of the way, when the hull was damaged by rocks. Men were hastily sent to the rescue and we all but sank. Sharp rocks had pierced the hull and we were stuck fast. This had probably been caused by the boatmen loading so much chinaware. By the southern bank of the New Rapids is what is called the Government Waterway (the character for waterway is pronounced in the level tone), while beside the northern is the Dragon Gate. The waters through Dragon Gate are particularly turbulent and fast, and there are many hidden rocks; the Government Waterway is more or less navigable, though it too has many sharp rocks. So this is considered the most dangerous stretch of the Gorges, and only light boats that aren't carrying anything can pass up or down stream. That the boatmen's search for profits led to this should be a caution to them.

I visited the Riverside North Temple. The temple looks directly across to Dragon Gate. There's a hot spring in a cleft in the rock below. Despite being shallow it never dries up, and a whole village depends on it. The women who draw water from it all carry three-legged pots on their backs made of a single piece of wood two feet long. At the side of the spring they use a ladle to scoop up the water, and when the bucket is eight parts full they turn round to sit on a nearby rock, tie the pot onto their backs, and set off. Generally speaking, within the Gorges everything is carried on the back, and mostly by women. And not just water; women also carry wine for sale in the same manner as they carry water. If you call them to buy some they kneel up to proffer it. The unmarried girls all put their hair up into love knots two feet high and insert as many as six silver hairpins, with an ivory comb as large as a hand stuck in behind.

Southern Song bowls in Dong ware (left) and Jianyang ware (right).

Fan Chengda, Lu's contemporary as an official and writer of travel journals (see Day 6/28) comments: 'When one reaches the New Rapids, which have the worst repute of any of the Three Gorges, if one wishes to avoid ascending or descending them one must trans-ship and go by land, negotiating the rapids with an empty boat. There are many inhabitants on both banks called Rapids Men who make their living solely by transporting goods past the rapids'.[72] But accidents could occur anywhere on the River. Off Nanjing Little 'had the misfortune to collide with a crockery-junk, the captain of which quickly ran his vessel ashore, and so saved her from sinking. . . . The bales of blue and white rice-bowls of which the cargo consisted, were quickly unladen and placed on the bank, the hole patched up and the cargo restored'. And Isabella Bird watched 'on two occasions junks fly down the rapids, strike rocks,and disappear as unconnected masses of timbers, as if exploded by dynamite'. Little wonder that Pére Amand David, best remembered for giving his name to a breed of rare deer, called the rapids 'effrayantes cataractes'.

Day 10/14 (23rd November)

We were detained at the post-house, so in the evening I took a small boat over to the south side of the River and climbed the hill to the Riverside South Temple. Renewal and repairs to it are not yet completed. There's a stele composed by a former Presented Scholar, Zeng Huadan [eleventh century], stating that after a landslide on the hill the resulting rock-fall had formed these rapids and incalculable numbers of boats had been wrecked. So an order had been issued forbidding navigation between the tenth and second months of the year. Zhao Cheng [mid-eleventh century], Prefect of Gui prefecture and Vice-Director of the Criminal Administration Bureau of the Department of State Affairs, reported the matter to the court, but it took eighty days work to clear a channel before the hazard was removed. This was in the third year of the Huangyou period [1051]. So the River, disrupted during the Tiansheng period [1023–31], was only then made passable again, though even to this day they haven't been able entirely to remove the hazard of the rapids. If advantage were taken of the period during the twelfth and first months when the water is low and the rocks are fully exposed one could, with a concerted effort, completely excavate and remove the sharp rocks. But the people living along the rapids all profit from the wrecked boats, selling off the planking on the cheap and hindering trade. They would be sure to hamper the labour, or else they would bribe the quarrymen to claim that the rocks were immovable. It will only be accomplished if we act in a decisive manner.

Quarrymen, from Cooper.

Furthermore, the reason that boats are wrecked is that they make the mistake of being over-laden. We should have a stone inscribed in large characters and set up in front of the post-house so that those who pass by would be sure to be on their guard. These two measures really must be discussed, and the authorities informed.

Lu You ends in a tone somewhere between concerned official who has the people's interests at heart and dyspeptic letter-writer to the newspapers, but perhaps such warnings as his were heeded. Little, seven hundred years later, says that at the more dangerous rapids in the winter months 'all boats and junks are, by order of the mandarins, obliged to discharge half their cargo . . . so that few accidents occur'. Such precautions were not always effective, however, and the wreckers were still benefiting in later centuries. Just before Cooper reached rapids beyond Lu You's final destination of Kui prefecture 'a large junk, laden with cotton . . . had struck on a sunken rock and gone down. . . . She was very much damaged, and even while her crew were busy at work about her, numbers of wreckers were deliberately pillaging her spars and cargo, while her owner, a Sz-chuan merchant, sat by utterly helpless.' The work of clearing channels and especially dangerous rocks went on through the centuries. When Cooper travelled this route in 1868 rocks 'were being blasted by way of deepening the bed of the river. The expense of the work, which had been in progress for several years, was defrayed by contributions levied on the owners of junks and cargoes passing up and down, and this contribution will be levied until the work is finished; when that will be it is difficult to say, as the several mandarins, under whose supervision it is carried on, reap a grand harvest of wealth from it.'

Day 10/15 (24th November)

It was only when the boatmen had brought off all the cargo that they could haul the boat through the rapids, but it needed repairs so we've changed boats. We left the New Rapids and passed White Dog Gorge, mooring the boat at the mouth of the Mount Xing stream.

I was then carried by litter to the Jade Void Grotto which is two miles or so from the banks of the River, and across a brook known as the Fragrant Stream, the source of which rises in Lady Zhao Village. The water tastes delightful, and is recorded in the 'Classification of Waters'. It's as bluish-green as eye-shadow. I called up a little boat to cross, and when we were over the stream and had gone a further third of a mile we came to the doorway of the grotto. It was tiny, only ten feet across, but once inside there was room enough to hold several hundred people, and as grand and magnificent as if one had entered a vast stately hall. The stone had formed into such things as canopies, banners, the magic mushroom, bamboo shoots, immortals, dragons, tigers, birds and beasts, in a thousand forms and ten thousand attitudes, and every one life-like. The most uncanny thing was the rock on the east side which was completely round like the sun, and the rock on the west side which was a semi-circle like the moon. I have seen nothing to match it in all the caves I've been to in my life. The names of Xie Shihou and Cen Yanqi had been written up in the Xining period [1068–77]; and there was also an inscription written by Chen Yaozi [b.970] which gives a thorough description of this grotto. He says it was first discovered by a hunter in the Tianbao period [742–55] of the Tang dynasty.

When we came to go home it was already night and the wind was so strong we couldn't carry our torches, but the moonlight was as bright as day. My boys and the monk

Small Yangzi tributary in the Gorges.

Shiquan all followed me carrying staves, quite unconscious of danger amidst the precipices and ravines.

Lady Zhao was said to have been born in the eponymous village. She was a tragic heroine, sent from the Han court in 33 BC to marry a barbarian khan as part of Chinese diplomatic efforts to shore up their northern frontier. She figured in many poems, stories and plays through the centuries, her grass-covered grave in the empty desert a poignant image. Mount Xing stream was another name for the Fragrant Stream, at the head of which lay Lady Zhao Village.

The New Rapids, so-called, had resulted from rock slides in the Han and Jin dynasties hundreds of years before, Fan Chengda tells us. The Jade Void Grotto, on the other hand, was said to have been discovered in the more recent past. In 746 a hunter had been led into it by a white deer. The Chinese have lost none of their fascination with strange rock forms, and you are to this day liable to see scaly dragons, mushrooms, nymphs and lions in limestone caves, sometimes improved with neon lighting and cement entrance ways.

Day 10/16 (25th November)

We reached Gui prefecture where I called on Jia Xuan, whose courtesy name is Zigong, the Prefect and a junior Court Gentleman Consultant; and Chen Duanyan, whose courtesy name is Minzhan, the Assistant Prefect and a senior Gentleman for Court Service. We lodged at the Monastery of Requited Kindness and Glorification of Filial Piety which is over a third of a mile from the town, but forlorn and bereft of monks. Though a prefectural town Gui has but three or four hundred households. It is perched on Recumbent Ox Mountain overlooking the River. Before the prefectural town lie the Renzhaweng Rapids, and within its walls there's not so much as a foot or an inch of level terrain. The sound of the rapids is constant, as if a raging storm were approaching.

Across the River is the King of Chu's City, but though it too lies in a mountain valley the terrain is more level than Gui prefecture. Some say that Chu was initially established here. The *Classic of Mountains and Seas* states that Emperor Qi [r.2197–87 BC] of the Xia dynasty enfeoffed Meng Chu at Danyang City, about which Guo Pu comments: 'This is south of Zigui county.' I suspect this might be the place. However, the *Records of the Historian* has it that King Cheng enfeoffed Xiong Yi at Danyang which, Pei Yin [fl.465–72] tells us, was at Branch River. I haven't investigated who is right.

'We came to Kwei,' Blakiston tells us, speaking of early April rather than late November when Lu You was travelling, 'where are a number more reefs caused by the inclination of the strata. There is also a pretty strong rapid, when the water is high, right opposite the place; and, to afford facilities for tracking up the boats along the steep bank, flights of steps and paths have been cut out in the solid rock, an arrangement which we observed not only here, but in many places on the river; and at other points chains have been fastened to the face of the vertical cliffs to assist in getting junks along, where there is no foothold on shore for trackers.' When he went past in August Fan Chengda's accompanying boat nearly capsized, with water coming through its windows; at that time of year the Renzhaweng Rapids occupied seven or eight tenths of the river.

The King of Chu in question was King Zhao (r.515–489 BC), who built this city in 506 BC. Chang and Smythe[73] demonstrate that since the original Danyang was moved to Branch River, and the name Danyang retained at the new location, all three of the authorities adduced by Lu You were right; but that he misquoted Guo Pu.

Day 10/17 (26th November)

There was an official reception at the Enjoyment of Flora Pavilion at Ocean View Hall. It's a rough terrain made up entirely of sand and rock. Governor Jia tells me that there are two annual harvest receipts to the prefectural granaries, in autumn and summer, of wheat, millet, and non-glutinous rice which amount to over five thousand piculs in toto. This is barely equivalent to one poorly off household in the Wu area.[74]

Fan Chengda learned that Gui prefecture only yielded an annual revenue of 20,000 strings of cash.

Day 10/18 (27th November)

We have just got hold of a clinker boat, but a small one. It's broad-bottomed and light, so well suited for going up the rapids.

Blakiston was similarly provided a little earlier since he had been travelling on a larger ship in the lower reaches: 'But we are in a new boat! And some five-and-twenty naked and half-naked fellows are dragging us along at a smart rate by a long plaited bamboo line, while I-chang [Xia prefecture] is fast fading behind us.'

Day 10/19 (28th November)

There was an official reception at the Homebound Hall.[75] I had wanted to travel onwards this evening but it was not to be. I paid a visit to the house of Song Yu [290?–222? BC] to the east of Zigui county. It's now been turned into a wine shop. It used to have the three characters 'Song Yu's House' inscribed on stone, but this has recently been removed by people of the prefecture to avoid a taboo name in the governor's family. It would be a shame if the house's provenance were forgotten because of this.

Song Yu was the third-century BC poet at the court of the state of Chu to whom is ascribed the 'The Summons of the Soul' (see Day 10/5).

Day 10/20 (29th November)

In the morning we left Gui prefecture through the Shaman Peak Gate, and visited the Celestial Blessings Abbey where we stayed a while. I examined a Tang dynasty stele of the first year of the Tianbao period [742] which bore the story of Emperor Minghuang's dream of Laozi, and had been erected by Liu Tao, the governor of Ba East. The strokes of the characters were very pure and refined. Along the side of the stele were recorded the names of the commandery officials and clerks of the time, and here too the characters were beautiful. There was also a stele erected in the Xiande period [954–60] of the Zhou dynasty by Sun Guangxian [d.968], the Administrative Assistant at Jingnan, in honour of the prefect of Gui, Gao Conghui.[76] Gao was a scion of the royal family of Nanping. Sun Guangxian was renowned as well, and the *National History* records his deeds. In the Five Dynasties period Gui and Xia prefectures were both subordinate to Jingzhu.

In front of the main hall stand cedars several hundred years old. And below the abbey lie the Bellowing Rapids, strewn with countless rocks.

Potential hazards of the Yangzi exposed at low water.

We had a meal at the Monastery of Numinous Spring-water, and then afterwards went aboard the boat and passed the Ye Rapids, which are also famous. The water was low and our boat light, and we had passed through them in a trice.

The first of the steles refers to Minghuang, Tang emperor during half a century of peace and prosperity. As we saw on Day 8/4, he was a supporter of Daoism; his famous dream underscored state sponsorship of the religion and it is not surprising to find that officials of the time had as it were signed up to the imperial enthusiasm for Daoism and its purported founder Laozi or Lord Lao.

The second stele that Lu saw recorded personalities of the Five Dynasties period; the Kings of Nanping, from whom Gao Conghui was descended, were little more than satraps of the minor dynasties of the period.

Day 10/21 (30th November)

From the boat we looked out towards the Stone Gate Pass. It is barely sufficient for a single man to get through, and is the most impregnable in the world.

In the evening we moored at Ba East county. The grandeur and beauty of the River and mountains far surpass that of Zigui, but commercial activity is sluggish in the extreme; there are only a hundred or so households in the township. From the magistrate's office downwards everything is built in thatch, without so much as a tile.

Wang Kangnian, the provisional county magistrate [of Ba East], Commandant of Zigui, and a junior Gentleman for Meritorious Achievement; and Du Dexian, Commandant and concurrently assistant prefect, and a junior Gentleman for Meritorious Achievement, called on me. They are both from Sichuan.

I paid my respects at the shrine-hall to Kou Zhun [961–1023], Duke of Lai, and climbed to the Pavilion of Autumn Winds to look down over the River and hills. Today has been heavily overcast with light snow, and the air swirled around. When I read the name of the pavilion again it made me feel despondent, and for the first time I

Remote View of Hills and Streams, detail of mountain-top pavilion, Xia Gui (fl.1190–1225). National Palace Museum, Taipei.

sighed that I had drifted to the ends of the earth. Then I climbed to the White Clouds Pavilion at the Pair of Cedars Hall. Below the hall there used to be cedars, now withered and dead, which the Duke of Lai had planted; but the mountains to its south, one overlapping another, have a beguiling beauty, and the White Clouds Pavilion is one of the world's most wondrous settings. It's surrounded by a host of mountains, tier upon tier, with dense forests of ancient trees, often two or three hundred years old, appearing amidst them. Beyond its balustrade a pair of waterfalls spurt into a rocky gully, leaping pearls and splashing jade that chill one to the bone. Down below, these form Compassion Creek which gushes on to join the River. In my journey from Wu into Chu I have travelled

In Front of the Waterfall, unsigned, attributed to Ma Lin (fl.1246).

more than one thousand seven hundred miles and passed through fifteen prefectures, but there's been no pavilion or belvedere that stands comparison with the White Clouds. And it lies just behind the county administration buildings! There's absolutely no business to conduct in Ba East, so if one were County Magistrate you could even sleep and eat in the pavilion. What boundless pleasure! So why is it that when a Magistrate is needed it's often two or three years before anyone is prepared to fill the post?

Ba East (Badong) from the Yangzi.

Ba East was the last town in Hubei; Blakiston described it as 'a small place without a wall, situated on rather steep sloping ground on the right bank; and on the opposite side stands a joss-house, at a considerable height above the river'. Little called it 'the unwalled district city of Pa-tung, in which a small coal trade alone exists'. The district magistrates described it as the poorest city in the province. Its main street was on a steep bank one hundred feet above the level of the river as Cooper passed in March, but at other seasons it was sometimes covered by water. It has now been rebuilt at a higher level since the old town will be submerged by the Three Gorges Dam.

Kou Zhun was famed as a forthright official. He served in Ba East early in his career, and became a Grand Councillor in 1004. When the Liao, the semi-nomadic state in north and north-east China whose dynasty had been established in 907 on the fall of the Tang, launched a major incursion Kou played a decisive role in steadying nerves. He urged Emperor Zhenzong to lead troops personally against the Liao, and then entered into diplomatic negotiations which led to the Treaty of Shanyuan (1005), securing Song authority, albeit over a diminished area in comparison with earlier major dynasties, and with tribute payments made annually to the Liao. The treaty proved to be the basis for comparative peace for a century until the Jurchen overcame the Liao (1122) and went on, as we have seen, to drive the Song out of north China. Kou was also a poet of some standing, his poetry the expression of private sorrow; his career ended in demotion and exile to minor posts. He was, however, posthumously rehabilitated and buried in the valley of the Song imperial tombs at Gongxian in Henan province. Kou had built the White Clouds Pavilion when he was county magistrate of Ba East. Lu You admired Kou and is drawing an unspoken parallel between his own position and that of the former Prime Minister's banishment to a remote posting, though there is a paradox, characteristic of Chinese literati, between his maudlin sense of being at the ends of the earth and his delight in its beauty and freedom from official duties.

Isabella Bird's boat through the Yangzi Gorges.

Day 10/22 (1st December)

We set forth from Ba East and the mountains grew increasingly wonderful and strange. The Master's Grotto was a single cave at the very highest point of the sheer cliff where no human foot could tread, yet it seemed as though it had a balustrade around it. I don't know who 'the Master' refers to. We passed the Three-branched Spring which comes out of a cave in the mountains. It had only two channels. The common saying has it that if there are three channels there'll be a bumper crop. Two channels means an average harvest. One channel, or no flow of water at all, spells famine.

We moored at Weary Rock. It's raining tonight.

Proceeding at the slow pace imposed by tracking and rowing, not to speak of the leisurely style in which he chose to travel, Lu You had opportunity to observe and to visit many more places than the nineteenth century, or indeed modern, voyager on the Yangzi. But Isabella Bird in her 'small house-boat of about twenty tons' was able to take in many of the strange formations: 'There are cliffs of extraordinary honeycombed rock, possibly the remains of the "potholes" of ages since, rock carved by the action of water and weather into shrines with pillared fronts, grottoes with quaint embell-ishments — gigantic old women gossiping together in big hats — colossal abutments, huge rock needles . . . while groups of stalactites constantly occur as straight and thick as small pines, supporting rock canopies festooned with maidenhair. Higher yet, surmounting rock ramparts 2000 feet high, are irregular battlemented walls of rock, perhaps twenty feet thick, and everywhere above and around are lofty summits sprinkled with pines, on which the snow lay in powder only.' Isabella Bird appears to have caught the Chinese enthusiasm for grotesque rock formations.

Peaks above the Yangzi.

Birds and boat.

Day 10/23 (2nd December)

We visited the Abbey of Coalesced Truth at Mount Shaman, and I paid my respects at the shrine of the Transcendent of Wondrous Accomplishments. The Transcendent is known to the world as the Goddess of Mount Shaman. Her shrine is directly opposite Mount Shaman, its peaks and ridges soaring into the firmament, the base of the mountain thrusting into the River. Judges of such matters consider that neither Mounts Tai, Hua, Heng nor Lu possess such marvels. But I couldn't see all twelve of its peaks; of the eight or nine visible the Goddess Peak is the most gracefully beautiful and astonishingly steep, a fitting abode for an immortal or transcendent.

The officiant told us: 'Each year on the fifteenth night of the eighth month, when the moon is bright, the music of strings and pipes moves back and forth on the summit, and the mountain gibbons all howl out, the sound only dying away with the dawn'. Half-way up the mountain behind the temple is a broad flat stone altar. There's a tradition it was here that Emperor Yu of the Xia dynasty met the goddess and she gave him magic charms. If viewed from the altar the twelve peaks look just like a screen.

This was a day when heaven's vault was bright and clear, with not the faintest haze in any direction other than a few wisps of white cloud on the Goddess peak, wafting and drifting to and fro around it for ages like phoenixes and cranes. It was strange.

There used to be several hundred rooks at the shrine which greeted travellers' boats and saw them on their way. As a poem by the Tang dynasty prefect of Kui prefecture, Li Yi [fl. late eighth century?], put it

A flock of rooks enjoys the remnants of the offerings.

But recently, in the first year of the Qiandao period [1165], they suddenly stopped coming and now there's not a single rook here. It's not known why.

We moored at Clearwater Grotto. The grotto is very deep and its rear exit gives out onto the back of the mountain, but it's pitch dark and has water flowing through it so one can rarely enter. When there's a drought here prayers for rain are generally answered.

A Goddess Carried Away on a Phoenix, Song dynasty, eleventh/twelfth century, ink on silk.

The Wushan (Shaman) Gorge, from Blakiston.

Ran Huizhi, the provisional Magistrate of Mount Shaman county and a senior Gentleman-litterateur, and Wen Shuji, the Commandant and a junior Gentleman for Meritorious Achievement, called on me.

> The accomplishments of the goddess of Mount Shaman were inscribed in the temple, according to Fan Chengda. She had assisted Emperor Yu in driving out demons and had cut through the rock to make a channel for the waters. But the charms she dispensed were not limited to the magical ones with which she helped the mythical Emperor drain the flood waters. She also shared her charms with the historical King Huai (r.328–299 BC) of Chu, and when he asked how he could see her again she replied, in an expression which became a euphemism for sexual intercourse: 'At dawn I am the morning clouds, at evening the passing rain'. A faint air of mystery and eroticism is implicit in Lu You's description.
>
> The rooks were back a few years later. Fan Chengda found they came to greet travellers' boats miles away and saw them off again for miles down-river. People threw food into the air and the rooks never failed to catch it. The locals called them 'holy rooks' or 'boat-welcoming rooks.'

Day 10/24 (3rd December)

In the morning we reached Mount Shaman, the county town of which lies within the Gorges and is a fine place. The commercial district surpasses that of both Gui and Xia prefectures. Across the River stand the lofty South Barrow Mountains. A thread-like road, which they call the 'hundred and eight turns', winds round to the very summit and is the main road to Shi prefecture. Huang Tingjian has a poem which refers to this place:

> One hundred and eight turns, as hand in hand we climbed.
> Now my dreams of going home are wound through a sheep's intestine.

Mountains beside the Yangzi.

In the county offices there's an ancient iron bowl, the bottom of which is pointed and shaped like one half of a pitcher, but very sturdy and thick. The inscription inside dates it to the Yongping period [58–75] of the Han dynasty. Where a piece is missing the iron is a lustrous black like fine lacquer, and the strokes of the characters have an appealing plainness and simplicity. A 'Dedication for a Bowl' written by Huang Tingjian has been inscribed on stone. In outline it says that 'in the first year of the Jianzhongjingguo period [1101] my younger brother Shuxiang, whose courtesy name is Sizhi, was transferred from Commandant of Fuling to be the acting official in charge of this county, and I came from Rong prefecture to lodge in the county office here. This dish had previously been used to plant lotuses. I washed and rinsed it and the written characters were revealed'.

I visited the ancient Subsidiary Palace of Chu, popularly known as the Palace of Slender Waists. It has a pool which was the site of palace banqueting in those days, but which is now almost entirely filled in. On three sides are desolate mountains, but to the south the view of the River and hills is spectacularly beautiful. There's also the General's Tomb dating from the Eastern Jin dynasty [317–420]. Behind the tomb a stele has sunk into the ground, and leans tottering forwards. Only half the wording remains.

Isabella Bird was not impressed with Wushan (Mount Shaman) as a place. It was grey and picturesque, its walls following the contour of the hills on which it was built, enclosing fields, orchards, and beautiful trees; but the town, though fairly clean, had no look of prosperity and was disappointing. The old town was demolished in 2002 and rebuilt on higher ground in anticipation of the Three Gorges Dam reaching its full height in 2009.

The Subsidiary Palace belonged to King Xiang of Chu (r.298–263 BC). A predecessor of his had a fondness for girls with slender waists, and his country ended up with women starving themselves; hence the other name for the palace.

Day 10/25 (4th December)

Late in the afternoon we reached the mouth of the Great Creek where the boat was moored. They produce fine pears the size of a half litre measure.

Day 10/26 (5th December)

We set out from the mouth of the Great Creek and entered the Qutang Gorge. Cliffs towered up on either side into the firmament, as smooth as if they had been sliced with a blade, and when we looked upwards the sky was like a ribbon of silk. The waters have already gone down and within the gorge were as smooth as a dish of oil. We passed the Holy Mother Spring, which is in a fissure up on the rock. If you shout from one side of it the spring gushes out; if you shout repeatedly the spring-water gushes out repeatedly. It's odd.

By evening we reached the Qutang Pass. In the Tang dynasty ancient Kui prefecture was linked to White Emperor City. Du Fu says in a poem:

> White Emperor and Kui prefecture are separate towns,

suggesting they were difficult to distinguish. The western gateway of the pass is directly opposite the Yanyu Reef. The Reef is composed of an agglomeration of loose rocks sticking out of the water several hundred feet. But the locals say that when the waters rise in summer and autumn they are several hundred feet higher than the Reef.

I went in through the pass in a litter and paid my respects at the Temple to the White Emperor. It has a most archaic atmosphere, with pines and cedars hundreds of years old. There are several steles, all erected while the Meng family ruled Shu [934–65]. In the courtyard are stalagmites for which Huang Tingjian wrote an inscription in the first year of the Jianzhongjingguo period [1101]. There's also the Hall of the Duke of Yue built by Yang Su [d.606] of the Sui dynasty; Du Fu composed a poem for it. Though it was destroyed the present hall, constructed in recent years, is still very imposing. Eastwards of the pass is East Village where Du Fu used to live.

Blakiston once more: 'Before coming to Quai-chow [Kui prefecture] there is another gorge to be passed. It is a short one, and known as 'Fung-siang', or Wind-box. Although the last, it is by no means the least in grandeur. One pass at its upper end is not over 150 yards across; cliffs rise towering above to a prodigious height, and large caverns have been scooped out by the mighty current, allowing fishing-boats lying in perfect security from the wind and weather.'

The Holy Mother was a popular goddess who presided at confinements and childbirth.

The biographer of Du Fu, William Hung (*Tu Fu: China's Greatest Poet*), has a different view of the poet's lines about White Emperor City and Kui; quoting Du Fu's lines above, he says: 'Historians generally took this to mean that there were two different cities, one adjacent to the other. Examining Tu Fu's [Du Fu] poems closely, I find, however, that he really applied the names, Fish-return, White Emperor, and K'uei-

Trackers' gallery along the Yangzi.

chou [Kui prefecture] to the same place. The line in question was meant to indicate only a historical difference. In his time, there was but one city, officially known as K'uei-chou, but still popularly known as White Emperor City.' But Lu You tells us in the next day's diary entry that Kui and White Emperor City in fact occupied different sites. He makes the question quite clear in a collection of anecdotes he composed under the title *Miscellanea from the Retreat of Study in Old Age*[77] in which he says: 'In the Tang dynasty Kui prefecture was at White Emperor City but the terrain was precipitous. So in our own dynasty, during the Taipingxingguo period [976–84] when Ding, Duke of Jin, [this is Ding Wei whom we shall encounter in the next day's entry] was serving as Fiscal Commissioner he transferred it to Rills West.' Fish-return gained its name, according to Hung, because 'tradition had it that breams, swimming upstream and reaching the section of the river below the city, would turn around and go downstream again'.

Fan Chengda, passing downstream in August 1177, sent someone ahead to see the state of the water at the entrance to the Qutang Gorge and found it just submerging the Yanyu Reef. The locals described this as the reef 'letting out its hair' which Fan thought even more dangerous than when it was 'like a horse'; by the following morning the level of the water was fifty feet above the reef. But though the gorge was 'smooth as a mat' when he went through it there was still turbulence round the reef. The reef was about a hundred feet long, sixty feet wide and one hundred and thirty feet high. It was blown up in 1959 to make navigation safer. Fan also had a variation on the Holy Mother Spring story: the spring gushed out when you called out 'I'm thirsty'.

Qutang (Fung-siang or Wind-box) Gorge, from Blakiston.

The Meng were the ruling family in Sichuan in the period between the Tang and the Song known as the Five Dynasties. The term which I have translated stalagmites is literally 'stone bamboo shoots'; I wonder if they were not perhaps fossilized trees

Yang Su, ennobled as Duke of Yue, had helped the founder of the Sui to establish his dynasty, and in 588 when he was based in Kui prefecture built the original hall called after him.

Du Fu lived in East Village in 766 and 767, in a particularly productive period of his poetry.

Day 10/27 (6th December)

In the morning we reached Kui prefecture. The prefectural town lies on sandy ground on the slopes of the mountain. The so-called Palace of Eternal Peace at Fish-return is now the prefectural granaries, while the prefectural administrative offices are north-west of the palace and south-west of the tomb of Lady Gan. They were relocated in the Jingde period [1004–8] by the Fiscal Commissioners Ding Wei [962–1033] and Xue Yan [953–1026]. Though a more level and ample site than White Emperor City it has lost its strategic value, and no longer holds the advantage of terrain. It lies to the west of the rills, and hence is also called Rills West. The locals call these mountain becks which flow into the River 'rills'.

South-east of the prefectural town are the Eight Formations boulders, a vestige of Zhuge Liang's [181–234] work. Loose rocks form lines like stretched ropes; every year when the River rises the waters are several hundred feet above these boulders, but when they subside the rocks of the Formations are as they were.

The Palace of Eternal Peace was built by Liu Bei and covered a vast area; in effect a town. About half a mile to the south lay the Eight Formations boulders, sometimes known as the Eight Battle Arrays. They were an arrangement of sixty-four piles of stone about five feet high. Perhaps, as David Hawkes[78] suggests, they were megalithic structures but they had long been ascribed to the heroic Prime Minister of Liu Bei's state of Shu, Zhuge Liang. The Formations were supposed to possess magical powers to defeat enemy forces. Certainly the water at Gui prefecture could rise fully a hundred feet, and in exceptional years many tens of feet higher.

Lady Gan was Liu Bei's wife, and mother of Liu Chan, the Last Ruler of Shu.

Ding Wei had served in Kui prefecture from 1000–4, and had then gone on to the highest political offices. Xue Yan was his successor in Kui. Between them they effected the removal of the town to the site at which Lu You had arrived.

The sand-banks were used later, as Isabella Bird observed, for manufactory. 'At low water there are great sand-banks below the city of Kuei-fu, or Kuei-chow Fu, where a number of salt boilers establish themselves for the winter months, who dig great brine pits in the sand and evaporate the product with coal.' She goes on to describe the city, though she did not enter because of hostility to foreigners: 'A great bank of boulders, a strong *chipa* [a race that could catch a boat even when there were no rapids], a highly cultivated region, the pleasant valley slopes of which rolled up into hills, pleasant farms, a general sunny smile, a grey-walled city of much picturesqeness, a great fleet of junks moored below it, a mat town to supply their needs, and we were at the city of Kuei-chow Fu.' Little was similarly taken with the place: 'a fine city, picturesquely situated on a bold slope, and . . . surrounded by high crenel-lated walls with turreted gateways, and four tiers of stone bunding on the river-front below; all in an unusually good state of preservation. Built out of the reach of summer floods, the foundations of its walls are a good hundred feet above our boat, and the wide sandy slope between is green and yellow with wheat and rape-seed. . . . At the foot of the bank and along the water's edge is the usual winter street of temporary mud-plastred houses with opium-booths, tea and other shops for the needs of the boat population.' Cooper called the place 'a city of the first grade . . . pleasantly situated on the left bank of the river'. But over the centuries, though the scenery might remain unchanged, foreign influence was apparent in more than gun-boats and missionaries. The crops of the area included by the late nineteenth century peas, beans, wheat, barley, Indian corn and potatoes, and the smoking of opium was widespread. Cooper goes on to add that Kui prefecture contained 'many fine joss-houses and temples. The country surrounding it is very fertile, producing opium and sugar in large quantities; the best coal in the province is also found in the district of which Qui-foo is the chief city'.

Kui prefecture, nowadays known as Fengjie, was one of the first Yangzi towns to be flooded by the waters of the Three Gorges Dam, its buildings razed and its population transferred to a new town five miles away. Some cultural artefacts such as the city gates were moved, most blasted, buldozed or, if they were lucky, looted. It was here in Kui, obscure and remote in the twelfth century, that Lu You disconsolately spent the next year. (Those who enjoy the concurrence of unconnected events will recall that twenty-three days after Lu You's diary ends Thomas à Becket was murdered in Canterbury Cathedral.) But Lu was transferred early in 1172 further up-river to posts in Sichuan. He later looked back on this Sichuan sojourn, its contact with the military, proximity to the frontier with Jin, and occasional tiger hunts, as the most exciting period of his life.

Lacquered leather travelling coffer, c.1250. Brooklyn Museum of Art, New York.

NOTES

1. Iain Macleod Higgins, *Writing East: the 'travels' of Sir John Mandeville*, University of Pennsylvania Press, 1997.

2. Ross E. Dunn, *The Adventures of Ibn Battuta, a Muslim Traveller in the Fourteenth Century*, University of California Press 1986.

3. The interpreter 'was saying totally different things as the fancy took him'. Quoted by Arthur Waley in Ch'ang-ch'un, *Travels of an Alchemist*.

4. See for instance S.A.M. Adshead, *T'ang China: The Rise of the East in World History*.

5. See Deborah Rudolph, 'The Power of Places: A Northern Song literatus tours the southern suburbs of Ch'ang-an' (*Journal of the American Oriental Society* 114 (1994).

6. Linda Walton, 'Diary of a Journey to the North', *Journal of Sung-Yuan Studies*, 2002.

7. Isabella Bird makes a tantalising reference to 'Lu Yew, a much-travelled mandarin of the twelfth century, the translated account of whose journey from Shanjin near Ning Po to Kueichow on the Upper Yangtze is a fascinating bit of literature', and she quotes a couple of sentences. But who made this translation and brought it to her attention, and what became of it I have been unable to discover.

8. Su Shi, *Shu Pu Yongsheng hua hou* 'Written at the end of a painting by Pu Yongsheng'. Quoted in *Tang Song Sanwen jingxuan* p.169. Mr Qi was Qi Shunchen.

9. Adapted from Shiba Yoshinobu quoting A.C. Moule, *Quinsai, with Other Notes on Marco Polo* (Cambridge University Press, 1957).

10. Shiba Yoshinobu p.59.

11. Xu Zizhitongjian, j.141.

12. Xu Yinong, *The Chinese City in Space and Time* p.100.

13. The best reading, which is followed by the 1976 Zhonghua shuju edition, is 'zi Yizhe' rather than 'zi Xinxiang'.

14. Chang and Smythe are mistaken in believing Tao was a maid.

15. Shiba Yoshinobu *op. cit.*

16. Lu You's Collected Poetry (Jiannan shigao j.2).

17. Lu You has made a mistake here. Emperor Wen was in fact the son, Emperor Wu the father.

18. The eighth-century Lu Yu (died 804) in his *Classic of Tea* specifically advises using mountain springs to brew tea, and says that 'well-water tea is quite inferior' (*The Classic of Tea*, tr. Francis Ross Carpenter).

19. The town I have translated as Concordia is Jianning in Fujian.

20. See *Tang Song ci jianshang cidian* (Nan Song, Liao, Jin) p.1792.

21. Hong Mai, *Rongzhai suibi* 4:3.

22. i.e. Golden Mount.

23. See for instance James M. Hargett, *op. cit.*, p.78.

24. See Shiba Yoshinobu for a description of sails (p.10). I translate fu as 'section' following Needham *op. cit.*, Vol. 4 Part 3 p.451. A section was 2 feet 3 inches in width, and the sail would therefore have been square: 58 ft wide and the same in height.

25. Quoting Richard M. Barnhart *Along the Border of Heaven*. Guo Xi is quoted by a writer on painting, Han Zhuo, in his *Shanshui chunquan ji* of 1121.

26. Kojiro Yoshikawa, *An Introduction to Sung Poetry* p.37.

27. The text uses the expression *youjie* 'right-hand lane'. Left and right lanes were honorific titles given to senior monks in the departments of Buddhist sutra translation that came within the purview of the Court of State Ceremonial, itself a branch of central government.

28. H. Chatley, 'Feng-Shui' in *Encyclopaedia Sinica*, quoted by Needham, *op. cit.*, Vol. 2 p.359.

29. Needham, *Science and Civilization in China*, Vol. 2, p.361.

30. Valerie Hansen, *op. cit.*

31. Michael Sullivan, *op. cit.*, p.141.

32. The Chinese *bu*, usually translated 'pace', was actually a double stride so I have translated 100 *bu* as 'two hundred paces'.

33. This is Ouyang Xiu's *Yuyi zhi*, whose title has been variously translated: James Hargett in his *On the Road in Twelfth Century China* gives it as *Chronicle of Going Into Service*; Chang and Smythe have *On Serving in a Distant Post*.

34. Chang and Smythe take this passge to refer to the Huiri monastery; Buton Watson translates in the same sense: 'Temple of the Compassionate Sun'. I can find no evidence for such an establishment; *ri* should be taken as 'in the days when'.

35. There is a difference of reading of *qing* (either 'clear' or 'green'). The 1976 Lu You Ji, which is based on the 1220 edition in Beijing Library, has 'green'. However most editions in the intervening centuries have 'clear'; and Fan Chengda also has 'clear' in his *Wuchuanlu* (9th month *bingwu* day).

36. Pen, the name of a river in Jiangxi, is transliteration rather than translation.

37. Xingren (*Prunus armenaica*) is correctly translated as apricot pits according to Nathan Sivin, *op. cit.*, p.277, rather than almonds.

38. Bi Yuan, *Xu Zizhitongjian*, j.141.

39. B. J. Ter Haar, *op. cit.*

40. When the original author uses the same expression (in this case 'antique ambience') twice within a few lines the translator is perforce obliged to follow suit.

41. Bai Juyi ji (*Zhongguo gudian wenxue jiben congshu*, juan 43, p.933).

42. Max Loehr, *The Great Painters of China*.

43. Michael Sullivan, *op. cit.*

44. Fan Chengda, *Wuchuanlu* entry for 8th month, *yiwei* day (22nd September 1177).

45. Valerie Hansen, *op. cit.*

46. Yijian zhi 4:2:5:547. Referred to in Valerie Hansen, p.66.

47. Shi Zhengzhi (not the same man that Lu You met on Days 8/3 and following) is quoted by Shiba Yoshinobu; the paddle-ships are referred to by Needham, *op. cit.*, Vol. 4 Part 2, section 27 p.422.

48. Xin Tang Shu, j.196 (p.5608 ff).

49. I follow the Chang/Smythe reading of the punctuation here, rather than that of Lu You Ji.

50. Burton Watson, *Su Tung-p'o: Selections from a Sung dynasty poet*.

51. Sima Guang's *Comprehensive Mirror for Aid in Government* (*Zizhitongjian*, presented to the throne in 1084) quotes Emperor Wu's orders; after 'in a long-range sortie' the orders continue: 'as far as Nanjing', which Lu You has omitted.

52. Xu Yinong, *op. cit.*

53. Shiba Yoshinobu *op. cit.*

54. Li Bo's title to the poem is dedicated to a man called Wei Bing of Nanling, a nearby district. Chang and Smythe appear to have mistaken the name as Wei

Nanling. They go seriously awry in their rendition of Huang Tingjian's couplet that follows.

55. In other words they were nominal changes on paper.

56. James Legge (*op. cit.* p.136) translates this excerpt as 'From Po-chung [Mountain] he surveyed the Yang [River], which, flowing eastwards, became the Han'.

57. See Valerie Hansen, *op. cit.*

58. The skipper Red-Whiskered Scullion is not easy to translate. Chang and Smythe take the latter part of the phrase 'zhangniansanlao' in the sense of skipper, but take the fore-going part as two separate entities: Red Head and Bearded Junior Head; Shiba Yoshinobu (*op. cit.* p.18 ff) interprets *zhangnian* and *sanlao* as two separate roles amongst the sailors. I believe the *xu* must stand for the fuller version *xu* meaning beard. Shiba quotes a Tang commentator's observation with reference to a Du Fu poem that 'the men of the Yangzi gorges call the one who holds the punt-pole at the prow and spies out the way through the water the *zhangnian* and the main helmsman the *sanlao*'.

59. Stuart Sargent, *Music in the World of Su Shi.*

60. Needham warns (*op. cit.* Vol. 4 Part 3 p.452, note b) of the notorious difficulties of interpreting ancient and mediaeval tonnage figures. He says that a ship of 200 'tuns and tunnage' would have been exceptionally large in fourteenth-century Europe; in the fifteenth century Prince Henry's caravels were about 50 tons; Columbus' *Santa Maria* was probably 280 tons.

61. This couplet of Du Fu's has been translated by William Hung in his *Tu Fu, China's Greatest Poet* (p.260) rather differently: 'Thus I was led out of the

mist of the river to the grassy path of your garden/ Where the sunflowers are nourished in the autumn dew.' As a parallel couplet, *tong* (to penetrate, reach through to) should, it seems to me, balance *jie* in the sense of 'connect, combine with'. An alternative translation, introducing the poet as the unspoken subject of the sentence, would be: 'In river mist I penetrate the grass along your path,/ Through autumn dews I reach the sunflowers in your garden.'

62. Archibald Little, *op. cit.* He travelled along the Yangzi in 1883.

63. Lyman P. Van Slyke, *op.cit.*

64. This translation perhaps strikes a jarringly modern note, but the term *kuangyi* means the sort of mental abnormality which the *Grand Dictionnaire Ricci de la Langue Chinoise* describes as 'changer de caractère sous l'empire de la folie'.

65. Generally the tombs of the Song upper classes, officials or merchants, were smaller and less elaborate than their Tang dynasty predecessors. That is perhaps why Zhang Shangyin's catches Lu's attention.

66. The King's House (Wangwu) Mountains are in Shanxi province in north China and were an important Daoist site.

67. Nathan Sivin, *op. cit.*

68. I am indebted to Chang and Smythe's notes for pointing me in the direction of some of these allusions.

69. Other readings have a light breeze or light cloud.

70. Ouyang Xiu visited the Yellow Ox in 1037 and mentions the stone horses.

71. The last word of this little poem is literally 'turned to silk floss', which is white.

72. Quoted in Shiba Yoshinobu, *op. cit.*, p.20.

73. Chang and Smyth, *op. cit.*. p.176, note 43.

74. 5,000 piculs was approximately 380,000 kilograms or 360 tons. Shiba Yoshinobu quotes the twelfth-century Lü Zuqian, writing of the mountainous Yanzhou area (modern Jiande): 'Leaving on one side the rice of high gluten content (*nuomi*), the tax rice paid in each year by all six counties only amounts to 8,751 piculs of rice of moderate gluten content (*gengmi*) (i.e. approx. 600 tons), or less than the quantity harvested by one rich commoner household in Huzhou or Xiuzhou'. Wu was Lu You's home area in east central China. These quantities (360 tons for poor households and 600 tons for rich) seem astonishingly high; but the huge discrepancies between Wu and other areas to the south and inland is well attested.

75. Chang and Smythe point out that *Guixiang*, translated here as Homebound, was originally *Kuixiang*, a place-name which was the fiefdom of the Viscount of Kui; the viscountcy ceased to exist in 635 BC.

76. Chang and Smythe argue convincingly that Gao Conghui is the correct reading rather than Congrang. The distinction need not detain us.

77. Lu You, *Laoxuean biji* j.5.

78. David Hawkes, *op. cit.*, p.186.

DRAMATIS PERSONAE

Lu You mentions more than four hundred people in the course of his diary, and most of these will be unfamiliar to Western readers. Some are historical characters famous in Chinese history or literature, others obscure contemporaries; indeed some are making their one and only appearance in the historical record in the lines of Lu's diary.

For those not familiar with Chinese nomenclature it is sufficient to know that most Chinese surnames are of one syllable, a few are double barrelled (such as Zhuge Liang in the last day's diary entry). The given name follows the surname; and traditionally Chinese of Lu You's class had both a personal name and a courtesy name. For instance Lu's own personal name was You, his courtesy name Wuguan. As we see in the diary, he frequently records both the personal and courtesy names of colleagues he meets along his route which, given the possibility in Chinese of similar or identical names, helps to determine exactly who they are. To complicate matters, in the Chinese text of the diary Lu You sometimes refers to others, particularly writers, by their literary soubriquet; for example the great eleventh-century poet Su Shi is often known as Su Dongpo or Su of the Eastern Slope. I have taken the liberty in this translation, where names appear in a variety of guises, of using the standard forms of people's names (surname and personal name), and so listing them in the Dramatis Personae which follows. I recognize that this diminishes variety but hope it also reduces confusion.

In the text of the translation each name on first appearance is followed, where known, by birth and death dates, or in the case of rulers by reign dates. Thereafter, where names reappear, no dates are given. Readers who wish to know more, or to remind themselves of an individual's background on subsequent occurrence, will find all names listed below in alphabetical order with brief biographical details. In describing people referred to by Lu You I have avoided mention of any names other than those already appearing in the diary; so it may be taken that a q.v. applies to anyone whose name occurs in these brief biographical notices. Readers familiar with the language will find the Chinese characters of the names helpful in identifying the players. Other names which occur in the commentary but not in the text of Lu You's diary are given in the index. For the sake of clarity, surnames, emperors and Buddhist monks' religious names appear in capitals in the following list. The dates of appearances in the Diary follow the names.

BAI Juyi 白居易 6/19, 8/5, 8/8
  (772–846), sometimes referred to in Chinese as Tutor to the Heir Apparent BAI Juyi, was the third of the great poets of the Tang after DU Fu and LI Bo. He espoused simplicity of language, but ranged in subject matter from poems of social satire, romantic love, friendship, and Buddhism, to the simple aspirations of the family man seeking quiet contentment, with a corresponding attention to the minutiae of daily life. These various aspects of his poetic persona must be seen against the

background of a successful official career; he graduated in 800 and, apart from the period 815–18 when he was banished for his outspokenness to a humble posting in River prefecture (where he built a cottage in the Lu Mountains which LU You visited on Day 8/8 of the Diary), BAI's career was a successful one; he served in the capital, in what is now Xi'an, in Luoyang, and as governor of Hangzhou and of Suzhou on the Grand Canal. He retired in 833, devoting himself thereafter to Buddhism, charitable work, and poetry. His poems were popular in his own time, and he took pains to ensure his work survived, with the result that 2,800 of BAI's poems are extant.

BAOLIANG 寶良 9/15 (eleventh century), a Buddhist monk who was a pupil of Zen Master FAYAN.

BAOYIN 寶印 6/19, 6/26, 6/27 (1109–90), Venerable and eminent monk of Golden Mount in Zhenjiang. He had the courtesy name Tanshu 坦叔 and came from Jia prefecture in Sichuan.

BAOYU 寶餘 7/7 (fl.1170), Venerable Buddhist, a native of Chu prefecture.

BAOZHI 寶誌 7/8 (419–514), also known as the Master ZHENJUE 真覺 of the True Way Forest; a Buddhist monk who in one account was found in a nest up an ancient tree. He couldn't say still, didn't eat regularly, and grew his hair long. His prophecies circulated widely, and were of course borne out. He also tried to exercise some restraint on the excesses of the rulers of his time. After his death he was interred on Mount Zhong in Nanjing and a pagoda erected in his memory. BAOZHI was still of topical interest when LU You was writing his diary. In 1161, when the Jin invasion south of the Huai river took place, he had manifested his powers, it was said, by causing the death of the enemy leader, WANYAN Liang. Emperor GAOZONG had acknowledged this by granting BAOZHI the designation 'Compassionate Response'.

BIAN Kun 汴壼 7/7, (281–328), a leading official under two emperors of the Eastern Jin dynasty (317–420), served together with YU Liang, and was killed in battle along with his two sons attempting to suppress a rebellion against his ruler.

BIAN Xu 汴肝 7/7 (d.328), a son of BIAN Kun who died in battle with his father.

BIAN Zhen 汴眕 7/7 (d.328), a son of BIAN Kun who died in battle with his father.

Buddhabhadra 佛馱跋陀尊者 8/8 (359–429), also written 佛陀跋陀羅, arrived in China from India in 406, and translated the Avatamsaka-sūtra into Chinese.

CAI Guang 蔡洸 6/17 (fl.1170), courtesy name Ziping 子平, was a County Magistrate.

CAI Jing 蔡京 6/2 (1047–1126) had the courtesy name Yuanchang 元長 and came from Fujian. A synopsis of his career is given in the commentary to Day 6/2. Under Emperor HUIZONG at the beginning of the twelfth century he restored many of the New Policies with which WANG Anshi had tried to reform Northern Song government and society, and in doing so proscribed and banished his opponents, many of whom were leading figures in the culture of the day. This, and his reputation for extravagance, earned him the obloquy of traditional Chinese historians.

CAI Kan 蔡戡 8/3 (fl.1170), whose courtesy name was Dingfu 定夫, was a Surveillance Circuit Judge.

CAI Zhun 蔡準 6/2 (eleventh century), the father of CAI Jing whose burial was considered too lavish.

CAO Bin 曹彬 7/11, 7/24 (931–99), the Song general who led his forces across the Yangzi to bring down the last of the minor dynasties of the Five Dynasties period, the Southern Tang under its poet-emperor, in 975; thus re-unifying China under the Song dynasty which had been declared in 960. He used the Southern Tang defector FAN Ruobing as his guide.

CAO Cao 曹操 6/23, 7/4, 8/19 and Commentary to 9/14 (155–220), like Emperor ZHAOLIE of the Sichuan kingdom of Han and the emperor of Wu, was a leader of one of the Three Kingdoms at the beginning of the heroic period of division in the early third century. Their shifting alliances provided later writers with dramatic plots. CAO Cao, the adopted son of a court eunuch, made his name in the suppression of a peasant rebellion in the 180s. He became a successful warlord who effectively ruled north China with the emperor as a figurehead. But his attempt to take southern China was blocked at the battle of Red Cliff on the Yangzi in 208 when he was defeated by SUN Quan (emperor of Wu) and LIU Bei (Emperor ZHAOLIE). When CAO died in 220 his eldest son succeeded him, deposing the last Han dynasty emperor and proclaiming himself the first emperor of Wei. CAO Cao was posthumously known as Emperor WU of the Wei dynasty.

CAO Mishen 曹彌深 8/7 (fl.1170), the follower of the Daoist HUANGFU who lived at the Clear Void Retreat.

CEN Yanqi 岑嚴起 10/15, an eleventh-century official.

CHAI Angong 柴安恭 7/9 (fl.1170), a doctor from Dragon Hill in Xing prefecture who ministered to LU's family.

CHANGZONG 照覺禪師常總 8/8 (1025–91) was from Sichuan and had been invited by WANG Shao to become abbot at East Forest in 1080. CHANGZONG later received imperial recognition, including the award of the title Zen Master ZHAOJUE.

CHEN Bing 陳炳 7/20 (fl.1170), Recorder of Grand Tranquillity county in Secured-nation; he had the courtesy name Dexian 德先 and graduated in 1166. When LU You met him he was working on instructions from the Judicial Commission, overseeing the collection of cash and bolts of silk as a Commissioner for Grand Ceremonials, an ad hoc duty assignment for a court official. CHEN was talented but severe in demeanour, and was said to be unsociable. He wrote in the ancient prose style, amongst other things on the Book of Changes, and was clearly drawn to matters mystic.

CHEN Boda 陳伯達 6/14 (fl.1170), an Instructor, courtesy name Jianshan 兼善.

CHEN Daguang 陳大光 6/6 (fl.1170); his courtesy name was Zichong 子充. He was an Assistant Magistrate and a grandson of the Censor CHEN Guan.

CHEN Dexin 陳德新 7/7 (fl.1170) was a Daoist priest whose courtesy name was Kejiu 可久. He came from Gusu (Suzhou) and LU You thought him a man of great perception.

CHEN Duanyan 陳端彥 10/16 (fl.1170), whose courtesy name was Minzhan 民瞻, was an Assistant Prefect.

CHEN Guan 陳瓘 (1057?–1122?), courtesy name Yinzhong 瑩中, was from Fujian. He graduated first of his year in 1079 and became an official of outspoken views as well as a distinguished scholar. He was at first taken up by ZHANG Chun with whom he later fell out. When ZENG Bu was a Grand Councillor CHEN was made a Censor, but ZENG came to distrust him and he fell from favour. As a Censor CHEN strongly denounced CAI Jing. His writings and calligraphy were admired for their individuality.

CHEN Ru 陳孺 9/18 (fl.1170) seems to have had no post at the time he met LU You, but held the prestige title of senior Court Gentleman for Instruction.

CHEN Shaofu 陳紹復 8/18 (fl.1170), an Assistant Prefect.

CHEN Tingrui 陳廷瑞 7/21 (fl.1170), a Daoist abbot.

CHEN Yaosou 陳堯叟 6/16 (961–1017) took his degree in 989 and went on to become an official with a reputation for compassion, intelligence and discretion. He was an expert on the state's equine policy, an important facet of military planning. LU You refers to him by his posthumous title of Wenzhong (Cultured and Loyal) 文忠. He was a brother of CHEN Yaozi.

CHEN Yaozi 陳堯咨 10/15 (b.970) came from a distinguished literati family, and took his degree in 1000, gaining first place. CHEN was remembered in later ages as an expert archer because of a story written about him by OUYANG Xiu: his archery was observed by an old oil seller who pointed out that his skill was nothing more than that of the steady hand and eye required in pouring oil into a narrow jar. CHEN was suitably deflated. He also suffered a set back in his early career when he corruptly tried to help a friend succeed in the government examinations. But CHEN later became a member of the prestigious Hanlin Academy and gained a reputation in military and civilian posts, promoting able but poorly connected officials, keeping local grandees in order, and carrying out water conservancy and defence projects. He was a brother of CHEN Yaosou.

CHENG Min 成閔 6/17 (fl.1170), Campaign Commander with the Qingyuan Army Military Commission.

CHENG Tan 程坦 8/3 (fl.1170), whose courtesy name was Lüdao 履道, was an Administrator in the Supply Commission.

CHENG Xiaoba 程小八 9/28 (fl.1170) was chosen as 'engager' by the boat owner ZHAO Qing in preference to WANG Baiyi.

CHU Chengshu. See CHU Yi.

Chu, Viscount of 楚子 7/19 (sixth century BC). He launched an attack down the Yangzi against the kingdom of Wu and conquered Jiuzi in 570 B.C.

CHU Yi 褚意 7/6, 7/9 (fl.1170), courtesy name Chengshu 誠叔, a Surveillance Circuit Judge, had been Commandant of Minqing in Fu prefecture. He had been successful in capturing brigands.

CHUDI 出帝 7/7 (r.943–7), emperor of another of the minor dynasties of the Five Dynasties and Ten Kingdoms period, his the Later Jin (936–47).

CUI Hao 崔灝 8/28 (d.754), drinker, gambler, womaniser and poet, lived during the long period of peace at the height of Tang dynasty prosperity. He was generally disapproved of, and his poetry was considered to verge on the lewd. He seems to have redeemed himself in later life by writing vigorous and natural poems inspired by his travels on the frontier. Amongst his works is a famous poem entitled 'Yellow Crane Tower'.

DAI Ziwei 戴子微 6/3 (fl.1170). A contemporary of LU You.

DING Baochen 丁寶臣 10/8 (1010–67) had the courtesy name Yuanzhen 元珍. He and his brother graduated together in the mid-1030s, and both achieved literary fame, being known as the Two Ding. DING Baochen was much praised by Emperor YINGZONG and was a great friend of OUYANG Xiu who wrote his epitaph.

DING Wei 丁謂 7/1, 10/27 (966–1037). He came from near Suzhou and graduated in 992. Between 1000 and 1004 DING served in Kui prefecture; while in Kui as a Fiscal Commissioner he transferred the administrative offices to a new site. DING went on to serve Emperor ZHENZONG in the highest offices. In 1019 he took power at the centre and the following year got rid of KOU Jun and became Grand Councillor. DING was enfeoffed as Duke of Jin 晋公 in 1022. But on RENZONG's accession in 1023 he was banished to provincial posts, though his career prospered and declined again under RENZONG. He was considered rather a slippery character, but is also known as a distinguished writer.

DINGHUAN 定圜 6/18 (fl.1170), Venerable Buddhist monk, of Jiao's Hill Monastery in Zhenjiang.

DONG, The Transcendent 董真人 8/9. DONG's given name was Feng 奉. He was an alchemist who lived in the Later Han dynasty (25–220).

DOU, Magistrate 竇長史 7/26. An eighth-century magistrate mentioned in the title of one of LI Bo's poems.

DU, Mr 杜公 8/28. A Governor of Mian prefecture of the mid-eighth century known to the poet LI Bo.

DU Dexian 杜德先 10/21 (fl.1170) was a Commandant and concurrently assistant prefect. He came from Sichuan.

DU Fu 杜甫 8/1, 8/11, 8/28, 10/26 (712–70), poet of the High Tang and generally considered China's greatest, though his pre-eminence was not established until the eleventh century. He has been seen as a realist and a people's poet, compassionate but also allusive. He was an impoverished aristocrat in a time of rebellion and upheaval, and held only minor posts. At one stage he was arrested and tried (but pardoned) for outspokenness. DU travelled widely through China, though he and his romantic contemporary LI Bo met only once. He had just been given an appointment in the Heir Apparent's household in 755 when a rebellion broke out which shook the foundations of the Tang dynasty. He managed to take his family to relative safety, but DU himself was captured by the rebels while trying to reach the Heir Apparent, by this time ruling from a north-western safe haven as Emperor SUZONG, and he was kept in the capital at Chang'an (now Xi'an) for a year. After escaping he managed to get to SUZONG and was given a post, but got into trouble again in 758 when defending a friend. DU Fu's poetry contains many themes both of daily life and of social and political concern which had not previously been considered fit subjects for verse; in part this was a return to the long established role of poetry as remonstrance, but DU combined the minutiae of personal life with broader national and historical issues. His last years were spent with his family in poverty and as dependants of richer relatives and patrons. But in the early 760s a number of friends in official positions were able to sustain him in Chengdu in Sichuan, and he spent 766 and 767 in Kui prefecture (LU You's destination on his journey) under the aegis of the local prefect. DU's last three years were spent travelling further south to Lake Dongting and up the Xiang River; he drowned in 770. The poems of his final years are considered masterpieces of technical perfection, allusive, sometimes complex in syntax, and exploiting a rich ambiguity.

DU Mu 杜牧 7/24, 7/25, 8/18 (803–52). One of the best-known of the Late Tang poets, particularly famous for his quatrains. His poems are sensual, colourful and less sombre than his ninth-century contemporaries.

DU Yu 杜預 7/19 (222–84/5) came from Xi'an and was a famous figure of the Three Kingdoms period. He contributed to the fall of Wu and a brief reunification of China, his success relying on strategy rather than military prowess; but he was essentially a scholar and historian.

FACAI 法才 8/8 (fl.1170), an abbot of a Buddhist monastery.

FACHUN 法淳 6/5 (fl.1170), a Buddhist priest whom LU You met.

FAN Chengda 范成大 6/26 (1126–93), courtesy name Zhineng 致能, was one of the leading poets of the twelfth century, admired for his bucolic poetry describing the life of farmers. He was also a successful official. One of his assignments was an embassy to the Jin capital in 1170 to renegotiate clauses in the peace treaty between north and south. He had worked with LU You in the capital some years previously and they were friends. FAN kept a diary of his journey to the Jin and of his travels down the Yangzi. In addition he wrote a gazetteer of his home county.

FAN Guang 樊廣 6/5 (fl.1170),whose courtesy name was Ziqiang 自強, was an Administrator. As LU tells us, he was the son of FAN Guangyuan and the brother of FAN Yi.

FAN Maoshi. See FAN Guangyuan.

FAN Guangyuan 樊光遠 6/5 (1102–64), courtesy name (by which LU refers to him in the Diary) Maoshi 茂實. He was the top graduate of his year but his views, particularly on morale in the army at a time when an armistice was under consideration, seem to have ensured that his career never prospered.

FAN Ruobing 樊若冰 7/11, 7/24 (943–94), a subject of the Southern Tang court who defected to the Song and gave advice to the Song general CAO Bin on a military crossing of the Yangzi.

FAN Yi 樊抑 6/5 (fl.1170), whose courtesy name was Zimu 自牧, was an Instructor. He was the son of FAN Guangyuan and the brother of FAN Guang.

FAN Zhineng. See FAN Chengda.

FAN Zimu. See FAN Yi.

FAN Ziqiang. See FAN Guang.

FANG Dao 方導 6/6 (1133–1201), whose courtesy name was Yiwu 夷吾, was the son of FANG Zi and studied under FAN Guangyuan amongst others. FANG rose to be a prefect and on the Military Commission of Huainan, the area south of the border with Jin.

FANG, Graduate 方進士 7/26 (eleventh century). FANG is mentioned in the title to one of MEI Yaochen's poems.

FANG Wude. See FANG Zi.

FANG Yiwu. See FANG Dao.

FANG Zi 方滋 6/5, 6/7 (1102–1172), whose courtesy name was Wude 務德, was a Vice-Director. He came from Zhejiang and had an official career spanning over forty years in many posts and over much of south China. He established a reputation for resisting tax increases, building sea defences and other measures to improve people's lives.

FAYAN 法演 9/15 (c.1022–1104) was an eleventh-century monk from Fifth Patriarch Mountain where the real fifth patriarch of the Zen sect had lived in the seventh century.

FEI Yi 費禕 8/28 (d.253). FEI Yi, otherwise pronounced FEI Wei, was a high official of the state of (Shu) Han in the period of the Three Kingdoms, much commended by ZHUGE Liang and renowned for his diplomatic, administrative and military skills. He was murdered by a defector from the state of Wei while drunk at a party. There was a tradition that when he became an immortal he rode a crane from a tower by the Yangzi near what is now Wuhan.

GAN, Lady 甘夫人 10/27 (second/third-century) was the wife of LIU Bei, the Emperor ZHAOLIE of the Shu Han dynasty which was based in Sichuan after the fall of the Han. She was mother of LIU Chan, the Last Ruler of Shu Han.

GAN Ning 甘寧 8/13 (fl.180–220) had the courtesy name Xingba 興霸. GAN was the 'storming general' who helped SUN Quan, the ruler of Wu during the Three Kingdoms period after the break-up of the Han dynasty. He was violent and cruel, but dashing, brave, a good tactician, with no interest in wealth but respect for his men.

GAO Conghui 高從誨 10/20 (tenth century) was a scion of the royal family of Nanping, a petty regime based in the middle reaches of the Yangzi in the Five Dynasties period. He recognised SUN Guangxian's talents and employed him.

GAO Qi 高祁 9/25 (fl.1170), a Magistrate.

GAO Shidong 高世棟 8/15 (fl.1170), a Supervisor of Taxes and subaltern.

GAOZONG 高宗 (r. 1127–62) was born in 1107, the ninth son of Emperor HUIZONG. When the Jurchen overran north China and captured his father and elder brother, by then Emperor QINZONG, he escaped south and proclaimed himself emperor in 1127. Over the next decade he rallied Song forces and refounded the dynasty, eventually basing its capital at Hangzhou. Despite his resistance to the Jurchen he finally compromised in the treaty of Shaoxing of 1141 which established the River Huai as the frontier between the states in north and south China, and imposed tribute payments on Southern Song. This gave rise to the suspicion that GAOZONG was not keen to see the defeat of the Jin and consequent return of his father and brother as the legitimate emperors. In 1162 GAOZONG, who was without sons, abdicated in favour of a descendant of the first Song emperor, and lived on until 1187.

GAOZU 高祖 6/22, 7/15 (r.420–2), emperor of the (LIU) Song dynasty.

GE, the Immortal. See GE Hong.

GE Hong 葛洪 7/20 (283–343). Otherwise known as the Immortal GE, GE Hong was an historical figure who turned from politics to the role of literary recluse and sought immortality through Daoist alchemical practices. He wrote the

Baopuzi (*He Who Embraces Simplicity*), completed around 320.

GE Xun 葛郇 6/18 (fl.1170) was a Notary of the Administrative Assistant to the Military Commissioner.

Great Emperor of the Wu. See SUN Quan.

GU family 古氏 8/19. A reference to GU Gengdao, a farmer friend of SU Shi's during his exile in Huang prefecture in the 1080s.

GU Yong 顧雍 7/26 (168–243) came from a distinguished southern family and was a trusted lieutenant of the ruler of Wu in the Three Kingdoms period, SUN Quan. As Prime Minister GU promoted the interests of the people and strengthened Wu. Personally he was taciturn, punctilious in observing the relationship of ruler and subject, but treated his colleagues and staff well.

GUAN Chong 管銃 6/9 (fl.1170), a County Magistrate.

GUAN Yu 関羽 8/13 (160–219), referred to in the Diary by one of his several appellations as GUAN Yunchang 関雲長, was one of the heroes of the romantic period of division which followed the collapse of the Han dynasty. He is said to have begun life as a bean-curd seller. He assisted LIU Bei, the founder of one of the Three Kingdoms states, resisted the blandishments of CAO Cao and was finally caught and executed by the third, SUN Quan. GUAN Yu was later deified and became a national cult, often known as the Chinese God of War.

GUO Pu 郭璞 6/28, 10/7, 10/16 (276–324) was a diviner, naturalist, alchemist, commentator and lexicographer. He wrote a commentary on the *Erya Dictionary* (*Examples of Refined Usage*) in the early fourth century.

GUO Shixian 郭師顯 7/12, 7/13 (fl.1170), a doctor.

GUO Shu 郭舒 9/8 (late second/early third-century), the subordinate of WANG Cheng who refused to follow WANG when the latter abandoned his post in the face of an assertive subordinate.

GUO Xiangzheng 郭祥正 6/4, 7/13, 7/17 (1035–1113?) had the courtesy name Gongfu 功甫 by which LU refers to him. He came from Dangtu in Grand Tranquility prefecture and held minor official posts under Emperor SHENZONG, but achieved fame as a poet. He was a friend of SU Shi and admired by WANG Anshi; another poet of the eleventh century, MEI Yaochen, considered GUO's poetry to be in the style of LI Bo of the Tang dynasty. But by the late eleventh century his poetry was generally denigrated.

GUO Zhen 郭振 7/6 (fl.1170), Military Commissioner for the Wutai Command and Campaign Commander for the Jiankang armies.

HAN Ju 韓駒 8/19 (c.1086–1136), courtesy name Zicang 子蒼. A poet whose official life spanned the fall of the Northern Song and the establishment of the dynasty in the south; he became governor of River prefecture.

HAN Kui 韓夔 8/26 (tenth century) was the nephew of HAN Xizai, and like him served the Southern Tang. HAN Kui was a Registrar and Proof-reader in the Imperial Library.

HAN Qinhu 韓擒虎 7/11 (538–92) was the Sui dynasty general entrusted with the task of bringing down the Chen dynasty. This he did when he captured Nanjing in 589 with five hundred cavalry, re-unifying China after the long period of division that had lasted from the early third century.

HAN Xizai 韓熙載 8/26 (902–70), an accomplished literary and artistic figure of the mid-tenth century, served the three emperors of the Southern Tang dynasty based at Nanjing. But his wild behaviour and fondness for women seem to have attracted the attention of his contemporaries as much as his statesmanship, and lack of seriousness made the Last Emperor question his suitability for the Prime Ministership. The painting of HAN's 'night revels' was said to have been made at the request of the Last Emperor to discover what HAN got up to.

HAN Yu 韓愈 8/23 (768–824) was a Tang forerunner of the Confucian revival known as Neo-Confucianism which came to maturity in the succeeding Song dynasty. He was a fierce critic of Buddhism, though the dissolution of their monasteries did not take place until some years after his death. HAN was also a considerable poet, and is particularly significant as a prose stylist who advocated a return to the Ancient Style of classical Chinese which took as its model the historical and philosophical writings of the fourth and third centuries BC. LU You greatly admired him

HE Chou 何稠 7/11 (late sixth/early seventh century) was a quick-witted youth, musical and with a practical bent. He was taken into the department dealing with palace construction and manufacturing where his inventiveness ranged from weapons to glazed pottery to baubles. He followed Emperor YANG of the Sui on his campaign to conquer Korea and displayed his skill with pontoon bridges. After the fall of the Sui

he was employed in the early Tang in the Directorate of Palace Buildings.

HE Shiqing 何世清 8/8 (early twelfth century), a brigand who with LI Cheng based himself in the Lu mountains in the disturbed period when the Jurchen had just invaded northern China and the Song were fighting to survive.

HE Shoucheng 何守誠 7/20 (fl.1170), an abbot residing at the Supreme Unity Priory.

HE Xiezhi 何頡之 8/19 (eleventh century), courtesy name Siju 斯舉, which is how LU You refers to him in the Diary. He was a poet and friend of SU Shi's and other writers of the late eleventh century.

HE Xunzhi 何洵直 10/6 (eleventh century), a Director. In the course of his official career he was involved in debate with LU You's grandfather LU Dian and others about ceremonial matters.

HE Zuoshan 何作善 7/6 (fl.1170), courtesy name Baixiang 百祥, Magistrate of Jiangning.

HOU Andu 侯安都 9/8 (506–63), a general sent by the emperor of the Chen dynasty (557–89), the regime which immediately preceded the re-unification of China in the late sixth century, to attack WANG Lin who was resisting the establishment of his new dynasty. WANG defeated and captured him.

HU Fen 胡奮 8/23 (third century), a general of the state of Jin who received orders to advance down the Yangzi and take Nanjing.

HU Kuo 胡适 8/3 (fl.1170), an Assistant Prefect.

HU Siqi 胡思齊 8/8 (fl.1170), the abbot of a Daoist establishment.

HU Zhen 胡振 10/7 (fl.1170), a County Magistrate.

HUAI Xu 懷敘 7/26, a third-century member of the court retinue, was reprimanded for failure to follow proper legal procedure.

HUAISU 懷素 7/13 (c.735–c.799), a Buddhist monk of the Tang dynasty who was one of the great masters of Chinese calligraphy. He created the Mad Cursive script in which he wrote his *Autobiography*, described as 'one of the most extraordinary calligraphic creations of all epochs' (Lothar Ledderose, *Ten Thousand Things*, Princeton University Press).

HUAN Wen 桓溫 7/17 (312–73) was a member of an important family of the third and fourth centuries in the state of Jin. His son was HUAN Xuan.

HUAN Xuan 桓玄 7/15, 10/3 (369–404) was a son of HUAN Wen by a concubine. He was an unruly subject of the Jin who declared himself emperor in 403. He was killed shortly thereafter.

HUANG Dalin 黃大臨 10/8 (fl.1095), elder brother of the poet HUANG Tingjian. He held minor office in the late 1090s, but was criticized for being too compassionate to which he replied that the job of a prefect was precisely to care for the people.

HUANG Qing 黃檠 10/8 (fl.1101), a nephew of HUANG Tingjian.

HUANG Shuxiang 黃叔向 10/8, 10/24 (fl.1101), a younger brother of HUANG Tingjian. He had the courtesy name Sizhi 嗣直. In 1101 he was transferred from the post of Commandant to that of an official in charge of a county.

HUANG Tingjian 黃庭監 8/4, 8/26, 8/27, 8/28, 10/6, 10/8, 10/24, 10/26 (1045–1105) was a poet and calligrapher, a younger contemporary and admirer of SU Shi. Introspective by nature, he is said to have sought to achieve a feeling of intense stillness; but his diction, avoiding the banal, sometimes falls into obscurity. HUANG was a great admirer of the eighth-century poet DU Fu. In the half century following HUANG's death a number of other poets to a greater or lesser degree followed his style and are known, from his birthplace, as the Jiangxi School.

HUANG Xiang 黃相 10/8 (fl.1101), a son of HUANG Tingjian.

HUANGFU Tan 皇甫坦 8/7 (fl.1170), a Daoist who lived at the Clear Void Retreat on Mount Lu, beneath Cloud-Disperser Peak. CAO Mishen was a follower of his.

HUAZHAO 化昭 6/18, 6/23 (fl.1170), Venerable Buddhist monk of Ambrosia Monastery in Zhenjiang.

HUI, Emperor 惠帝 7/7 of the Western Jin dynasty reigned 290–306.

HUIMING 惠明 7/15 (fl.1170), an abbot from Pingyang in Wen prefecture.

HUIYONG 慧永 8/9 (332–414) was a Buddhist monk and relative of HUIYUAN. The story was told of him that a tiger used to visit HUIYONG in his room; if others were frightened he would tell it to go off into the hills, but it would come back after the visitor had left and once more lie down tamely.

HUIYUAN 慧遠 8/7, 8/9 (334–416) was an eminent Buddhist monk and scholar who, according to tradition, had founded the White Lotus Society, a group of monks and laymen paying devotion to Amitabha Buddha and hoping to be reborn in the Western Paradise. HUIYUAN moved to the Lu Mountains in 373 where he established the East Forest Monastery.

HUIZONG 徽宗 7/20 (1082–1135), eighth emperor of the Song dynasty under which LU You lived. He reigned 1101–25, presiding over a faction-ridden court which at the same time attained the highest aesthetic standards, and was himself a distinguished painter and calligrapher, and promoter of court painting. His capital of Kaifeng was among the leading cities of the world, and the garden he created there attained a notoriety in Chinese history for the network of collectors he organised to exact rare and unusual plants and stones to embellish it. HUIZONG's rule ended with the loss of north China to the Jurchen; he and his son Emperor QINZONG, the last of the Northern Song emperors, were taken prisoner and died in the north. Another son, Emperor GAOZONG, organised resistance in the south and established the Southern Song.

JI Shao 嵇紹 7/7 (253–304) was an official of the Western Jin dynasty (265–317) who died defending his emperor in battle after others had fled, his blood spattering the emperor's tunic. The emperor ordered that the blood should not be washed off because it was JI's.

JI Xun 紀旬 5/19 (fl.1170), an Assistant Magistrate.

JIA Xuan 賈選 10/16, 10/17 (fl.1170), whose courtesy name was Zigong 子公, a Prefect.

JIANG 姜 6/7 (fl.1170). A doctor who was summoned to see LU's family.

JIANG Shi 姜詩 10/7 (first century AD) lived under the Eastern Han. He and his wife, née PANG, were known for their filial devotion to his parents.

JIANG Yan 江淹 5/19 (444–505) served as an official for a series of minor dynasties in the period of division, but is best remembered as a writer.

JIANG Yi 蔣誼 6/14 (fl.1170), Assistant Prefect under LI Anguo when LU met him.

JIANG Yuanlong 蔣元龍 6/15 (fl.1170), courtesy name Ziyuan 子雲, a gentleman from Chang prefecture who told LU about grave robbing in the area.

JING 漢景帝 10/7 (second century BC), emperor of the Han dynasty who reigned 156–141 BC.

Jingda, Prince of Qi 齊王景達 7/4 (tenth century) was a general and member of the Southern Tang royal family. In 956 he led twenty thousand troops across the Yangzi at Melon Jetty but was defeated by the future Emperor TAIZU of the Song with the loss of the Southern Tang's best troops. Jingda thereafter avoided engaging with the enemy wherever possible.

JUBAI 居白 6/5 (fl.1170), a disciple of the Buddhists MAIOJI and FACHUN.

KONG Ji 孔覬 6/14 (fl.466) came from Shanyin, LU You's hometown. He was highly intelligent, but a heavy drinker and not one to fawn on his superiors. He held high office but was often drunk, though it was said of him that the one day he was sober in the month was more effective than other people's twenty-nine days sober and one day drunk. He was eventually executed in a failed rebellion.

KOU Zhun 寇準 10/21 (961–1023), Duke of Lai was a leading statesman of the early Song, famed as a forthright official. He became a Grand Councillor in 1004. He played a decisive role in resisting the Liao incursions from north and north-east China, and his diplomatic skills led to the Treaty of Shanyuan (1005) which secured Song authority over most of north China for a century and more, albeit in a diminished area compared with earlier major dynasties and with annual tribute payments to the Liao. But his career ended in demotion and exile to minor posts. KOU was also a poet of some standing.

Lao, Lord 老君 8/4, 10/20, also known as Laozi 老子. He was a philosopher to whom is accredited the composition of the Daodejing or The Way and its Power. In due course he became the supreme deity in the Daoist pantheon. His legend places him anywhere between the sixth and fourth centuries BC.

Last Ruler of the Southern Tang dynasty. See under LI Yu.

LI Anguo 李安國 6/14 (fl.1170), a Prefect.

LI Bai. See LI Bo.

LI Bian 李昪 7/9 (889–942) was born XU Zhigao 徐知誥, but changed his name to LI to bolster his claim to be the successor to the Tang dynasty emperors whose surname it had been. He reigned as Emperor LIEZU from 937–42, calling his state the (Southern) Tang. He was the grandfather of the poet-emperor and Last Ruler of the Southern Tang, and a friend of SONG Qiqiu.

LI Bo 李白 6/16, 7/4, 7/9, 7/11, 7/13, 7/15, 7/17, 7/18, 7/21, 7/23, 7/24, 7/26, 7/27, 8/2, 8/4, 8/16, 8/19, 8/23, 8/26, 8/28, 8/30, 9/11, 10/3, 10/11 (701–62), otherwise known as LI Bai, is considered one of the greatest of Chinese poets. He is thought of as the antithesis of his Tang dynasty contemporary DU Fu: the former romantic, extravagant, unconventional, with a strong interest in Daoism; the latter controlled, profound but equally passionate. LI was probably of Central Asian origin, but his family settled in Sichuan when he was a child. He never

took the examinations for government service, spending much of his life travelling and drinking. He was briefly given a post under Emperor MINGHUANG as a sort of poetic adviser, but left after a couple of years (742–4) for some indiscretion. About 744 he and DU FU met. LI was in some way associated with the rebels who rose against MINGHUANG in 756, and was exiled to Yelang in the far south of China, though he was pardoned before he had reached his destination. Tradition has it that he drowned while proffering a drink to the reflection of the moon in the Yangzi. There are more than a thousand poems extant in his collected works.

LI Cheng 李成 8/8 (early twelfth century), a brigand who with HE Shiqing based himself in the Lu mountains in the disturbed period when the Jurchen had just invaded northern China and the Song were fighting to survive.

LI Deyu 李德裕 6/23 (787–849) had the courtesy name Wenrao 文饒 by which LU refers to him. He was a statesman of the Tang dynasty who served under several emperors and became Grand Councillor in 833. He and his father, who had also been a leading statesman, were involved in the factional struggles of the period which went under the name of their principal contenders, LI and NIU Sengru.

LI Gonglin 李公麟 7/8 (1049–1105/6), whose personal name was Boshi 伯時, is often referred to by his soubriquet as LI Longmian 李龍眠. He was a painter best known for his figure-drawing in ink alone; his landscapes and paintings of horses were also famous in the Song. There was a family connection with LU You whose grandfather, LU Dian

(1042–1102), had recommended LI Gonglin for appointment in the bureaucracy.

LI Jiaming 李嘉明 7/27, a court musician under the Southern Tang dynasty during the tenth century.

LI Jing 李靖 6/22 (571–649), referred to in the Diary as Duke of Wei, and after whom a hall was named, was a general who had been ennobled with this title for his role in helping to found the Tang dynasty.

LI Jinsu 李晉肅 8/28 (eighth century) is mentioned in the title of a poem by DU Fu.

LI, Old Mother 李媼 7/17 (fl.1170). She was eighty by Chinese reckoning in 1170, so was born in 1091. She had acute hearing and sight, and had acquired occult arts.

LI Shouzhi 李守智 8/4 (fl.1170), an abbot of a Daoist abbey who had once belonged to an affluent family.

LI Yangbing 李陽冰 8/28 (fl. mid-eighth century) was a Tang calligrapher, particularly noted for his small seal script with its 'iron wire' line. He served as a prefect, rising in the bureaucracy to the position of Director of Palace Buildings 將作監 and was therefore referred to as Director LI 李監 (LI Jian), as does LU You in the Diary. (Chang and Smythe mistakenly thought LI Jian was a person).

LI Yi 李貽 10/23 (fl. late eighth century?). He has not been identified, but Chang and Smythe believe he may have been LI Yisun 李貽孫 who was a Prefect of Kui prefecture in the late eighth century.

LI Ying 李膺 (fl.1170), Director of the Audit Bureau.

LI Yu 李煜 7/7 (937–78; r.961–75), the Last Ruler of the Southern Tang dynasty.

He was the third and last emperor of the Southern Tang state which controlled the lower Yangzi area in the mid-tenth century; his father and he gradually lost ground to the Song, and the Southern Tang fell in 975. LI Yu was taken into captivity, dying (probably poisoned) a few years later. LU You is disparaging about his abilities as a ruler, but LI, who presided over a cultured court, was a great lyric poet, some of his best work composed after he had been deposed.

LI Zhi 李植 6/3 (fl.1170), Assistant to County Magistrate WU Daofu.

LI Zonge 李宗諤 7/1 (964–1012) was sent as Deputy Receiving Officer with DING Wei to greet the four statues of imperial personages.

LIANG Ji 梁冀 9/4 (d.159) was a mighty subject of the Han, a maker and un-maker of emperors during the middle years of the second century. He is said to have amassed an immense fortune; over three hundred of his dependants suffered in his fall.

LIAORAN 了然 8/8 (mid-twelfth century), abbot of a Buddhist establishment.

LIAOZHENG 了証 8/29, 9/13, 10/2, 10,8 (fl.1170), a Buddhist monk from Sichuan with whom LU travelled on part of his journey.

LIEZU, emperor of the Southern Tang dynasty. See under LI Bian.

Lingzhao 靈照 8/29 (fl.1170), a daughter of LU You's who had her pulse taken by Dr ZHAO Sui.

LIU Bao 劉寶 7/4 (twelfth century) was one of YUE Fei's generals. After YUE's execution he dismissed his troops and went into retirement. (Chang and Smythe have mistaken LIU for a sixth-century man of the same name).

LIU Bei 劉備 6/23, 8/14, 8/18, 9/14, 9/14 (r.221–3), otherwise known by his imperial title Emperor ZHAOLIE 昭烈. He was a descendant of the ruling family of the Han and established a short-lived dynasty in Sichuan at the beginning of the period of division after its fall in 220. As one of the Three Kingdoms it bolstered its legitimacy by using the name Han, but is known to history as the Shu Han (Shu was a name for Sichuan) to distinguish it its predecessor. ZHAOLIE, along with the other contenders for supremacy, CAO Cao and the emperor of Wu and their advisers, became the stuff of heroic legend.

LIU Binke. See LIU Yuxi.

LIU Chengzhi 劉程之 8/9 (352–410), one of whose courtesy names was Yimin 遺民 by which LU refers to him in the Diary. After early service as an official he strenuously declined further offers and joined the Buddhist monk HUIYUAN who was living at the East Forest Monastery in the Lu Mountains. He is recorded as a lay follower of HUIYUAN, and listed as one of the so-called Eighteen Worthies or Wise Men.

LIU, Commander 劉帥 9/21, 9/23 (fl.1170) was in charge of the escort from Kui prefecture which met LU You in E prefecture (Wuhan). His mother was Mme. ZHUO, the Grand Lady of Anding Commandery.

LIU Gong 劉珙 9/18 (1122–78), whose courtesy name LU You gives as Gongfu 恭父 (共夫 according to the *Zhongguo renming dacidian*), was a Prefect at the time LU met him. He had got on the wrong side of QIN Gui, but ended his career with high honours.

LIU Gongfu. See LIU Gong.

LIU Guangshi 劉光世 8/13 (1089–1142), a general who fought with notable lack of success against the Liao (1122), and later against the invading Jurchen (1129–37). His almost unrelieved incompetence was rewarded by not falling out with QIN Gui and the peace party, and enjoying office and favour for the remainder of his life.

LIU Quanbai 劉全白 7/17 (fl. second half of the eighth century), a poet taken up in his youth by LI Bo whose epitaph LIU wrote in 790, many years after LI's death. LIU served as an official (he was Prefect of Lake prefecture in 794) and was closely connected with YAN Zhenqing and the literary circle of the period.

LIU Tao 劉瑫 10/20, an eighth-century governor of Ba East.

LIU Wei 劉煒 7/7 (fl.1170), Commandant of Wukang in Hu prefecture and a protegé of QIN Xuan.

LIU Ying 柳楹 6/9, a twelfth-century county magistrate.

LIU Yuezhi 柳約之 10/3 (d.404) was loyal to the Jin dynasty and brought his forces down-river on hearing that HUAN Xuan, who had usurped the throne in the previous year, had died.

LIU Yun 劉筠 8/26 (971–1031). His official posts were mostly at court where he received YANG Yi's recommendation. LIU was one of those who worked on the National History, and he was eventually appointed a Hanlin Academician. He is said to have been of uncompromising character. In his poetry he followed ninth-century models, and was also famed for his richly embellished Parallel Prose, his name often coupled with that of YANG Yi.

LIU Yuxi 劉禹錫 7/11, 7/19, 7/23, 9/16, 10/3 (772–842) is often referred to as

LIU Binke 劉賓客 (Adviser to the Heir Apparent LIU), as does LU You in the Diary. He was a leading poet of the first half of the ninth century, often bracketed with BAI Juyi who admired LIU's work; and a prose stylist in the Ancient Style which he helped to revive.

LIU Zhongbao 劉仲寶 7/6 (fl.1170), a doctor.

LIU Zongyuan 柳宗元 8/26 (773–819), or LIU Liuzhou 柳柳州 as LU You calls him in the Diary since he was once Prefect of Liu prefecture. Together with HAN Yu he promoted the Ancient Style which two centuries later became established as the orthodox prose style.

Louzhide Tathāgata 婁至德如來 9/14. This is Rucika, the last of the thousand Buddhas of our present kalpa. A Tathāgata is Buddha in his corporeal manifestation.

LÜ Dabian 呂大辨 10/5 (fl.1170), a County Magistrate.

LÜ Meng 呂蒙 9/14 (178–219) was a general of the Three Kingdoms period after the collapse of the Han who, together with ZHOU Yu, defeated CAO Cao.

LU Qiwang 陸齊望 6/5, LU Zhi's grandfather and therefore an ancestor of LU You; a Director of the Imperial Library in the Tang dynasty.

LU Su 魯肅 8/18 (172–217), courtesy name Zijing 子敬 by which he is referred to in the Diary. He came from a rich family in the last years of the Han dynasty, and helped ZHOU Yu who recommended him to SUN Quan. LU served the kingdom of Wu well, advising alliance with LIU Bei against CAO Cao.

LU Xun 陸遜 7/19 (183–245) was one of the heroic figures of the Three Kingdoms period. As a general of the state of Wu in the south-east he won a great victory in 222 over LIU Bei, emperor of Shu Han, and served as Prime Minister of Wu from 244-245.

LÜ Yan 呂嵒 8/28, 10/5 (755–805), more popularly known by his courtesy name as LÜ Dongbin 呂洞賓 or the Patriarch LÜ 呂祖, was a historical character who briefly served as a minor official under the Tang dynasty until the peasant rebellions of the ninth century encouraged him to seek a life of reclusion where he found the Way. He was inducted into the mysteries of alchemy, magic formulae and swordsmanship, becoming an immortal who amongst his attributes could travel great distances instantly. His cult was popular from the twelfth century; he eventually became one of the Eight Immortals of the Daoist pantheon. In many of the stories told about him he shows a teasing playfulness.

LU Yanyuan 陸彥遠 7/13 (twelfth century), a paternal kinsman of LU You's.

LÜ Yuan 呂援 6/6 (fl.1170), the Assistant Prefect of Jingnan (Jiangling). His courtesy name was Yanneng 彥能.

LÜ Zhaowen 呂昭問 7/19 (fl.1170), a magistrate.

LU Zhi 陸贄 6/5 (754–805) was an intimate of Emperor DEZONG of the Tang, and later an important Chief Minister, a reformer with incisive views whose memorials were much admired. He fell from power in 794. LU You, who claimed descent from LU Zhi, refers to him in the text of the Diary by his posthumous name Xuan 宣.

LU Zhonggao 陸仲高 5/26 (1113–74), was a second cousin of LU You's.

Lun, Prince of Shaoling 邵陵王綸 8/30 (d.551) played a role, with WANG Sengbian and others, in the struggle for supremacy in mid-sixth century China.

LUO Shu 羅述 10/3 (d.404) was loyal to the Jin dynasty and brought his forces down-river on hearing that HUAN Xuan, who had usurped the throne in the previous year, had died.

LŬQIU Xiaozhong 閭丘孝終 8/19, courtesy name Gongxian 公顯, who had been Governor of Huang prefecture in the eleventh century.

MAI Tiezhang 麥鐵杖 7/11 (d.612) led the campaign of 612 to bring Korea under Chinese control. He was killed in battle at the Liao River.

MAO Dake 毛達可 6/15 (fl.1126) was a protegé of CAI Jing. He served as governor of Jingkou and Hangzhou, and in the latter capacity tried to help the CAI family preserve some of its vast wealth when CAI Jing fell from power as the Jurchen invaded.

MAO Dezhao. See MAO Wen.

MAO Wen 毛文 6/6 (twelfth century), LU You's former tutor, a childless scholar who became ill and blind. His courtesy name was Dezhao 德昭.

MEI Yaochen 梅堯臣 7/4, 7/26 (1002–60), courtesy name Shengyu 聖俞, one of the leading poets of the mid-eleventh century, perhaps best known for the realism, particularity and sometimes unusual diction of his poems.

MENG 孟 10/26. The family name of a minor dynasty which from 934 to 965 ruled Shu, more or less the present province of Sichuan, during the disjointed period of the so-called Five Dynasties between the Tang and Song.

MENG Chu 孟除 10/16. A feudal lord of High Antiquity.

MENG Haoran 孟浩然 8/28 (689–740) was a leading poet of the first half of the eighth century, the High Tang. He lived a retired life until the age of forty, at which point he came to the capital in Chang'an (the modern Xi'an) to take the civil service examinations. He failed, and thereafter served as a minor unranked official before dying of an ulcer. He travelled extensively in south-east China and his poetry, often specific and personal, contains delicate descriptions of nature.

MENG Jia 孟嘉 7/15 (mid-fourth century), who served as an official of the Jin dynasty in the fourth century, is best known for his riposte at a dinner given by HUAN Wen when his hat came off.

MI Fei 米芾 7/3 (1051–1107) had the courtesy name Yuanzhang 元章 by which LU refers to him in the Diary. MI was a poet, calligrapher and connoisseur, but above all a painter. His wet ink produced atmospheric landscapes, much imitated in later centuries as one of the hallmarks of scholarly, as opposed to artisanal, painting.

MI Heng 禰衡 8/30 (c.173–98), was a brilliant, eccentric and arrogant young poet of the period of division at the end of the second and beginning of the third centuries. He was shunted between one or other of the leading figures of the day, managing to insult them all while remaining an arbiter of literary taste; his best known extant work is a prose-poem on a parrot. Eventually he overstepped the mark and was executed.

MIAOJI 妙濟 6/5 (fl.1170), an elderly nun whom LU met.

MIAOTUAN 妙湍 7/2 (fl.1170), Venerable Buddhist in charge of the monastery at Yizhen who came from Chang prefecture.

MING 齊明帝 6/15 (r.494–8), emperor of the Qi dynasty in the period of division;

the short-lived Qi lasted from 479–502.

MING 宋明帝 6/14 (r.465–72), emperor of the fifth century (LIU) Song dynasty, the surname of whose ruling family was LIU.

MINGHUANG 明皇 8/4, 10/20 (685–762), the Brilliant Emperor, was also known as Emperor XUANZONG 玄宗 of the Tang dynasty. He reigned 712–56 during one of the heights of Chinese civilization, an era of expansion of trade and territory; of unprecedented contact with the outside world; of poets, painters and musicians; of an influential legal code; of pottery and the first porcelain and the origins of printing. His reign ended in disaster, however, when a general of barbarian extraction invaded and the emperor was forced to flee the capital. Though he returned, he was supplanted by one of his sons and forced to abdicate. His name is forever associated in Chinese minds with his love for one of his concubines about which there were many poems, the most famous that of BAI Juyi.

Mystic True Man 玄真子 8/16 (c.730–c.810) was the soubriquet of an eighth/ninth-century official called ZHANG Zhihe who retired from political life to become a recluse. He was expert on the early Daoist texts, painted, played the drums, drank, composed songs, and went fishing. He was a friend of the calligrapher and statesman YAN Zhenqing.

NIU Dake 牛達可 9/24 (fl.1170), Superintendent in the office of the Hubei Military Commission.

NIU Sengru 牛僧孺 8/9, 8/24 (778–847), enfeoffed with the title by which LU You refers to him, Duke of the Commandery of Qizhang 奇章郡公, was a major figure of the ninth century who held various posts up to Chief Minister and is remembered as leader of one of the cliques in the factional struggles of the late Tang.

OUYANG Fa 歐陽發 10/6 (1044–89), son of OUYANG Xiu and Vice-Director of the Directorate of Imperial Manufactories which supervised Directorates of Coinage in various prefectures.

OUYANG Xiu 歐陽修 7/18, 10/3, 10/7, 10/8, 10/9, 10/11 (1007–72) was a dominant figure of eleventh-century China. He was a statesman who spanned the period between the reforms of the 1040s and the more sweeping programme that attempted to transform society from the late 1060s; he was also a political theorist, Neo-Confucian thinker and historian. But his presence was felt most directly for centuries after his own time in prose style: he was the most influential of those who revived the classical prose of the fourth and third centuries BC. OUYANG was also a poet, essayist, and collector of anecdotes.

PAN Shu 潘恕 7/5 (fl.1170), an Assistant Prefect.

PANG, Miss. See JIANG Shi.

PEI Xiu 裴休 8/9 (786–859) graduated in the 820s. He held various provincial commands as a Military Commissioner, and served as Prime Minister from 852 to 856. PEI was a devout and knowledgeable Buddhist, contributing to the building of monasteries. He was also a distinguished calligrapher with a distinctive style.

PEI Yin 裴駰 10/16 (fl.465–72), wrote a commentary on the Records of the Historian (Shiji) in which he quoted extensively from earlier scholars.

PENG, Master 彭郎 8/1, an imaginary character created by the popular imagination with a play on the homophone for 'billowing waves' 澎.

QI, Emperor 夏啟 10/16. Emperor QI of the Xia dynasty is traditionally said to have reigned 2197–87 BC.

Qi, Prince of. See Jingda, Prince of Qi.

QI Shunchen 戚舜臣 5/19 (996–1052), a painter from Chang prefecture on the Grand Canal north of Suzhou mentioned by SU Shi, and known for his depiction of water. He served as a Prefect, gaining a reputation for kindness to the poor and for destroying heretical shrines, and ended as a member of staff of the Bureau of Forestry and Crafts. Shunchen was in fact his courtesy name. QI's personal name was Wenxiu 文秀.

QIAN Tong 錢同 7/13 (fl.1170), whose courtesy name was Zhonggeng 仲耕, was an Assistant Prefect.

QIN Bohe. See QIN Xuan

QIN Guan 秦觀 8/18 (1049–1100), courtesy name Shaoyou 少游, was one of the so-called 'Four Great Disciples' of SU Shi, and a friend. He is said to have been an ambitious and complex personality. QIN wrote lyric poetry, though this didn't always find favour with his mentor. His regular poetry was criticized by contemporaries for a kind of effeminate weakness, and was called by one 'maiden's poetry'. SU Shi helped QIN to a post in government, but he was exiled to the south when SU fell into disfavour, and thereafter his poetry became maudlin. Despite all this he had an outgoing personality and a masculine appearance with a heavy beard for which he was nicknamed 'Bearded QIN'. LU You's mother had dreamed of QIN when she was giving birth to him, and so LU's personal and courtesy names were adapted from QIN's.

QIN Gui 秦檜 (1090–1155) graduated in 1115 and by 1127, when the Jurchen attacked and the Northern Song collapsed, he had risen to a rank of some significance. But because he voiced his objection to the Jin establishing a puppet Chinese ruler in north China he was taken off to the north, along with Emperor HUIZONG (who had abdicated) and his son QINZONG, by the Jurchen. Here he seems to have won the trust of the Jurchen ruler's younger brother, and in 1130 was allowed to return to the Song which was by this time in retreat in south China. QIN was made a Grand Councillor by the Southern Song in 1131, and soon afterwards Prime Minister. He lost his position in 1132 but was restored in 1134. He held power for some nineteen years thereafter, and in difficult circumstances as the Song tried to retain its control over at least a part of the country. QIN managed both to exploit and to sacrifice a number of generals and political allies; most notably he had the energetic and successful young general YUE Fei executed as a sop to the Jin. He retained the confidence of Emperor GAOZONG, and the Shaoxing peace treaty signed in 1141, though it involved the ceding of territory, the payment of an annual tribute from Song to Jin, and diplomatic language which made manifest the subordinate status of Song, preserved the dynasty in the wealthiest part of China for another one hundred and fifty years. QIN was made a duke, and posthumously a prince; but he received short shrift from traditional patriotic historians.

QIN Xuan 秦塤 7/6, 7/9 (fl.1170), whose courtesy name was Bohe 伯和, was a

Vice Director and grandson of QIN Gui, the Prime Minister who had made a peace treaty with Jin. QIN Xuan had graduated in the same year as LU You.

Qingyeji Tathāgata 青葉髻如来 9/14. A Tathāgata is Buddha in his corporeal manifestation.

Qizhang, Duke of. See NIU Sengru.

QUAN Siyan 權嗣衍 9/18 (fl.1170), an Assistant Prefect.

RAN Huizhi 冉徽之 10/23 (fl.1170) was a Magistrate holding a provisional appointment.

RENCONG 仁聰 8/9 (fl.1170), an abbot from Fujian in charge of a Buddhist house near the Lu mountains.

RENZONG 仁宗 6/26, 7/26 (1010–63; r.1022–63), emperor of the Northern Song dynasty. When he first came to the throne a regency was established, but he assume the government himself in 1033. Debilitating wars in the late 1030s and early 1040s with the Western Xia, who controlled the passage to Central Asia along the Silk Road, gave the Liao in north-east China the opportunity to impose annual tributes on the Northern Song in 1043. RENZONG sanctioned a programme of reform from 1043, but this petered out in the face of opposition.

RUI Ye 芮曄 5/26 (1115–72), courtesy name Guoqi 國器, was Director of Studies at the National University in the capital, Hangzhou. He had previously served in the south of China in the Fiscal Commission.

SENGJIA 僧伽 6/22 (628–710), a Buddhist monk who came from Central Asia to the Chinese capital at Chang'an during the Tang dynasty and travelled in the Yangzi region.

SHEN Chiyao. See SHEN Shu.

SHEN Huaiming 沈懷明 6/14, a fifth-century general of the (LIU) Song dynasty.

SHEN Liao 沈遼 5/19, 7/25 (1032–85), courtesy name Ruida 睿達, came from a distinguished literary family. He held various official posts, leading at one stage to his imprisonment. After this he withdrew from public life and concentrated on poetry and calligraphy; his Regular and Running scripts were praised by WANG Anshi and ZENG Bu.

SHEN Shu 沈樞 5/29 (fl.1170), personal name Chiyao 持要. He was an Examiner when LU met him, an office under the Secretariat whose functions remain unclear.

SHEN Xia 沈夏 7/6 (fl.1170), a Vice-Minister in the Court of Imperial Treasury and Overseer-General of Revenues for the Two Huai.

SHEN Ying 沈瀛 6/14 (fl.1170), courtesy name Zishou 子壽, produced a volume of his recent works for LU You to see.

SHENZONG 沈宗 8/8 (r.1068–85), emperor of the Song dynasty under which LU You lived.

SHI Duanyi 石端義 5/26 (twelfth century), a Tea and Salt Intendant in Guangnan in the south of China; of cruel disposition and eventually hoist with his own petard.

SHI Hao 史浩 5/19 (1106–94), courtesy name Zhiweng 直翁. A distinguished official who was instrumental in putting Emperor XIAOZONG on the throne when GAOZONG abdicated in 1162. SHI became a Grand Councillor, in which post he called for the rehabilitation of YUE Fei, the young general executed in 1141 as a sop to the Jin. He later fell from grace for his opposition to another attack on the north, and came to govern

LU You's home town of Shaoxing, though he returned to senior positions at court in due course.

SHI Mizheng 史彌正 6/17 (fl.1170), whose courtesy name was Duanshu 端叔, was an Administrator in the Overseer-General's department.

SHI Zhengzhi 史正志 8/3, 8/4, 8/10 (fl.1170), whose courtesy name was Zhidao 志道, was a Supply Commissioner and Vice-director in the Ministry of Revenue.

SHI Zhidao. See SHI Zhengzhi.

SHIQUAN 世全 8/29, 9/13, 10/2, 10/15 (fl.1170), a Buddhist monk from Sichuan with whom LU travelled on part of his journey.

SHIZONG 周世宗 7/1, 7/4, 7/12, 8/28 (r.955–9), emperor of the (Five Dynasties) Zhou dynasty which lay in north China along the Yellow River; by 959 it had extended its territory south from the River Huai to the Yangzi at Southern Tang expense.

SHUNGUANG 舜廣 8/26 (fl.1140–mid-1170s) was the Buddhist monk in charge of the Dhūta Monastery in E prefecture (the modern Wuhan) from about 1140, having come south from the old capital at Kaifeng which had been overrun by the Jurchen.

SONG Minqiu 宋敏求 7/13 (1019–79), whose courtesy name was Cidao 次道, graduated in 1039. He went on to senior posts, taking part in the compilation of the New Tang History, and writing a number of other works of a historical nature. His library was reputed to have 30,000 fascicules, with all of which he was familiar.

SONG Qiqiu 宋齊丘 7/9, 7/23 (c.886–959), courtesy name Zisong 子嵩, by which LU refers to him in the Diary. He served as Chief Minister to the minor Five Dynasties period state of Wu and its successor in the Lower Yangzi area, the Southern Tang. He had been a close friend of the founder of the Southern Tang, XU Zhigao who later changed his name to LI Sheng, when they both served Wu. SONG was known for being ill-tempered. LU You wrote SONG's biography in his History of the Southern Tang (Nan Tang shu).

SONG Yu 宋玉 10/19 (290?–222? BC) was one of a group of third-century BC poets at the court of the state of Chu in the middle Yangzi. He is said to have been a romantic and rather dissolute character, but in reality little is known of him.

SONG Zisong. See SONG Qiqiu.

Spontaneity. See ZHAO Mr.

SU Che 蘇轍 8/17 (1039–1112), the younger brother of the poet SU Shi and himself one of the most distinguished prose writers of the period. He and his brother were placed high in the civil service examinations of 1057, and SU Che went on to have a successful official career, though he suffered the vicissitudes of an opponent of WANG Anshi's New Policies. His prose style was admired in his own day, and has been a model of classical writing ever since.

SU Shen 蘇紳 6/26 (c.996–1043), courtesy name Yifu 儀甫. He was a proponent of reform over a wide range of subjects, rising to become a Hanlin Academician. His recommendations led eventually to his demotion to provincial posts.

SU Shi 蘇軾 6/4, 7/13, 8/4, 8/17, 8/18, 8/19, 8/28, 10/5 (1037–1101) was one of the leading intellectual figures of the eleventh century, poet in most of the genres then current, prose-writer, politician of the conservative anti-reform party, painter, commentator on the classics. He is an exemplar of the Confucian scholar-official who was also a devout Buddhist with a strong interest in Daoism. His poetry draws on the tradition of moral seriousness of DU Fu and the romantic energy and lack of restraint of LI Bo, but it is his humour, stoicism in adversity and moral courage which have appealed to generartion after generation of readers. SU was a member of the family which produced the three great prose writers of the Song: he, his father SU Xun and his brother SU Che. He and his brother graduated in 1057; he held a minor post until his father's death in 1066, after which he observed the customary three year mourning period. In the 1070s he was in provincial jobs, but in 1079 was arrested for slandering the emperor. Though released he was banished to Huang prefecture from 1080-1084 (where LU You visited some of the sites associated with SU on Days 8/18 and 8/19 of the Diary). With the return to power of the conservatives he held more responsible posts from 1086 to 1093, both in the capital at Kaifeng and in the provinces, but was again banished to the south in 1094 when the reformist New Policies party returned to office. In 1097 he was banished still further, to the very limit of Chinese southern control on the island of Hainan, but restored to favour in 1100 and was on his way north when he died in 1101.

SUN Dechu 孫德芻 7/25 (fl.1170), an Assistant Prefect.

SUN Guangxian 孫光憲 10/20 (d.968) was a scholar, historian and poet. His talents were recognized by GAO Conghui, and he served under a minor dynasty of the Five Dynasties. But he successfully transferred his allegiance to the Song as it took control of the Yangzi area.

SUN Quan 孫權 6/23, 8/13, 8/17, 8/19 (182–252) ruled the lower Yangzi and much of south-east China in the first decades of the third century, in effect a warlord, and it was not until 229 that he declared himself emperor. It is as Great Emperor of the Wu dynasty that he is referred by LU You. SUN was one of the heroes of the period of division that began with the collapse of the Han dynasty. He was especially skilled in choosing capable advisers. In 208 he and his commander ZHOU Yu, together with LIU Bei who ruled Sichuan, defeated an attack by the ruler of north China, CAO Cao, at the battle of Red Cliff. The various intrigues, alliances, deceptions and acts of bravery have been recorded in official history and in novel form.

TAIWU 元魏太武 7/4 (r.423–52), emperor of the Toba Wei dynasty. In the mid-fifth century China was divided between the Wei dynasty in the north, whose nomadic rulers had sufficiently sinicized themselves to change their surname to Yuan and move their capital south of the Yellow River to Luoyang; and the Song dynasty whose rulers were named LIU. In fact the division of China at this period was not far different from that in LU You's time between the Jin in the north and the Song dynasty under which he lived in the south.

TAIYI 太易 9/14, an eighth-century Buddhist monk known to DU Fu.

TAIZONG 宋太宗 7/1, 7/21, 8/8 (r.976–97), the brother of the founding emperor of the Song dynasty. He succeeded his brother as the second emperor in circumstances which may have been more nefarious than traditional historians have acknowledged.

TAIZU 周太祖 7/7 (r.951–3); ruler of the Later Zhou dynasty in the Five Dynasties and Ten Kingdoms period; not to be confused with Emperor TAIZU of the Song dynasty.

TAIZU 宋太祖 7/1 (r.960–76). ZHAO Kuangyin 超匡胤 was a general serving the short-lived Zhou dynasty until he usurped the throne and declared himself emperor of a new dynasty, the Song. This proved to be enduring, and by the reign of his brother and successor it had established control over the greater part of China.

TANG family 湯氏 7/17 (twelfth century); the TANGs were living on the site of XIE Tiao's house; no further details.

TANG Bin 唐彬 8/23 (235–94), a general of the state of Jin in the third century who received orders to combine with WANG Jun and other commanders to advance down the Yangzi and take Nanjing.

TANG Heng 湯衡 9/24 (fl.1170), Administrator for the Military Commission.

TANG Lü 唐履 10/8 (fl.1101), a Daoist.

TANG Wenruo 唐文若 10/5 (1106–65), courtesy name Lifu 立夫 by which LU refers to him in the Diary, served in a number of provincial posts, earning a reputation for dealing with flooding. Promoted to positions at court, he put forward proposals for increasing preparedness for war. When WANYAN Liang invaded in 1161 he argued that leading ministers should take command along the Yangzi.

TANG Zhuan 唐璪 7/5 (fl.1170) was serving, when LU met him, as a member of the subsidiary capital's Regency and a Senior Compiler in the Imperial Archives.

Tao 綯 6/7, 6/13 (fl.1170), one of LU You's sons.

TAO Fan 陶範 8/9 (late fourth century), a Prefect.

TAO Zhizhen 陶之真 6/17 (fl.1170), a junior Gentleman for Court Service who appears to have had no substantive position at the time LU You met him.

Tong 統 6/9, 7/2, 8/26 (fl.1170), one of LU You's sons.

WANG, Mr 王公 8/28. A Prefect of Hanyang of the mid-eighth century known to the poet LI Bo.

WANG Anshi 王安史 7/4 (1021–86). WANG was the great reforming statesman of the eleventh century whose far-reaching programme of measures covered financial, military and political institutions. He was also a distinguished poet and prose writer. WANG was in power from 1069–74 and again from 1075–6, but the repercussions of his reforms and the factional fighting which they provoked were felt until the end of the Northern Song.

WANG Baiyi 王百一 9/28 (fl.1170), a dismissed 'engager' in charge of helmsmen who tried to kill himself.

WANG Cha 王察 7/2 (fl.1170), a Prefect.

WANG Che 王屮 8/26 (d.505), courtesy name Jianqi 简棲, lived under the Southern Qi dynasty. He had been included in Selections of Refined Literature (Wenxuan) compiled by the sixth-century Crown Prince Zhaoming of the Liang. He wrote in Parallel Prose.

WANG Cheng 王澄 9/8 (d.313) served as an incompetent prefectural Governor under the Western Jin dynasty (265–316) who fled his post in the face of an assertive subordinate.

WANG Dun 王敦 7/19, 7/20 (266–324) was an early fourth-century general who served the Eastern Jin; but when the Eastern Jin ruler tried to curtail the power of the WANG family he rose in revolt, captured Nanjing, slaughtered many of the leading citizens and appointed himself Prime Minister. With his army based up-river at Wuchang he controlled the court from afar. His enemies took their opportunity to attack him when he fell ill, but he managed through his underlings to launch a counter-attack on Nanjing. This petered out when he died, and his army dissolved.

WANG Hun 王渾 7/11 (223–97), the general whose signal WANG Jun ignored when the latter went on to capture Nanjing and bring an end to the Wu dynasty in 280.

WANG Jingze 王敬則 6/15 (d.498) had humble origins and was illiterate; but his mother, who was a shamaness, predicted his rise to fame. WANG served the Southern Qi dynasty, which ruled south China, as a local governor and established a reputation for being tough on crime in his district and a decisive man of action. But he fled in the face of reports of an enemy advance; toadied to superiors and was arrogant to subordinates. He was eventually killed in battle as he treid to lead a force against government troops.

WANG Jun 王浚 7/11, 8/23 (206–85), the general who ignored WANG Hun's signal and went on to capture Nanjing and bring an end to the Wu dynasty in 280, and with it the period of the Three Kingdoms, briefly re-unifying China.

WANG Junyi 王君儀 9/26 (early twelfth century) was a native of Yan prefecture and had been taught by LU You's grandfather. He was an expert on the Book of Changes; none of his writings are extant. His nephew was WANG Shidian.

WANG Kangnian 王康年 10/21 (fl.1170) was a provisional county magistrate and Commandant. He came from Sichuan.

WANG Lin 王琳 9/8 (526–73). On the fall of the Liang dynasty in 557 WANG refused to acknowledge the new Chen dynasty. HOU Andu was sent by the Chen ruler to attack him, but was defeated by WANG.

WANG Quan 王權 7/13 (fl.1170) was the Magistrate for Dangtu county.

WANG Rong 王戎 8/23 (234–305), a general of the third-century state of Jin who received orders to advance down the Yangzi and take Nanjing.

WANG Sengbian 王僧辯 8/30 (d.555) served the Liang dynasty, playing a role in the military and political machinations of the mid-sixth century.

WANG Shao 王韶 8/8 (1030–81), whose courtesy name by which LU You refers to him was Zichun 子純, advocated a forward policy against the Western Xia state which during the eleventh century controlled the north-western corridor out of China on the Silk Road. He had some success in the 1070s, while he held military appointments, in gaining the submission of the Qiang tribes on the western border and was made Deputy Commissioner for Military Affairs. Dismissed in 1077, he received a provincial appointment, and shortly before his death in 1081 turned to Buddhism and created a Garden of Meditation. WANG invited CHANGZONG to become abbot at East Forest in 1080.

WANG Shidian 王師點 9/26 (fl.1170), a
junior legal officer; and nephew of
WANG Junyi.

WANG Wei 王維 6/16 (699–761) was one
of the leading poets of the High Tang
perod. He is particularly admired for his
quietist verse with its deceptive
simplicity, profoundly influenced by
Buddhism, but he also wrote urbane
court poetry while serving under
Empreor MINGHUANG. He had a
successful official career; captured by the
rebels who drove out MINGHUANG in
756, he nevertheless managed to avoid
opprobrium. WANG was also a landscape
painter to whom was later ascribed a
role in the development of scholarly, as
opposed to artisinal, painting. In later life
he turned part of his estate into a
Buddhist monastery.

WANG Xiu 王秀 6/25 (1120–post-1170),
the military man LU You met who came
from Bo prefecture and had been
engaged in military operations against
the Jin which had gone unrecognized.

WANG Xuan 王煊 7/5 (fl.1170) was a
Supervisor of Military Granaries when
LU met him.

WANG Yucheng 王禹偁 8/18, 8/19
(954–1001), courtesy name Yuanzhi
元之 by which LU You refers to him. He
was an outspoken official of the early
Song who suffered for this on occasion;
he was a forerunner of those who
advocated reform in the eleventh
century. He admired the poets DU Fu
and BAI Juyi and his reputation as a poet
rests on his plain and natural freshness,
an early departure from the ornate style
of the Late Tang and Five Dynasties. In
prose too he was a forerunner of the
Ancient Prose style which was revived in
the eleventh century.

WANG Zhiyi 王知義 6/20 (fl.1170), a boat
owner of Jia prefecture in Sichuan.

WANYAN Liang 完顏亮 6/25, 7/17
(1122–61; r.1149–61), was known as
Prince Hailing (WANYAN was a tribal
name), but was the fourth emperor of
the Jurchen Jin dynasty which had
overrun north China in 1127. He had
ambitions to complete the conquests
begun forty years previously, and in
1161 launched a large-scale attack to the
south. He inflicted a heavy defeat on the
Song forces led by YE Yiwen at Melon
Island on 8 November 1161, but his
army was defeated at Coloured Stone,
after which his own troops murdered
him.

WEI 韋太守 8/23, eighth-century Governor
of Jiangxia whose name appears in the
title of a poem by LI Bo. He was perhaps
the same man as WEI Bing 韋冰 of
Nanling to whom LI Bo presented
another poem (Day 8/26) when he was
in Jiangxia, though this WEI has been
identified as WEI Jingjun 韋景駿; the
annotators of LI Bo's Complete Works know
not on what basis.

WEI Bing of Nanling 8/26 (mid-eighth
century), an official known to LI Bo.

WEI Pi 魏丕 (919–99), a soldier sent by the
Song court to their enemy the Southern
Tang.

WEI Tai 魏泰 10/5 (c.1050–1110), courtesy
name Daofu 道輔, was a brother-in-law
of ZENG Bu. He had no official career,
never having got a degree because he
nearly killed an examiner, though he was
recommended for appointment by
influential backers in the late eleventh
century. Instead he retired into private
life, though remaining a friend of several
leading officials of the late eleventh and
early twelfth centuries, including

ZHANG Shangying. He wrote a number of miscellanies.

WEN 宋文帝 6/15, 7/4 (r.424–53), emperor of the (LIU) Song dynasty. See also TAIWU of the Toba Wei dynasty, his contemporary. Toba Wei ruled north China, (LIU) Song the south.

WEN 梁文帝 6/15 (r.550–1), emperor of the Liang dynasty, another of the short-lived dynasties of the period of division. He was a son of Emperor WU of the Liang, and brother to Emperor YUAN and to the anthologist Crown Prince Zhaoming.

WEN Shuji 文庶幾 10/23 (fl.1170) was a Commandant. No further details.

WEN Tingyun 溫庭筠 7/19 (798–868?), courtesy name Feiqing 飛卿. WEN was a leading poet of the Late Tang who belonged to a declining aristocratic family and whose official career was blocked by the eunuchs holding sway in the Tang court in the ninth century.

WENREN Boji. See WENREN Gang.

WENREN Boqing. See WENREN Fumin.

WENREN Fumin 聞人阜民 6/5 (fl.1170), courtesy name Boqing 伯卿, was an Instructor. He was the son of WENREN Zi.

WENREN Gang 聞人綱 6/6 (fl.1170). He was a Presented Scholar; in other words he had taken his degree but had not yet been assigned a job. His courtesy name was Boji 伯記. He was a private tutor in the household of FANG Zi, and had known LU's former tutor MAO Dezhao.

WENREN Maode. See WENREN Zi.

WENREN Yaomin 聞人堯民 7/3 (fl.1170) was a Supervisor of Taxes. He was a nephew of WENREN Zi.

WENREN Zi 聞人滋 6/5 (twelfth century), courtesy name Maode 茂德, the father of WENREN Fumin, was an expert on ritual and ceremonial.

WU, emperor of the Wei dynasty. See CAO Cao.

WU 武帝 8/23 (r.265–89), emperor of the Western Jin dynasty, an effective and cultured ruler who nevertheless lost control of the increasingly powerful aristocratic families, bequeathing his successors a divided kingdom into which northern barbarians found it easy to penetrate.

WU 梁武帝 6/15 (r.502–49), emperor of the Liang dynasty and father of Emperor WEN.

WU 吳 8/11 (fl.1170), an Administrator in the Supply Commission. LU does not provide his other names or identifying particulars.

WU of Han 漢武帝 7/27 (r.141–87 BC), emperor of the Han dynasty, sometimes known as Han Wudi. He presided over a vast expansion of China into the western regions along the Silk Road, south into what is now northern Vietnam, and east into Korea. Chinese armies penetrated as far as the Pamirs, and trade flourished. The prosperity of Han Wudi's reign was marred, however, by factional fighting amongst the powerful aristocratic families around the emperor.

WU Bogu 吳博古 7/15 (fl.1170), courtesy name Minshu 敏叔, was an Instructor at a prefectural school.

WU Daofu 吳道夫 6/3 (fl.1170), a County Magistrate.

WU Daozi 吳道子 8/8 (c.689–c.758), a court painter who was reputed the greatest of Tang artists. He executed wall-paintings in the Buddhist monasteries and Daoist temples of the capital Chang'an (the modern Xi'an) and the subsidiary capital of Luoyang, as well as secular figure painting and landscapes. None of his work survives.

WU Li 吳澧 6/12 (fl.1170), a Magistrate.

WU Yin 吳隱 6/3 (fl.1170) who had been a merchant of no education but who developed powers of divination based on the Book of Changes. His name might perhaps be rendered WU the Hermit.

WU Yuan 伍員 10/10 (late sixth century BC), otherwise known as WU Zixu 伍子虛 by which name LU refers to him in the Diary, was a citizen of the ancient state of Chu in the central Yangzi area. His family was killed by the King of Chu and he then travelled to the eastern state of Wu to assist its king in attacking Chu, eventually falling foul of the king of Wu and committing suicide in 483 BC.

WUKONG 悟空 7/7, a tenth-century Zen master.

XIE An 謝安 7/8 (320–85) was a great-great uncle of the poet XIE Lingyun, and himself a statesman who saved the foundering Jin dynasty and helped southern China to withstand the nomad pressure to the north. His sang froid on hearing that his army had defeated the northern invasion of 383 is as familiar to Chinese as that of Sir Francis Drake's before the Spanish Armanda is to the English.

XIE Lingyun 謝靈運 6/15 (385–433), was one of the leading writers of his time, learned, a calligrapher, a painter, a nature poet and a Buddhist thinker. He was also a member of one of the great aristocratic clans, inheriting the title of Duke of Kangle 康樂 by which name LU You refers to him in the Diary. XIE served in office, but in the complicated politics of the period eventually suffered banishment and execution.

XIE Shihou 謝師厚 10/15, an eleventh-century official.

XIE Shiji 謝師稷 8/23, 8/24 (fl.1170), an Assistant in the Tax Transport Bureau; also refrerred to as Fiscal Commissioner XIE.

XIE Tiao 謝朓 7/11, 7/17 (464–99), courtesy name Xuanhui 玄暉, by which LU You refers to him in the Diary. XIE was a member of one of the leading families of the fifth century and held high office under the Qi dynasty, but died in prison. He was a poet and calligrapher.

XIE, Fiscal Commissioner. See XIE Shiji.

XIN Dafang 辛大方 10/8 (fl.1095), son of XIN Hong and known to HUANG Tingjian. No further details.

XIN Hong 辛紘 10/8 (fl.1095), father of XIN Dafang and known to HUANG Tingjian. No further details.

XIONG Ke 熊克 6/17 (fl.1170), an Instructor at a prefectural school.

XIONG Yi 熊繹 10/16 served King Cheng (r.1104–1068 BC) of Zhou. His enfeoffment in the Yangzi valley led ultimately to the formation of the state of Chu.

XU, Mr 徐先生 7/20, a twelfth-century Daoist from the Wan Hills with medical and mystical skills who taught CHEN Bing.

XU Bohu 許伯虎 6/14 (fl.1170), courtesy name Ziwei 子威, had been a fellow student of LU You's in his youth and was a Revenue Manager when they met again.

XU Fu 徐俯 7/11, 7/18 (c.1086–1140) whose courtesy name, by which LU refers to him, was Shichuan 帥川. He was a poet and nephew of HUANG Tingjian whose style he followed at first, though in later years he seems to have wanted to cast aside meticulous embellishment in favour of naturalness.

XU graduated in 1132 and went on to hold a number of bureaucratic posts.

XU Kai 徐鍇 8/26 (920–74) lost his father when young, and while his mother taught music and had little time to attend to the young XU he taught himself to write. He was soon taken up by the Southern Tang and given a post commensurate with his literary and academic bent. He appears to have grieved to death at the collapse of the Southern Tang.

XU Rong 徐容 6/23 (fl.1170), whose courtesy name was Zigong 子公, was an Instructor in Grand Tranquillity prefecture.

XU Wen 徐溫 7/1, 8/26 (d.927). He had been an illiterate seller of salt who rose by cunning and murder to be a Grand Councillor and prince of one of the petty states of the Five Dynasties period (907–60). He was revered as the Honorary Ancestor of the Southern Tang, in other words posthumously regarded as the founder of that Five Dynasties regime.

XU Wuzi 徐務滋 6/18 (fl.1170), a Surveillance Circuit Judge.

XU Zhigao. See LI Bian.

XU Zhu 徐注 10/5 was from Zhen prefecture. He had written a colophon for the inscription LU You was shown by a Daoist; no further information.

XUANZONG, Emperor. See under MINGHUANG.

XUE, Magistrate 薛明府 9/12, an eigth-century magistrate whose name appears in the title of one of DU Fu's poems.

XUE Yan 薛顔 10/27 (953–1026). While in Kui as a Fiscal Commissioner he transferred the administrative offices to a new site.

XUN, Zen Master 佛燈珣禪師 7/23 (early twelfth century); XUN of the Buddha Lamp who was furious that young monks were avoiding the rigours of the cold by lining their clothes with reed floss.

YAN, Duke of Lu. See YAN Zhenqing.

YAN, Zen Master 顔禪師 9/15 (twelfth century), a Zen Master of the Sauvastika Retreat who had taught ZUZHU.

YAN Zhenqing 顔眞鄉 8/9 (709–85), an important minister under the Tang dynasty who took part in the suppression of the rebellion which broke out in 756 and overwhelmed Emperor MINGHUANG's rule. But YAN, who was generally known by the title with which he was ennobled as the Duke of Lu, was most famous as a calligrapher. Examples of his writing still serve as models for aspiring calligraphers.

YANG 隋煬帝 6/16, 7/11 (r.605–17), emperor of the Sui dynasty. The Sui (589–618) reunified China after the period of division and built part of the Grand Canal along which LU travelled. In 612 Emperor YANG also tried unsuccessfully to invade Korea.

YANG Chong 楊沖 6/18 (fl.1170), an Adjutant Revenue Manager.

YANG Pu 楊溥 7/1 (r.920–37) was emperor of a short-lived dynasty, the Wu (919–37),which ruled Huainan, an area between the Huai and the Yangzi rivers.

YANG Shizhong 楊師中 7/25 (fl.1170), a Prefect.

YANG Shouzhong 楊守忠 8/26 (tenth century) served the Southern Tang dynasty as Deputy Military and Surveillance Commissioner for Wuchang and Administrator of Military and Prefectural Affairs.

YANG Su 楊素 10/26 (d.606) helped the founder of the Sui (589–618) establish his dynasty. He was ennobled as Duke of Yue.

YANG Xingmi 楊行密 7/25 (late ninth/early tenth century), Prince WU of the state of Wu 吳武王 in the period when the Tang Dynasty was collapsing. He began life as a brigand who won the loyalty of his men; was made, *faute de mieux*, a military appointee of the Tang court and a prince from 892–906; posthumously, when his son declared himself an emperor as the Tang fell, YANG was made founding emperor of the state.

YANG Xun 楊恂 7/15, 7/17 (fl.1170), courtesy name Xinbo 信伯, was a Supernumerary Instructor in the prefectural school at Dangtu.

YANG Yi 楊億 8/26 (974–1020) graduated in 992 and held various posts, including Hanlin Academician, at court where he won a reputation for his robust prose style and agility of thought.

YANG Youyi 楊由義 8/18 (fl.1170) was a Prefect and an Auxiliary in the Imperial Archives.

YANWEI 顔威 7/23 (twelfth century), a Venerable Buddhist who had studied under the Zen Master XUN of the Buddha Lamp.

YE Anxing 葉安行 10/7 (fl.1170) whose courtesy name was Lüdao 履道, was a Prefect.

YE Fen 葉棻 7/13 (fl.1170), was an Assistant Prefect.

YE Heng 葉衡 5/25 (1122–83), courtesy name Mengxi 夢錫, graduated in 1148. He was a distinguished official of the Southern Song period who served under Emperors GAOZONG and XIAOZONG as an able economic expert and administrator who made some original proposals for expanding agriculture.

YE Mengxi. See YE Heng.

YE Qingchen 葉清臣 5/19 (d. c.1051), courtesy name Daoqing 道卿. He spoke in favour of the reformers of the 1030s, and as a local official undertook a number of irrigation schemes.

YE Yiwen 葉義問 6/25 (1098–1170), whom LU refers to in the Diary by his courtesy name of Shenyan 審言, graduated in 1128 and went on to hold a number of posts before running up against the peace party under Grand Councillor QIN Gui. After QIN's death his career resumed, and he was instrumental in bringing down QIN's followers. In 1160 he warned against the likelihood of a Jin attack, and when this did indeed happen the following year YE was put in charge of defensive arrangements. But he proved incompetent against the Jurchens under WANYAN Liang, and was quickly removed from command.

YU, Emperor 夏禹 10/9, 10/23 (reigned traditionally 2205–2198 BC), emperor of the Xia dynasty, and known in Chinese mythology as YU the Great. He was the great engineer who mastered the waters by hydraulic conservancy.

YU Chu 喻樗 6/12 (d.1180), courtesy name Zicai 子材. After graduating in 1129 he had served early in his career in Sichuan on the border with Jin, as well as holding posts at court. But YU disagreed with the policy of making peace with Jin and consequently fell into disfavour, resigning to live at home. His official career resumed on the death of QIN Gui, the Grand Councillor who promoted the peace policy, and he went on to hold a number of middle-ranking jobs. But YU was best known as a writer on Neo-

Confucianism. He was a Director when LU met him.

YU Di 于頔 6/5 (d.818) came from Luoyang and served as a governor in provincial cities where he established a reputation for getting rid of heretical sects and for irrigation work. He was also a dreaded Surveillance Commissioner. By 798 he had been appointed a Military Commissioner, in which capacity he put down a revolt against the Tang. He was later a Grand Councillor and Minister of Works; though he came under a cloud he managed to retire as an Adviser to the Heir Apparent with a dukedom.

YU Liang 庾亮 8/5 (289–340) served the Jin dynasty in the period of division, governing the central Yangzi area from 334-340.

YU Zicai. See YU Chu.

YUAN, Emperor 梁元帝 9/18 (r.552–5), emperor of the Liang dynasty. He was the seventh son of the long-lived Emperor WUDI of the Liang whose scholarship, compassion, Confucian virtues and devotion to Buddhism ended in invasion and rebellion. One of WUDI's sons was the anthologist Crown Prince Zhaoming; another Emperor YUAN. YUAN seems to have combined Daoism, vindictive cruelty and scholarly interests in equal measure. He abdicated in 555, but his son lasted only one year before the Liang were supplanted by the Chen dynasty.

YUANZONG, Emperor 南唐元宗 7/7, 7/12, 7/27 (r.943–61), second of the three emperors of the Southern Tang dynasty, and father of the Last Ruler, the poet-emperor.

YUE Fei 岳飛 8/4, 8/13 (1103–42) was the dashing young general who helped to rally Song forces in the face of the Jurchen invasion and stemmed their advance. Indeed he launched a counterattack northwards which had some success. But the peace party, fearing the tide would turn again, reached a compromise with the Jin; the terms included payment of 'danegeld' by Song and YUE Fei's recall; he was executed shortly thereafter.

YUNCHANG 蘊常 7/3 (fl.1170), Venerable Buddhist of the Yongqing Monastery.

ZENG Bu 曾布 6/26 (1036–1107), courtesy name Zixuan 子宣. ZENG, whose brother was the prose writer ZENG Gong, began as a confidante of the reformer WANG Anshi and promoted a number of WANG's New Policies, becoming a Hanlin Academician. He later fell out with WANG and his supporters over opposition to some of these policies and was banished to a provincial post. When ZHANG Chun came to power under Emperor SHENZONG ZENG returned to the centre and on SHENZONG's death backed the prince who became Emperor HUIZONG. This not surprisingly led to further promotion, but he fell out with his powerful co-equal CAI Jing and ZENG ended in provincial banishment where he died.

ZENG Huadan 曾華旦 10/14 (eleventh century), a Presented Scholar who graduated in 1049 and in 1051 had written a stele that LU You saw.

ZENG Ji 曾幾 6/9 (1084–1166), whose posthumous name, by which LU You refers to him in the Diary, was Wenqing 文清, was an official who advocated no compromise with the Jurchen invaders and therefore fell foul of Grand Councillor QIN Gui. But ZENG was more significant as a poet, admiring DU Fu of the Tang dynasty and HUANG Tingjian in the generation older than himself. ZENG was the mentor and principal early influence on LU You's own poetry.

ZENG Pan 曾槃 5/19 (fl.1170), a Commandant (something akin to a local police chief).

ZENG Yuanbo 曾原伯 5/19 (fl.1170), personal name Feng 逢, was the father of ZENG Pan.

ZHAI Qinian 翟耆年 6/26 (twelfth century), courtesy name Boshu 伯壽, was a contemporary of LU You whose father had served under Emperor HUIZONG before being ousted by QIN Gui. The biographical dictionary *Zhongguo Renming Dacidian* mistakenly classifies ZHAI as living under the Yuan dynasty.

ZHAN Daozi 詹道子 5/26 (fl.1170), whose personal name was Kangzong 亢宗. He was a Senior Writer, responsible for editorial work in the Palace Library.

ZHANG Fu 章甫 8/28 (fl.1170), courtesy name Guanzhi 冠之, was a poet and calligrapher, and apparently an eccentric character. He chose the soubriquet Easily Satisfied.

ZHANG Gang 張綱 6/14 (1083–1166), whose posthumous name was Wending 文定. He was said to be a man of rectitude, and another of those whose careers were stalled while QIN Gui was in power.

ZHANG Guanzhi. See ZHANG Fu.

ZHANG Jian 張堅 6/14 (fl.1170) was a Supernumerary Assistant Prefect serving with LI Anguo and JIANG Yi when LU met them. ZHANG was the son of ZHANG Gang.

ZHANG Jun 張浚 8/1 (1096–1164) was famous as a general who resisted the Jin following their attack on the Northern Song capital of Kaifeng. In the following years he and YUE Fei held off Jin advances and suppressed rebels within the territory controlled by the Southern Song. His opposition to the peace policy of QIN Gui meant that he was demoted to provincial posts for almost twenty years. ZHANG was brought back in 1161 when the Jin under WANYAN Liang launched an attack south, but he is blamed for the major defeat at Jin hands (Battle of Fuli in 1163). ZHANG resigned in 1164. Amongst his titles was Duke of Wei 魏公 by which LU You refers to him in the Diary.

ZHANG Lei 張耒 7/11, 7/19, 8/9, 8/16, 8/17, 8/18, 8/19 (1054–1114), courtesy name Wenqian 文潛, by which he is referred to in the Diary. He was an upright and honest official, admired by SU Shi and his brother SU Che. ZHANG wrote a prose miscellany as well as poetry, some of it about farming, in a plain and natural style in the tradition of BAI Juyi.

ZHANG Mao 張茂 10/5 (twelfth century), son of ZHANG Shangying.

ZHANG Shangying 張商英 10/5, 10/9 (1043–1122), whose courtesy name was Tianjue 天覺, also known as Zigao 子高, was a high official of the second half of the Northern Song dynasty. He graduated in the 1060s and held a number of posts, though his career suffered in the late 1080s and 1090s from his espousal of the New Policies of WANG Anshi. When the young Emperor ZHEZONG assumed power in 1093 after a regency ZHANG's star was in the ascendant again. Under HUIZONG he joined the Hanlin Academy, and in 1102 the Department of State Affairs; but though at first he worked closely with CAI Jing they had fallen out by 1106 and ZHANG was sent off to remote postings. In 1110 he came back as Prime Minister and undid CAI's policies. He lasted at the top only a year or two. Alongside this distinguished official career ZHANG was a literatus, Daoist scholar and lay Buddhist.

ZHANG Shi 章浞 6/3 (fl.1170) was supervisor of the Xiu prefecture general customs post.

ZHANG Shunmin 張舜民 8/5 (c.1034–c.1110), who is referred to by his courtesy name Yunsou 芸叟 in the Diary, opposed WANG Anshi's New Policies. In 1081 he was attached to the campaign against the Western Xia and wrote poetry describing it. He held a number of jobs, including an embassy to the Liao in north-east China and postings to the north-west, after the return to power of the conservatives in 1086. When Emperor HIUZONG came to the throne in 1101 ZHANG became a Remonstrance Official and gained some notoriety for putting up sixty papers dealing with the northern areas in his first seven days in office. He was out of favour again when the reformers were back in power. ZHANG was reputed a straight-talking official. He composed a 'Record of a Transfer South' and 'An Embassy to the Liao', and also wrote poetry and lyrics

ZHANG Shuqian 張叔潛 5/26 (fl.1170), whose personal name was Yuan 淵, graduated in 1163 and was a Junior Compiler when LU met him, a post concerned with the compilation of historical and other records within the bureaucracy.

ZHANG Tan 張郯 8/23 (fl.1170), whose courtesy name was Zhiyan 之彦, was a Prefect.

ZHANG Tinggui 張庭圭 8/26 (c.664–734), courtesy name Wenyu 温玉, was a famous Tang dynasty calligrapher and high-ranking official. He was renowned for his Eight Part and Clerical style calligraphy.

ZHANG Wei 張謂 8/28 graduated in 743 and was a senior official under the Tang in the second half of the eighth century. He was author of a book on the local customs of Changsha south of Lake Dongting.

ZHANG Wen 章汶 6/17 (fl.1170), was an Assistant Prefect.

ZHANG Xian 張先 6/6 (990–1078), whose courtesy name was Ziye 子野, graduated in 1030. He was a minor official but a lyric poet of some importance.

ZHANG Yu 張遇 8/13, a brigand leader in the late 1120s following the collapse of the Northern Song.

ZHANG Yunsou. See ZHANG Shunmin.

ZHANG Zhenfu 張真甫 7/17 (twelfth century), a Drafter who had written a stele for repairs to a shrine.

ZHANG Zhihe. See Mystic True Man.

ZHANG Zigao. See ZHANG Shangying.

ZHAO, Mr 趙先生 7/20 (late tenth/early eleventh century) from Reed Port Town. After illness in youth and dreams which linked medicinal herbs, dietary requirements and esoteric scripts, he became a Daoist priest with the name Spontaneity. Despite state sanction of his standing as an ordained divine, something of mystery clung about him even in death.

ZHAO Cheng 趙成 10/14 (mid-eleventh century), a Prefect of Gui prefecture and Vice-Director of the Criminal Administration Bureau of the Department of State Affairs.

ZHAO Dezhuang. See ZHAO Yanduan.

ZHAO Qing 趙青 9/17, 9/28 (fl.1170), a boat owner from Jia prefecture.

ZHAO Shikui 趙師夔 6/5 (fl.1170), a Supernumerary Assistant Prefect.

ZHAO Sui 趙隨 8/29 (fl.1170), a doctor.

ZHAO Yanduan 趙彥端 5/29 (1121–75), personal name Dezhuang 德莊, was a member of the Song imperial family, whose surname was ZHAO. He graduated in 1138 and became a well-known writer of lyric poetry as well as an official.

ZHAO Yun 趙蘊 9/24 (fl.1170), Administrator for the Military Commission.

ZHAO Ziming 趙子覭 7/13 (fl.1170) was a Military Supervisor.

ZHAOJUE. See under CHANGZONG.

ZHAOLIE, Emperor. See LIU Bei.

Zhaoming 梁昭明太子 7/25 (501–31), whose name was XIAO Tong 蕭統, was Crown Prince of the Liang dynasty. He was a literary patron and son of Emperor WUDI of the Liang, but died before his father. *Selections of Refined Literature* (*Wenxuan* 文選), an anthology divided into poetry and prose and further subdivided into genres, was compiled under his aegis, a work that became a model for later makers of anthologies.

ZHEN Jizhi 甄季之 10/3 (d.404) was loyal to the Jin dynasty and brought his forces down-river on hearing that HUAN Xuan, who had usurped the throne in the previous year, had died.

ZHENG Duancheng 鄭端誠 6/9 (fl.1170), a doctor.

ZHENJUE. See BAOZHI.

ZHENZONG, Emperor 真宗 8/8 (r.997–1022), emperor of the Song dynasty under which LU You lived.

ZHIJIAN 志堅 10/10 (fl.1170), a Buddhist abbot.

ZHONGLI Quan 鍾離權 10/5, a Tang dynasty contemporary of LÜ Yan who acquired magic formulae and became an immortal; though other accounts say he lived under the Han dynasty.

ZHOU 周 7/17 (fl.1140–70), an old Daoist from Wei prefecture who by 1170 had lived in the Black Mountains for thirty years.

ZHOU Bian 周昪 8/3 (fl.1170), a Prefect whose courtesy name was Qiangzhong 強仲.

ZHOU Cao 周操 7/12 (fl.1170), personal name Yuante 元特. He was an Auxiliary Academician of the Hall of Exemplary Conduct.

ZHOU Qiansun 周謙孫 9/14, 9/15 (fl.1170), a Magistrate.

ZHOU Yan 周郔 6/9 (fl.1170), a Commandant (a local chief of security).

ZHOU Yu 周瑜 8/19, 8/23 and Commentary to Day 9/14 (175–210) (also referred to as Master ZHOU) was a heroic commander of the state of Wu in the period of division after the fall of the Han dynasty. Under his ruler SUN Quan, and in alliance with LIU Bei of the state of Shu, he helped to defeat CAO Cao's ambitions to conquer south China.

ZHOU Yuante. See ZHOU Cao.

ZHOU Zhan 周湛 7/26, an eleventh-century Supply Commissioner who cleared a channel in the Yangzi. He was a capable administrator, known for his photographic recall of the names of the officials under him and for his marksmanship as an archer.

ZHU 朱 10/7, an eleventh-century Prefect and member of the Bureau of Forestry and Crafts. He has been identified as ZHU Qingji 朱慶基 who was Prefect of Xia prefecture in 1035.

ZHU Dunru 朱敦儒 7/9 (1081–1159),
courtesy name Xizhen 希真. ZHU was a
lyric poet, much of whose later work in
the fist decades of the Southern Song
laments the times in which he lived.
For the first fifty years of his life ZHU
was a private citizen in north China,
declining opportunities to take up an
official post. But after the debacle of
Jurchen invasion and the loss of the
north he drifted south and a few years
later, in 1135, was given the equivalent
of an honorary degree; various jobs in
the capital and provinces followed. He
was too close to members of the pro-
war faction, however, condemned for
his aberrant views, and sacked in 1146;
though it is a measure of the
complexities of the politics of the
period that ZHU was then taken up by
the leading appeaser QIN Gui,
accepting a job teaching painting and
calligraphy for which he was later
ridiculed. On QIN's death in 1155 ZHU
was dismissed once more.

ZHU Lingbin 朱令贇 7/27 (tenth century)
was the Jiangnan Commander-in-Chief
of the Southern Tang who was defeated
by Song forces in 975 when they
brought an end to the dynasty for which
he was fighting.

ZHU Ziqiu 朱自求 6/5 (fl.1170) was an
Assistant Prefect in provisional charge of
a Commandery.

ZHUGE Liang 諸葛亮 10/27 (181–234)
was the heroic Prime Minister of LIU
Bei's state of Shu Han. He had lived in
retirement on Sleeping Dragon
Mountain, and only with difficulty been
persuaded by LIU Bei to take up the
burdens of state. He served LIU and his
ineffective son so loyally and astutely
that he is considered a paragon of those
virtues. His proclamations before the
launching of attacks against the state of
Wei in 227 and 228 are famous pieces
of classical prose.

ZHUO Mme 卓氏 9/23 (d.1170), mother
of Commander LIU, held the honorary
title of Grand Lady of Anding
Commandery 安定郡太夫人.

ZUZHU 祖珠 9/14, 9/15 (fl.1170), a
Venerable Buddhist from Nanping
Military Prefecture.

BIBLIOGRAPHY

A full and formal bibliography would not be appropriate to a work that hopes to appeal to a general readership. I have listed here merely those books which are cited in the body of the text, and suggested some further reading for those who might be stimulated to pursue avenues opened onto the Yangzi and the history and art of the Song dynasty. Early travels to China by Arabs or by Europeans such as Marco Polo I will leave the reader to discover from others more competent to make recommendations. At the end I give a brief list of those works in Chinese, including the Ru Shu ji text, on which I have drawn most directly; and some books in Chinese specifically on Lu You.

General

Adshead, S.A.M, T'ang China, The Rise of the East in World History, Palgrave Macmillan 2004.

Barnhart, Richard M., Along the Border of Heaven (Sung and Yuan Paintings from the C.C. Wang Family Collection), The Metropolitan Museum of Art, New York 1983.

Bird, Isabella (Mrs Bishop), The Yangtze Valley and Beyond: an account of journeys in China, chiefly in the province of Sze Chuan, John Murray 1899.

Blakiston, Thomas W., Five Months on the Yang-Tsze, and notices of the present rebellion in China, John Murray 1862.

Bonavia, Judy, The Yangzi River and the Three Gorges, Hong Kong Guidebook Company 1995.

Carpenter, Francis Ross, The Classic of Tea, The Echo Press 1974.

Chang Chun-Shu, 'Notes on the composition, transmission and editions of the Ju-Shu chi', Bulletin of the Institute of History and Philology, Academia Sinica, Vol.48, No. 3, 1977.

Chang Chun-Shu & Smythe, Joan, South China in the Twelfth Century (Lu You's Travel Diaries), The Chinese University Press HK 1977.

Clunas, Craig, Art in China, Oxford University Press 1997.

Cooper L.L, Travels of a Pioneer of Commerce, John Murray 1871.

Elvin, Mark, The Pattern of the Chinese Past, Eyre Methuen 1973.

Franke, Herbert, Diplomatic Missions of the Sung State 960-1276, Australian National University Press 1981.

Geil W.E., A Yankee on the Yangtze, Being a narrative of a Journey from Shanghai through the Central Kingdom to Burma, London Hodder & Stoughton 1904.

Hansen, Valerie, Changing Gods in Medieval China (1127–1276), Princeton University Press 1990.

Hargett, James M., On the Road in Twelfth Century China: The Travel Diaries of Fan Chengda (1126–93), Stuttgart 1989.

Hawkes, David, A Little Primer of Tu Fu, Oxford University Press 1967.

Ho Peng Yoke, Goh Thean Chye and Beda Lim, 'Lu Yu, The Poet-Alchemist', Occasional Paper 13, Faculty of Asian Studies, The Australian National University, Canberra 1972.

Hucker, Charles O., *A Dictionary of Official Titles in Imperial China*, Stanford University Press 1985.

Hung, William, *Tu Fu, China's Greatest Poet*, Russell & Russell 1969.

Legge, James, *The Shoo King, Tribute of Yu, The Chinese Classics Vol III Part 1*, Hong Kong 1865.

Kojiro Yoshikawa, translated by Burton Watson, *An Introduction to Sung Poetry*, Harvard University Press 1967.

Kracke, E.A. Jr, *Translations of Sung Civil Service Titles, Classification Terms and Governmental Organ Names*, San Francisco CMC 1987.

Little, Archibald John, *Through the Yang-tse Gorges, or Trade and Travel in Western China*, Sampson Low, Marston, Searle & Rivington 1888.

Loehr, Max, *The Great Painters of China*, Phaidon 1980.

Lynn, Madeleine, *Yangtze River, The Wildest, Wickedest River on Earth*, Oxford University Press (HK) 1997.

Murck, Alfreda, *Poetry and Painting in Sung China. The Subtle Art of Dissent*, Harvard University Press 2000.

Needham, Joseph, *Science and Civilization in China*, Cambridge University Press: Vol. 2 1956; Vol. 4 Part 2 1965; Vol. 4 Part 3 1971.

Nienhauser, William H. Jr, *The Indiana Companion to Traditional Chinese Literature*, Bloomington 1986.

Ortiz, Valerie Malenfer, *Dreaming the Southern Song Landscape: The Power of Illusion in Chinese Painting*, Brill 1999.

Reischauer, Edwin O., *Ennin's Travels in T'ang China*, The Ronald Press, Harvard University 1955.

Rudolph, Deborah, 'The power of places: A northern Sung literatus tours the southern suburbs of Ch'ang-an', *Journal of the American Oriental Socity* 114 (1994).

Sargent, Stuart, 'Music in the World of Su Shi', *Journal of Song-Yuan Studies* 32, 2002.

Schjöth F, *Chinese Currency, The Schjöth Collection of the University of Oslo*, Norway 1929.

Shiba Yoshinobu, translated by Mark Elvin, *Commerce and Society in Sung China*, Michigan Abstracts 1968/1970.

Sickman, Lawrence and Soper, Alexander; *The Art and Architecture of China*, Pelican History of Art, Penguin Books, 1956.

Siren, Oswald, *Chinese Painting*, The Ronald Press Company, New York, 1956.

Sivin, Nathan, *Chinese Alchemy: Preliminary Studies*, Cambridge, Massachusetts 1968.

Strassberg, Richard E., *Inscribed Images: Travel Writing from Imperial China*, Berkeley: University of California Press 1994.

Sullivan, Michael, *An Introduction to Chinese Art*, Faber and Faber 1961.

ter Haar, B.J., *The White Lotus Teachings in Chinese Religious History*, Brill 1992.

Valder, Peter, *The Garden Plants of China*, George Weidenfeld and Nicholson 1999.

Van Slyke, Lyman P., *Yangtze: Nature, History, and the River*, Addison-Wesley Publishing Company Inc 1988.

Waley, Arthur, *The Poetry and Career of Li Po*, George Allen and Unwin 1950.

Waley, Arthur, *Ch'ang-ch'un: the travels of an alchemist (the journey of the Taoist Ch'ang-ch'un from China to the Hindukush at the summons of Chingiz Khan)*, George Routledge & Sons, Ltd 1931.

Watson, Burton, *Su Tung-p'o: Selections from a Sung Dynasty Poet*, Columbia University Press 1965.

Watson, Burton, *The Old Man Who Does As He Pleases: Selections from the Poetry and Prose of Lu Yu*, New York: Columbia University Press 1973.

Watson, William, *The Arts of China 900-1620*, Yale University Press 2000.

Willetts, William, *Foundations of Chinese Art*, Thames and Hudson 1965.

Winchester, Simon, *The River at the Centre of the World*, Penguin 1996.

Worcester G.R.G., *The Junks and Sampans of the Yangtze*, Naval Institute Press, Annapolis, Maryland 1971.

Xu Yinong, *The Chinese City in Space and Time*, University of Hawai'i Press 2000.

Map

The map has benefited principally from the information contained in the relevant pages of the *Zhongguo lishi ditu ji* 1974/1982; the Alphabetical List of Geographical names in Sung China by Hope Wright (published by Sung-Yuan Research Aids in 1956 and 1992); and the computer skills of Mr. Geoffrey Arias.

Works in Chinese

Standard works of reference in Chinese, biographical, geographical, Buddhist, Daoist, linguistic and historical have been widely used, and I do not itemize them here. Internet resources have also on occasion proved useful, particularly in checking biographical references; though it is surprising how often an obscure twelfth-century individual shares the same name as, say, the current manager of a shoe factory in a remote Hubei industrial town. General works on China, Song dynasty history, art and specialized points of difficulty such as weights and measures are not listed. Here I provide only those works in Chinese on which I have drawn directly in my text.

Bai Juyi ji (Collected Works of Bai Juyi), Bai Juyi (772–846), in Zhongguo gudian wenxue jiben congshu, Zhonghua shuju 1979.

Guoxue jiben congshu 1931, based on Jiguge edition, as re-issued by the Guangzhi shuju of Hong Kong in 1963). Ru Shu ji is juan 43 (pp.264–98).

Congshu jicheng chubian, Vol. 3190 for Ru Shu ji.

Lu You ji, Lu You (1125–1210), Zhonghua Shuju 1976. Vol. 5 contains most of Lu You's prose collection Weinan Wenji, of which Ru Shu ji is juan 43–8.

Rongzhai suibi (Tolerant Study Notebooks), Hong Mai (1123–1202), Kunlun chubanshe 2001.

Song Shi (History of the Song Dynasty), Tuotuo (Toghto) (1313–55), Zhonghua shuju 1977.

Tang Song ci jianshang cidian [Nan Song, Liao, Jin], (Anthology of Tang and Song Lyrics; Southern Song, Liao and Jin), Shanghai cishu chubanshe 1988.

Tang Song sanwen jingxuan (Selections from Tang and Song prose), Wang Shuizhao, Jiangsu guji chubanshe 2002.

Wenwu No. 9 (1976) pp.87–8 (for discussion of a Lu You inscription).

Wuchuanlu (Record of a Boat of Wu), Fan Chengda (1126–93), Congshu jicheng chubian.

Xin Tang Shu (New Tang History), Song Qi (998–1061), Ouyang Xiu (1007–72) et al. Zhonghua shuju 1975.

Xu Zizhitongjian (Continuation of the Comprehensive Mirror for Aid in Government), Bi Yuan (1730–97), Yuelu shushe 1992.

Yijian zhi, Hong Mai (1123–1202), Congshu jicheng chubian 1937.

Zhongguo youji wenxueshi (*History of Chinese Travel Literature*), Mei Xinlin and Yu Zhanghua, Xuelin chubanshe, Shanghai 2004.

Zizhitongjian (*Comprehensive Mirror for Aid in Government*), Sima Guang (1019–86), Zhonghua Shuju 1956/1996.

Works on Lu You

Lu You Ci, xinshi jiping, Wang Shuangqi, Zhongguo shudian 2001.

Lu You juan, Gudian wenxue yanjiu ziliao huibian, Zhonghu shuju, Beijing 1962.

Lu You nianpu, Yu Beishan, Zhonghua shuju, Beijing 1961.

Lu You pingjuan, Liu Weichong, Zhengzhong shuju, Taiwan 1966.

Lu You pingzhuan, Qiu Minggao, Nanjing daxue chubanshe 2002.

Lu You yanjiu, Zhu Dongrun, Zhonghua shuju, Beijing 1961.

Lu You zhuan, Zhu Dongrun, Shanghai guji chubanshe 1979, republished with minor additions by Hainan chubanshe 2002.

Lu You, Qi Zhiping, Wenxue yanjiushe, Hong Kong (no date).

INDEX

Note: Page numbers in *italics* refer to the captions to the illustrations. Where references to the names of people mentioned in the text, and included in the Dramatis Personae, are very brief they are not included in the index.

ACKNOWLEDGMENTS

In returning after many years' absence to a study of classical Chinese, and to a re-reading of Lu You's Diary, I am reminded of a remark by Shi Kuang of the Spring and Autumn period (770–481 BC) with which Lu You was himself much taken. Shi Kuang once said that 'To study in old age is like carrying a torch as you travel through the night'. Indeed, Lu called his book of collected anecdotes *Miscellanea from the Retreat of Study in Old Age* (*Laoxuean biji*). I hope that my journey through the night will shed a little light on the richness of Chinese civilization for other Western readers.

That journey has been made particularly enjoyable by my participation in an informal Classical Chinese reading group held at Oxford University under the aegis of Dr Robert Chard. Though the whole range of classical Chinese literature falls within its purview, not just that of the Song dynasty, it has provided me with a stimulus and a wider grasp of the Chinese language than I could otherwise have aspired to. But its ever-shifting membership bears no responsibility for the errors of judgement and deficiencies of knowledge in this work.

I have also benefited greatly from the library resources of the School of Oriental and African Studies at London University and those of Durham University.

Days 19–23 of the seventh month of the Diary were first published in *Renditions* No. 62 (Autumn 2004), pp. 17–23. They are reprinted here, with minor variations, by kind permission of the Research Centre for Translation, The Chinese University of Hong Kong.

I am much indebted to Mr Geoffrey Arias who gave unstinting help in preparing on computer the map which may be found on the endpapers of this book. Chinese scholars have done much work over the centuries on identification and location of historical place-names, but to make sense of the Diary it was necessary to produce a map specifically tailored to the route of Lu You's journey.

I feel a particular sense of gratitude to my publisher, John Nicoll, for his faith in this book and for his advice, and to my editor Michael Brunström for his skilled and dedicated contribution to bringing it to fruition.

Finally, my wife deserves my thanks in many ways, not least for showing that fine balance of scepticism at the possibility of an outcome, and encouraging interest in seeing it, which has provided the spur to bring this translation into print.

Philip Watson

Picture acknowledgments
Photographs on pages 2–3 20, 21, 22 (above), 25, 26, 30, 32, 35, 37, 38 (above), 39 (below), 41, 45, 48, 49, 50, 52, 55, 58, 59, 67, 69, 70, 78, 101, 105, 106, 109, 111, 113, 122, 124, 137, 148, 161, 168, 170, 173, 176, 177, 179, 181, 189, 191, 194, 196, 199, 201 (above) copyright © Philip Watson.

The Publishers have made every effort to contact holders of copyright works. Any copyright holders we have been unable to contact are invited to contact the Publishers so that a full acknowledgment may be made in subsequent editions. For permission to reproduce the images on the following pages, the Publishers thank those listed below.

Page 62: Freer Gallery of Art, Smithsonian Institution, Washington DC, Gift of Charles Lang Freer, F1908.171; page 83: The Nelson-Atkins Museum of Art, Kansas City, Missouri. Purchase: Nelson Trust, 32-159/2; page 93: From William Watson, *The Arts of China to AD 900*. (New Haven, Yale University Press, 1995); page 115: Metropolitan Museum of Art, New York, Frederick C. Hewitt Fund, 1921 (21.76); page 157: The Nelson-Atkins Museum of Art, Kansas City, Missouri. Purchase: Nelson Trust, 31-84.